A Sourcebook
of Interactive Methods
for Teaching with Texts

David A. Hayes
The University of Georgia

Allyn and Bacon
Boston London Toronto Sydney Tokyo Singapore

To Rosalie and Jim

Library of Congress Cataloging-in-Publication Data

Hayes, David A.
　A sourcebook of interactive methods for teaching with texts /
　David A. Hayes.
　　p.　　cm.
　Includes bibliographical references and index.
　ISBN 0-205-13306-1
　1. Teaching.　　2. Teacher-student relationships.　　I. Title.
LB1027.H385　1992
371.1'02–dc20　　　　　　　　　　　　　　　　　91-30633
　　　　　　　　　　　　　　　　　　　　　　　　CIP

Printed in the United States of America
10 9 8 7 6 5 4 3 2 1   95 94 93 92 91

Contents

Preface

A Sourcebook of Interactive Methods for Teaching with Texts is a reference book for planning instructional encounters with students. Intended to serve the day-to-day needs of the classroom teacher, it describes and illustrates methods of teaching the content of subjects commonly taught in school. The methods are gathered from the literature on teaching and grouped according to the function they fulfill in the classroom: teaching effective study behavior, enhancing comprehension of subject matter, developing conceptual vocabulary, building organization skills in reading and writing, and presenting subject matter visually. The grouping scheme is but one of several possibilities for presenting the methods, and most of the methods accomplish purposes beyond those of the group in which they are placed here. The opening chapter provides the rationale for devoting this book exclusively to instructional procedures and sets forth general guidelines for applying them in the classroom.

Each group of methods is introduced with a brief explanatory comment and a statement of objectives. Individual methods are cast in uniform format in order to provide accessibility and to facilitate critical comparison among them. By this format, each method is presented in two parts. The first part explains, describes, and discusses the method in expository fashion. The second part illustrates the method as it plays out in a fictitious lesson.

The presentation of each method opens with a statement that specifies its instructional purposes. The introduction continues with information to explain why the method works and to indicate the grade levels and subject areas for which the method is most appropriate. (With modification, most of the methods may be applied across the grade levels and in teaching any school subject that makes significant use of textual materials.) Following this introduction, the method's procedure is spelled out step by step. The description of the method is capped with a short discussion of its strengths and limitations.

For each method presented, an example shows how procedures unfold in an imaginary classroom situation. A brief prologue sets the scene by indicating the subject, grade level, and teacher's objective. As the imaginary lesson proceeds, the steps of the method become apparent in the give and take between the teacher and students. The classroom dialogue makes significant reference to a text that is, as in most actual classrooms, central to the lesson. This text and other materials integral to the lesson are available for the reader to inspect.

The resemblance between the texts of the example lessons and actual texts used in teaching is intentional. In most of the example lessons, the texts are simulations of texts used in real classrooms. With the few exceptions noted as follows, the stories and textbook segments of the example lessons are my own work, fashioned especially to permit clear and concise portrayal of the lessons. For illustrative texts not my own, I am indebted to the following individuals: Sue Baskin for her story, "The Rise and Fall of 'Dutchy'"; Laurel Boykin for her editorial, "Teen Pregnancy a Problem," which originally appeared in *Smoke Signals,* the student newspaper of Oconee County, Georgia, Middle School; Joyce Maxwell for her descriptive passage, "I Am Texas"; Tom Morton for a lengthy excerpt from "Decision on Dieppe: A Cooperative Lesson on Conflict Resolution," which appeared in *History and Social Science Teacher;* and Harry I. Stein for a passage on the multiplicative inverse from *Refresher Mathematics with Practical Applications,* published by Allyn and Bacon. I am also grateful to the following publishers: Harcourt Brace Jovanovich for permission to reproduce William Wordsworth's poem "Strange Fits of Passion Have I Known"; Henry Holt and Company for permission to reproduce Robert Frost's poem "Fire and Ice"; and Washington Square Press for permission to reproduce an anonymous translation of Giovanni Boccaccio's tale "Neifile's Story (The Sixth Day)" from *The Decameron.*

For suggestions given to me during the development of the manuscript, I am grateful to colleagues and students too numerous to name individually. For word processing the manuscript, I thank Joy Reeves and Delia Weston. For constructive criticism of the original manuscript, I thank Judith Irvin of Florida State University, Marcia Modlo of Vestal Central Schools (New York), and Susan Whitten of Concord Public Schools (Massachusetts).

I am most appreciative of the genuinely nice people at Allyn and Bacon who transformed the manuscript into the finished volume. Steve Gold immediately understood the purpose of a book of this sort, saw value in it, and initiated the events of its publication. Mylan Jaixen remained upbeat and encouraging as he offered insightful advice about putting the manuscript into publishable form. Deborah Reinke meticulously attended to the many details associated with the publication process. Lynda Griffiths, at TKM Productions, carefully edited the manuscript and took pains to accommodate my amendments, even as the book was being typeset. To Steve, Mylan, Deborah, and Lynda go my deepest thanks.

Procedure in Teaching

Virtually every time a teacher prepares a lesson, the question arises: How shall I teach this lesson? Once a decision about what to teach has been made, a procedure for teaching it has to be planned. Merely telling students about a subject seldom results in durable learning, nor does assigning students to read the pertinent sections of the course textbook. To be effective, a lesson has to do more than thrust information upon students. An effective lesson structures the flow of information so that it captures students' interest and holds their attention; it encourages students to connect the information with other things they know; it provides activity that elicits thoughtful interaction among students; it motivates students to act on the material to be learned with deliberation and imagination; and it prepares students to apply its facts and ideas in other situations. How to accomplish all of this is the challenge that the teacher faces with each lesson. No matter how expert in the subject and no matter how richly supplied with instructional materials, the teacher still has to work out the procedure by which to engage students with the subject matter.

Procedure gives coherence and direction to instruction. It establishes the structure within which the teacher, students, and materials come together. The way it brings them together shapes the pattern by which the subject unfolds. Procedure defines the role of the teacher—whether to be directive, facilitative, or consultative. It specifies the steps the teacher is to take, and it provides alternative actions to be taken under a variety of contingencies. Procedure spells out what students are to do. It indicates how they are to be positioned vis-à-vis the subject matter, how they are to interact with the teacher and with one another, and what kinds of products they are to generate. Procedure indicates the proper place of materials—whether they are to serve as principal information source, instructional amplifier, or catalyst for learning. In short, it is procedure that structures students' classroom experiences so that they achieve the learning objectives that the teacher sets for them.

Teaching means, essentially, the procedure of teaching, for it is through procedure that students are brought to consider a subject's ideas and to apply its principles constructively. Lessons most likely to stimulate productive reflection and foster transfer to novel circumstances are the ones whose procedure is thoughtfully planned and skillfully implemented. Planning an instructional procedure calls for appraising the appropriateness and relative likelihood of success among several procedures that could possibly be used. In every situation there are conditions that limit what the teacher can do. Choice of procedure may be limited by such factors as subject matter, ability and maturity of students, philosophy of the school, and attitudes of the community. Having a broad knowledge of instructional procedures allows the teacher to adjust lesson planning to a variety of conditions. To increase the likelihood that a procedure will work, the teacher has to implement it in light of broad knowledge about teaching. This knowledge may be summarized in a relatively short list of guidelines for teaching:

1. Know the purposes to be served by instruction. *The application of any instructional procedure assumes that its purposes are already determined. Procedures are but means for achieving these purposes. Purposes set the direction of instruction and provide the basis of the procedure. With purposes in mind, the teacher can sort the relevant from the irrelevant and give due emphasis to most important information. Being clear about instructional purposes helps keep the teacher from misleading students about what is expected of them. The purposes of instruction indicate the criteria for evaluating its success.*

2. Prepare. *Most of a lesson's successfulness can usually be attributed to the teacher's preparation. By thinking through the lesson in advance, the teacher can formulate a plan and gather appropriate materials. The plan encompasses measures for introducing the subject matter, for incorporating it into productive activity, and for extending students' understanding. The plan anticipates what students may do at each phase of the lesson and provides alternative courses of action where problems might arise. Giving forethought to the lesson, the teacher can take account of junctures at which materials can be introduced most effectively.*

3. Provide appropriate materials. *Most instructional procedures entail the use of materials such as texts, audiovisual aids, study guides, and so on. To be useful, materials are commensurate with both the purpose of instruction and the capability of students to understand and use them profitably. For example, in a lesson whose purpose is to teach students about the features of persuasive discourse, students are provided with a written argument that exemplifies these features in language they can understand. Attempting to teach students to read argumentation makes little sense if they have no argument to read. Attempting to teach them with an argument they cannot understand not only makes little sense, it makes for an exercise in frustration.*

4. Minimize interference and distraction. *A lesson is structured to direct the ways that students attend to and think about subject matter. It controls the instructional situation so that students concentrate on the essential attributes of the subject. Opportunities are afforded for students to reflect on these attributes and to give expression to them. The teacher steadily keeps the focus on the subject matter, refraining from introducing information that competes with the focus and keeping out static that would take students' attention away from the focus. Intense concentration on the subject matter is especially important during students' initial attempts to learn concepts that are new to them.*

5. Give students a rationale. *Students tend to fare better at almost any task when they know the reasons for what they are doing. Just as the teacher's knowing the purpose for a procedure helps set the direction for a lesson, knowing the reasons for taking up a particular topic or for undertaking an assigned task helps students stay on course toward meeting instructional goals. Knowing the reasons for studying the topic and doing the tasks of a lesson helps students weigh the relative importance of different information and allocate their attention accordingly. It is essential for thinking constructively about the material presented and transferring what is learned to other situations.*

6. Let students see the overall scheme of the subject matter, but have them deal with it in manageable parts. *Students who can see the overall organization of the subject matter are less likely to be overwhelmed by it. Discernment of subject matter's organization allows students to act on it appropriately. When they can see how its parts fit together and contribute to the overall lesson, they can know how to allocate their attention. Presenting subject matter part by part allows students to keep up with the lesson as it unfolds. And it allows them to experience a sense of completion as each part is finished. Importantly, providing a scheme with discernible elements facilitates students' borrowing from the scheme and transferring its elements to further learning and problem solving.*

7. Model learning and using subject matter. *What students see the teacher do can be as important as what they hear the teacher say. When a procedure has the teacher act in ways that correspond to study behavior, students are given the opportunity to witness the teacher simulate what they are supposed to do with the subject matter on their own. Through direct observation, students learn how to perform academic tasks and act on the subject matter. When students see the actions that the teacher takes, they gain confidence that these actions are the correct ones to be taken in individual study.*

8. Keep students aware of what they are doing and how they are doing it. *Reminding students constantly to pay attention to themselves as learners prepares them to apply the subject matter in novel contexts. By having students ask themselves how they are learning and applying the subject matter, as they are learning and applying it, the teacher encourages students to develop a sense of reflective awareness. It is from paying attention to their own acts of learning and applying subject matter that students derive rules for transferring it to new situations. They learn to predict possible difficulties in its application and to figure out ways to surmount those difficulties. They also learn how to evaluate the quality with which they apply the subject matter.*

9. Respond to students' attempts to understand and learn. *Interacting with students about the facts and ideas of a subject is the essence of teaching. By responding to students' attempts to deal with facts and ideas, the teacher raises their consciousness about the subject and about how they may take control of it. Of the responses that the teacher may offer, most significant are those of encouragement and correction. When the teacher affirms that students are acting on the subject matter appropriately, students attend to those acts with deliberation and refine them for future use. When the teacher points out inconsistencies, omissions, and errors, students know where to adjust their efforts to understand and learn. Both encouragement and correction serve the purpose of informing future applications of the subject matter.*

    This book is intended to serve the teacher who faces questions about how to engage students with subject matter. It presents a variety of methods for meeting a wide range of instructional purposes. The opening section describes methods for presenting subject matter in ways that simulate effective study practices. The thrust of these methods is twofold: to present subject matter so that students can understand and learn it and to demonstrate to students how to study and deal with subject matter problems independently. To a degree, the methods presented in other sections accomplish the same ends. The methods presented in the section on rendering subject matter comprehensible offer ways to clarify concepts and to extend students' knowledge so that they can understand and learn more readily in future encounters with the subject. The sections presenting methods for building conceptual vocabulary and for teaching about the organizational aspects of reading and writing also offer procedures for extending knowledge and understanding. These procedures are especially useful for developing knowledge students need for communicating about subject matter. Methods for taking a visual-spatial approach to presenting subject matter allow students to see relatedness in the elements of the content and to grasp those elements all at once.

    Each method offers a distinct way of interacting with students about the information and ideas of school subjects. As the methods are described here, significant reference is made to textual sources, which play a central role in most formal instruction. Accompanying the description of every method is an example intended to illustrate how the method might unfold in the give and take of a lesson. Clarity necessitates presenting the methods as they might be implemented under ideal conditions. The methods are intended to serve as heuristic procedures to be considered in light of particular circumstances and modified accordingly. They are suggestions offered to the teacher who faces the question: How shall I teach this lesson?

Modeling Study

Teaching is a transaction in which the teacher enables students to know, and perhaps to do, things they could not efficiently come to know or do on their own. The teacher's part of the transaction is to share information about the subject and to demonstrate how that information is used to explore ideas and confront problems. The students' part is to follow the teacher's direction, attend to the information presented, and observe how the teacher makes use of it. In the transaction, how to learn and use the subject matter is no less important than the subject matter itself. The teacher makes apparent to students what a person knowledgeable in the subject does in handling its content. By adopting the teacher's approaches to the subject matter, students equip themselves to learn and use it independently as the teacher does.

Modeling study is a matter of exhibiting the kinds of behavior in which one engages in order to understand and learn. The teacher models such behavior by taking steps in teaching that approximate the steps one would take in studying. In this way, the teacher shows students how to act strategically with the subject matter. Acting strategically means acting planfully. By observing the teacher acting strategically with the subject matter, students can see how one formulates plans and implements them with deliberation in order to achieve goals specified for understanding and learning subject matter. By imitating the teacher's overt acts of instruction, students learn to deal with subject matter productively. Not only do they learn the steps to be taken in independent study, they acquire the attitude that studying is formulating and implementing plans with deliberation.

Numerous methods have been advanced for teaching subject matter and study skills simultaneously. With these methods, there is no sacrifice of traditional objectives that stress the delivery of subject matter. They are heuristic methods in that they are, at the same, time methods of teaching and models of studying. They have the teacher present subject matter in ways that simulate effective study behavior. The steps of presenting subject matter correspond to the steps of studying. By these methods, students are engaged in activities that have them:

- *Assume a questioning attitude*
- *Take stock of what they know about the subject*
- *Clarify their purposes for studying*
- *Formulate plans for studying at the global as well as local level*
- *Make predictions about what they will find out*
- *Monitor their own progress*
- *Adjust the study strategy as self-evaluation and subject matter demand*

- *Elaborate on subject matter by making judgments, comparing and contrasting, seeing causes and effects, and forming hunches*
- *Make connections both within the subject matter and to other knowledge related to it*

This section presents instructional methods that foster these study behaviors as well as deliver subject matter.

1

Listen-Read-Discuss

Listen-Read-Discuss (L-R-D) is a broadly applicable technique that promotes under-standing of subject matter, self-monitoring, and critical thinking. It also increases students' confidence about participating in class discussions.

L-R-D facilitates productive classroom interaction. In the interaction, students recognize troublesome parts of the material and attend to them carefully. By dealing consciously with problem areas, students learn to monitor their own study processes more effectively. Critical thinking skills are enhanced as students read analytically and ask questions in class. Because L-R-D is flexible, it can be modified to fit most class discussions and levels of text difficulty. L-R-D can be used in all academic subject areas, especially those that rely heavily on texts and text-related activities.

Procedure

The teacher begins with a portion of a text that is clear and well organized. The text is presented in a format comfortable for the teacher (usually lecture) for about half the class period. Following this, students read the page or pages covering that material. Then the teacher leads a discussion aimed toward clarifying the text and stimulating interest. The discussion is organized around three questions: What did you understand best of what you heard and read? What did you understand least? And what questions or thoughts did this material raise for you? The questions and thoughts need not be restricted to the topic specifically discussed, but may include related issues. The teacher models self-monitoring and critical thinking by expressing personal thoughts and uncer-tainties about the material.

Discussion

L-R-D brings about the desired triangulation of teacher, text, and students. It exposes students to the lesson's content in three different ways: the teacher's lecture, the text's presentation, and the class discussion. Redundancy in covering the material serves students across the range of academic ability. More capable students gain a thorough understanding of the subject matter, whereas lower-ability students keep up with the material as it develops. To a large degree, students influence the flow of the lesson. Obviously, this method can be quite time consuming. Also, exceptionally bright students may feel restricted by the L-R-D format.

EXAMPLE

A high school science class is studying the human circulatory system. The lesson in progress is preparatory to teaching students how the heart works. The teacher is concerned with introducing the heart's general purpose and teaching basic terms for describing the gross anatomy of the heart. Concluding a brief lecture, the teacher assigns students to read a portion of the text that deals with the same material covered in the lecture.

Teacher: . . . These, then, are key terms for referring to the parts of the heart. We have seen where the parts are on the diagram I have sketched here at the board. Now let's see how our text describes the heart. Let's read the section entitled "Structure of the Heart."

When it appears that students have finished reading, the teacher engages students in a discussion that elicits from them comments about what they understand and do not understand and that provokes thought about related matters, particularly matters to be addressed in future instruction.

Teacher: What seems most striking to you about the heart? What's clearest in your mind about what you've heard and read about the heart?

Ronnie: That it really seems to be not one self-contained body part but several very special parts. That each is so special, yet needs all the other parts.

Beth: Yes. And what really helps me visualize these parts is knowing the things their names mean in Latin. It makes sense that the entry chamber would be called an "atrium," like in a house. And without even looking at a diagram, I can just see that "little ear" of an auricle.

Craig: It's like Beth says. It's amazing that the heart has all these special parts that depend on each other to work right.

Melissa: That's the way pumps are. They're more than things whose handle you pump or button you push and water or whatever just flows. They have special parts inside that have to be there for them to work.

Mike: Every part has a special purpose that the other parts don't. They have their own thing to do.

Teacher: So you seem to be saying that you appreciate the heart's complexity as a pumping mechanism. You refer to it as *a* pump. A pump. (The teacher is trying to get students to remember that the heart is two pumps.)

Melissa: (missing the teacher's intention) Oh sure, it's only one kind of pump. Maybe it's not a pump like you ordinarily think of pumps, but it's still a pump. It pumps the blood.

Teacher: There's no question that the heart pumps the blood. But you're saying the heart is *a* pump.

Ronnie: Oh, I get what you mean. The heart is really *two* pumps.

Teacher: Right.

Ronnie: One pump sends blood to the lungs and one sends blood to the rest of the body.

The teacher again describes the action of the heart and traces the flow of blood to and from the lungs and to and from the body, stressing that the heart is two connected pumps that work together. The teacher takes an opportunity then to express a personal sense of wonderment and in doing so fosters in students curiosity that encourages further exploration of the heart.

Teacher: Marvelous. The heart is a marvelous organ. You can know all the parts and that they coordinate their action, but *how* it all happens in the first place is a marvel to me.

Craig: Do you mean the source of the heart's power? Like what provides the energy to make it work? It's like you've said many times, things don't just happen without causes.

Teacher: Well, we can explain the heart's electricity—the energy sources of that electricity and the way the body works to make the electrical impulses to the heart regular. It's a marvel to me that it all works together so well, with such precision. What's really the marvel of marvels is that it ever came to be.

Beth: (interrupting) Let's go back to what you were saying about the heart's electrical energy. I'm curious. Just where does the electricity come from? And what's the circuitry like that regulates the electricity that powers the heart?

Structure of the Heart

The human heart is actually two pumps connected together. Each pump has arteries taking blood away and veins bringing it back.

One of the pumps sends the blood to the lungs, where the blood picks up oxygen. When this blood returns to the heart, the second pump sends it out through the arteries to deliver the oxygen to the various organs in the body and to pick up carbon dioxide. When it comes back to the heart through the veins, the first pump sends it back to the lungs for more oxygen and to get rid of the carbon dioxide. This goes on, over and over and over.

Each half of the heart has two kinds of chambers. There is a thin-walled chamber above called the *atrium,* a Latin word meaning "entrance hall." The blood enters there first. This kind of chamber is also called an *auricle,* a Latin word meaning "little ear." It hangs down over the heart like a dog's ear. Beneath the atrium is a *ventricle,* a Latin word meaning "little hollow." It has thick, muscular walls. There are four parts altogether: A right atrium, a right ventricle, a left atrium, and a left ventricle.

Source

Ula Price Casale and Anthony Manzo. (1985). Listen-read-discuss: A content reading heuristic. *Journal of Reading, 28,* 732–734.

2

Directed Reading-Thinking Activity

The Directed Reading-Thinking Activity promotes reading as an active thinking process. Well known as the DR-TA, it encourages students to establish their own purposes for reading. It emphasizes making predictions and looking for proof in the text to support students' predictions.

The DR-TA has students simulate important questioning behaviors of effective readers. In a game-like activity, students set purposes for reading, predict events and outcomes, and seek to verify their predictions. These are motivating, direction-giving behaviors. They get students started, keep them on track, and push them vigorously to the end of a reading. Students gain confidence as readers as they declare their own ideas, reflect their own experiences, and inject their own associations into the activity.

The DR-TA can be used with students at any grade level. Although it may be used with an entire class, it is best used in groups of 8 to 12 students. Groups of this size allow a variety of predictions and interpretations to be made in the activity, yet allow significant participation by every student. The DR-TA is used most effectively with narrative material, especially short stories. Pictures, graphs, and diagrams in the reading material offer clues for making predictions, and so are positive features in this activity. The DR-TA is ideal for history and language arts/English classes, which typically present students with a great deal of narrative literature.

Procedure

The teacher begins the activity by arousing interest in the topic, by relating it to previous lessons or to students' first-hand experience. Students' attention is then drawn to the reading material with the teacher's direction to look at the title or heading and any illustrations in the selection. Students are told not to read yet, but to think about the title or heading and the illustrations and to predict what the selection will tell. Here, the teacher might say something like, "Just by looking at the title and pictures, can you guess what this story (or textbook section) will be about?"

The teacher then records students' predictions on the chalkboard, a chart, or overhead transparency. *All* predictions are recorded, no matter how obviously incorrect or zany they may be. By accepting all predictions as they are given, the teacher welcomes active participation by all students and encourages risk taking that is necessary for developing divergent thinking. After students have offered all the predictions they can generate, the teacher directs them to read the first segment of the selection. The length of this segment may vary up to 500 words or so, according to the maturity and reading proficiency of students. When it appears that students have completed reading this segment, the teacher has students review their predictions.

As students confirm or reject their predictions, the teacher places a check beside confirmed predictions and lines through rejected predictions. Rejected predictions are not erased. Some predictions cannot be conclusively confirmed or ruled out until the entire selection has been read, and these provide fodder for productive discussion as the activity proceeds. During review of predictions, the teacher seizes opportunities to have students cite evidence in the text to support their interpretations. Once predictions have been reviewed, the teacher elicits further predictions. The teacher asks students to make their predictions on the basis of their reading so far and, again, records *all* predictions offered, no matter how far-fetched.

This cycle of predicting-reading-checking predictions continues as the class reads the selection, segment by segment. With all predictions left on the chalkboard, whether confirmed or rejected, the teacher points out to students that they have done what good readers do during reading–make many predictions, some of which are subsequently confirmed and some of which are not. The teacher may wish to cap the activity with an assignment that makes use of predictions not born out in the reading. With these predictions, students can write alternate versions of the story, or, taking a direction suggested by these predictions, students may write sequels. Once students learn the technique, they can become "recorders" in small groups as the teacher oversees the entire lesson.

Discussion

Students enjoy the DR-TA. Its game-like quality invites all students to participate actively. It encourages students to speculate, and all the speculations they express are recognized and valued. Incorporating every student's contributions into the discussion motivates students to take risks as readers and thinkers. This kind of behavior is essential to the development of critical reading and thinking skills.

As attractive as the DR-TA is, its use is largely restricted to instruction with narrative reading material, since it is this type of material whose content lends itself to prediction as it unfolds. Other kinds of materials, such as expositions and arguments, typically present the thrust of their content in advance and then elaborate and explain it, cutting short opportunities for making divergent predictions. Another restriction is on the number of students that may be productively included in the activity. Fewer than 8 participants tends to curtail the number and diversity of predictions; more than 12 tends to allow reticent students to turn the activity over to the more assertive members of the group.

EXAMPLE

A high school journalism class is reading stories that describe and promote interest in the culture of a region or locality. The teacher's objective is to increase students' sensitivity to the anticipatory stance of readers.

Teacher: Here's a story sure to appeal to residents of the community where it is set. Let's have some fun with it. Let's do what readers of stories do–guess what's coming up next. Before we actually read the story, let's try to guess what the story is about just by looking at the picture and the title.

Sandy: From the title, I'd say this is a story about a place ruled by a duke. That's what a "dutchy" is, you know.

Several: (groans and laughter)

Teacher: (writing on the board) All right: "A place ruled by a duke." Good guess.

Jean: Isn't that spelled d-u-c-h-y?

Teacher: Usually. But who knows? It may be alternatively spelled here for a particular effect. In any case, in this activity *all* speculations are accepted. So don't hold back.

Jean: Well, OK. It *is* in quotation marks. Then maybe this is about a place ruled by a person who's not actually a duke, but *is* a powerful person.

Carol: Right. All these stories take place in America, so this one will too. The guy who runs it is of Dutch descent.

Paul: It's a place run by an oil magnate.

Elaine: Or a super rich owner of a gold mine.

Lynn: Or a cattle rancher.

Eric: The picture is of a soldier. So there's going to be a war told about.

Tom: Yeah—a war that takes place between rival factions within the "dutchy."

Linda: To gain control over it.

Sarah: The story is going to be about how a Dutchman came to power but how he was eventually overthrown in a war.

George: The uniform is the kind they used to wear a hundred years ago. That's *when* the story happens—about a hundred years ago.

On the chalkboard, the teacher has jotted down all of these possibilities based on the picture and title:

a place ruled by a duke

usually spelled d-u-c-h-y

ruled by powerful person, not a duke

takes place in America

place run by Dutch

place run by oil magnate

place run by gold mine owner

place run by cattle ranchers

a war

a war between rival factions

a war to gain control of dutchy

how the dutchman came to power and was overthrown 100 years ago

The teacher then directs the students to read the story's first segment.

Teacher: Interesting possibilities. Let's read to find out how close your guesses are. But just read the first paragraph. Do *not* read beyond the first paragraph.

Tom: You mean we have to stop reading just after the beginning?

Teacher: Right. We're going to do some more predicting after we have a little more to go on. When you've finished reading the first paragraph, look up. Let's check our initial guesses. Which of our predictions appear to be correct?

The teacher and students read silently.

George: The story took place in 1898. That's about a hundred years ago.

Teacher: (placing a check mark beside the prediction) Right.

Linda: It could still be about a place run by a powerful person, even a Dutchman.

Elaine: But we're incorrect about it being dominated by oil or gold or cattle.

Teacher: Should we eliminate those possibilities then?

All: Yes.

The teacher draws a line through these predictions.

Paul: The story's probably not about a war between rival factions. The soldier in the picture is a veteran of the Confederacy.

Teacher: Where does it say he's a Confederate soldier?

Paul: Right here: "A proposal to commission a statue in honor of those brave Elberton soldiers who died while serving the Confederacy."

Teacher: OK. I'll mark it out.

Others: But this story is not about a war. Draw a line through those predictions.

Teacher: Now that you have more to go on, what would you guess will happen in the story?

Eric: Dutchy is the name of the granite-finishing plant.

Sandy: The story will tell about the building of Dutchy granite finishing and about its demise after the need for it passed.

George: No. This story is about the statue. I think the people will give it the name "Dutchy."

Elaine: And it will deteriorate with acid rain falling on it.

Paul: Or the black people in the community will demand that a memorial to the Confederacy be taken down.

Linda: They will knock it down.

The students offer several additional predictions, all of which are recorded on the chalkboard:

> Dutchy a granite-finishing plant
>
> building a granite-finishing plant and its demise
>
> about a statue

the statue named Dutchy

the statue deteriorates from acid rain

black people demand statue be removed

black people knock it down

Dutchy a hero

unpaid granite carvers take back the statue

statue becomes too great an attraction for Elbertionians

taken down by townspeople

Then the teacher directs students to read the next two paragraphs, for which students check their predictions and, following that, make further predictions. The cycle of activity continues until the story is completed and all predictions are either confirmed or rejected.

Teacher: Would you just look at all of those predictions on the board!

Paul: Yeah. But look at all the ones with lines through them.

Teacher: That's all right. When we read, we make a whole lot of predictions that don't pan out.

The Rise and Fall of "Dutchy"
by Sue Baskin

In 1898, the ladies of the Confederate Memorial Association gathered for one of their weekly meetings. A proposal to commission a statue in honor of those brave Elberton soldiers who died while serving the Confederacy in the Civil War was entered. The ladies voted unanimously in favor of the project. It was to be a major undertaking. Although Elberton possessed plenty of natural materials—granite—there were no facilities available to produce the monument, so a granite-finishing plant was constructed. The granite carvers worked long and hard to complete the statue.

Finally the big day arrived. On July 15, 1898, hundreds of people came from all over the county to witness the unveiling. There was a festive air to the proceedings in Public Square, with speeches and lively band music filling the spectators' ears. Then, at last, the cover was pulled away. A gasp, and then a grumble rippled through the crowd. Atop the 15-foot pedestal stood a 7-foot soldier. His face was round and held no expression; he gave the impression of being "short and squatty," as one bystander put it. And to top it off, he was dressed in a uniform that looked suspiciously like that worn by the *Union* army. Someone said, "He looks like an old Dutchman," and the nickname "Dutchy" stuck.

"Dutchy" was a disappointment to the people of Elberton. Gradually, public sentiment against him grew until finally, on August 14, 1900, several of the townspeople took some ropes and pulled him down from the pedestal in Public Square, breaking his legs in the process. Though no one admitted being a party to it, most of the citizens of Elberton were not sorry to see him go. *The Elberton Star* even went so far as to claim that "Dutchy" had fallen while trying to get down from his pedestal and go get a beer. On August 16, after several groups of people had come to pay their "last respects," he was buried face down, a military disgrace, at the base of the pedestal from which he had fallen.

Over the years, "Dutchy" became a town legend. In 1982, the Elberton Granite Association received permission from the City Council to "exhume" the statue. So, April 19 arrived and people gathered once again to see "Dutchy" unveiled, though in a much different manner than before. The diggers found him buried about five feet down, behind the new Confederate monument. With a crane, they lifted him from his grave to the back of a pickup truck. The truck, with a police escort, took "Dutchy" to a nearby carwash and gave him a bath. After a more intensive cleaning by a local specialist, he was taken to the Elberton Granite Museum and Exhibit, where he now lies in state, awaiting the repair of his legs. When this is completed, "Dutchy" will take a place of honor in the museum, for, after all, the efforts made in 1898 to produce him also launched a multimillion dollar industry that has become the lifeline of Elberton. Maybe "Dutchy" is a hero after all.

Source

Russell G. Stauffer. (1969). *Directing reading maturity as cognitive process.* New York: Harper and Row.

Related Readings

J. Thomas Gill and Donald R. Bear. (1988). No book, whole book, and chapter DRTAs. *Journal of Reading, 31,* 444–449.

Martha Rapp Haggard. (1988). Developing critical thinking with the directed reading-thinking activity. *The Reading Teacher, 41,* 526–535.

3

Reciprocal Questioning

Reciprocal Questioning (ReQuest) is a game-like activity for engaging students with a story in such a way as to motivate them to finish reading it on their own. It encourages students to formulate their own questions and to set their own purposes for reading.

In the activity, the teacher and students take turns asking and answering questions. The teacher's behavior provides students with a model for developing their own questions and for responding to questions put to them. Because the teacher-student interaction is direct, students are encouraged to go along with the procedure. For the reading at hand, students' curiosity is aroused and they want to complete the reading in order to satisfy that curiosity. Over time, students develop an active inquiring attitude that leads to higher levels of thinking about their reading.

ReQuest is appropriate for students of all ages. It is very effective for use with students who have the ability to read but lack interest. Optimally, ReQuest is used on a one-to-one basis, though it can also be used with small groups of three or four students. It is most suitable for language arts/English and reading classes. Narrative material is usually best for creating interest and affording opportunity to speculate about the content. ReQuest can be adapted, however, for teaching with other kinds of texts used in the content areas.

Procedure

Having identified a student who can read but who apparently does not, the teacher selects a story that that student would probably like and could easily read. The teacher tells the student about the story and suggests that the two of them read it together. The teacher explains that as they read, they will pause to ask each other questions. Each may ask the other to repeat or to rephrase questions, but an attempt has to be made to give an answer. Responding with statements such as "I don't know" is not allowed.

The teacher and student then silently read enough of the story to provide for an exchange of questions. The teacher turns the book face down and invites the student to ask the first questions. When the student has asked as many questions as possible, the teacher asks questions. The teacher not only asks literal-level questions but also models asking questions that call for thoughtful answers. For uncertain answers, it is permissible to look back in the text.

The cycle of silent reading and reciprocal questioning continues until the student is hooked by the story. At that point, the teacher asks the student to predict the story's outcome. The student independently reads the remainder of the story to see if the prediction is sustained.

Discussion

ReQuest provides personalized attention to students who are drifting along, daydreaming, or becoming disinterested in reading. Not only do they interact with the teacher one-to-one, but they get to turn a classroom tradition around and interrogate the teacher for a change. As a result, their hypothesizing as well as questioning behaviors are likely to improve. Obviously, this is a method that can be easily modified. ReQuest may proceed on a peer basis student-to-student. It may also be adapted for paired studying in preparation for tests of content area material.

ReQuest's chief strength is also its major limitation. It is intended for use with individuals and small groups, leaving other students who may be present to work independently.

EXAMPLE

A fourth-grade reading teacher notices that every day during free reading period Debbie sits staring out the window. Knowing Debbie's interests and reading ability, the teacher has picked out a story that Debbie would probably like–if she will read it.

The teacher sits down beside Debbie.

Teacher: I've been thinking about you, Debbie, and the things you've told me you like. I know you like animals, especially furry baby animals.

Debbie: Yes, I do. I'd really love to have a kitten or a puppy.

Teacher: I know. I don't have a kitten or puppy to give you, but I do have a story I'd like to share with you. It's about a kitten.

Debbie: Oh?

Teacher: And a little girl like you.

Debbie: Oh?

Teacher: The story's title is "The Little Black Kitten."

Debbie: I like the title, but you know how stories are–not always what their title cracks them up to be.

Teacher: I'd love to read it *with* you. I know how we could make a game of the *way* we read it.

Debbie: Sounds like it might be fun.

Teacher: It is. Look, let's read just this much of the story (pointing to the end of the second paragraph). Then we'll ask each other questions about what we've read. You ask me questions first, and then I'll ask you questions, OK?

Debbie: OK.

The teacher and Debbie silently read.

Teacher: Debbie?

Debbie: What's the little girl's name?

Teacher: Vanessa.

Debbie: What's she doing?

Teacher: She's taking a morning walk with her parents.

Debbie: Where are they going?

Teacher: I'm not sure they are going anywhere in particular. The story says they are heading to the lake at the end of the street.

Debbie: OK. I don't have any more questions. It's your turn.

Teacher: What time of year do you guess it is?

Debbie: The story doesn't say.

Teacher: Well, what would you guess?

Debbie: It's probably spring, but it could be summer or early fall. The weather's nice enough that they can be outside early in the morning.

Teacher: That's a good answer. Does Vanessa have a brother or sister?

Debbie: The story doesn't say she does, not yet anyway.

Teacher: Whose kitten do you think it is?

Debbie: It probably belongs to the Martins.

Teacher: Why do you say that?

Debbie: Because they'd just walked past the Martins' house when the kitten came along.

Teacher: Now let's read on. Let's read down to here (pointing to the end of the third paragraph). Then we'll ask each other some more questions.

They read silently.

Debbie: It *was* the Martins' kitten.

Teacher: Where does the story say that?

Debbie: Right here: "Mom said, 'Vanessa, the kitten belongs to the Martins.'"

Teacher: That's what she says. And it makes sense. They noticed the kitten as they were passing the Martins'.

Debbie: Now I get to ask questions. Who said that the kitten will have to be left off at the Martins'?

Teacher: Vanessa's mother.

Debbie: What did the kitten do when Vanessa tried to leave it?

Teacher: It wouldn't stay. It kept on following them.

Debbie: Why did they let the kitten follow them?

Teacher: The Martins weren't home and Vanessa and the kitten were having fun playing together. Besides, there didn't seem to be any choice. The kitten was going to follow them anyway.

Debbie: Those are my questions. It's your turn.

Teacher: Those were good questions. That last question was really a good one. Let me see if I can come up with such good questions. Why was Vanessa not keeping up with her parents?

Debbie: Her mind was on the little black kitten. She'd rather play with it than walk with her parents.

Teacher: Why did the kitten keep following them?

Debbie: Because it liked Vanessa. She played with it. The kitten knew that Vanessa liked it, too.

Teacher: The story does seem to say that, in so many words. Now let's think about what's *going* to happen in this story. How would you guess that it will turn out?

Debbie: The Martins will come home and see how much Vanessa and the kitten love each other. They'll say they've already got a cat, so Vanessa can keep the kitten.

Teacher: That's a pretty good guess. Things could very well turn out that way. Let's go ahead, now, and read the rest of the story to see how close your guess is.

The Little Black Kitten

Early one morning Vanessa was taking a walk with her Mom and Dad. They were strolling to the lake at the end of the street. They had just passed the Martins' house when Vanessa stopped to visit a kitten that had scampered up behind her. It was furry and black. "Come along, Vanessa," her Dad called to her. But she liked the kitten and wanted to talk to it and pet it.

Vanessa picked up the kitten. Clutching it in her arms, she ran after her parents. When they came to the lake, Mom and Dad sat down on one of the benches there and gazed at the shimmering water. Vanessa played with the kitten.

On the way home, Vanessa and the little black kitten walked behind Mom and Dad. Mom said, "Vanessa, the kitten belongs to the Martins. When we walk by their house you will have to leave the kitten there." At the Martins' house, Vanessa tried to make the kitten stay. But the kitten insisted on following. Vanessa knocked at the door. The Martin family was not at home, so there was no choice but to let the kitten follow along. At home, Vanessa played with the little black kitten for hours. She wanted to take the kitten inside. But Mom said, "No. When the Martins come home they will look for the kitten." When Vanessa went in for lunch, Mom said, "Maybe the kitten will go home now."

Later, there came a knock at the door. Standing at the door was Mrs. Reeves, the neighbor from across the street. She said, "You need to take better care of your kitten. It might run out into the street. And it looks hungry." Mom explained to Mrs. Reeves, "The kitten followed us home this morning. It belongs to the Martins."

Mrs. Reeves said, "The kitten is in your care. You have a responsibility to take care of it." The kitten came up onto the porch and began to purr at Mrs. Reeves' ankles. Paying the kitten no mind, Mrs. Reeves turned and walked back across the street.

Mom and Vanessa took a saucer of milk to the little black kitten. "It does look hungry," Mom said. After the kitten lapped up the milk, both Mom and Vanessa played with the kitten.

When the Martins' station wagon passed by and pulled into their driveway down the street, Vanessa knew the time had come for her to return the little black kitten. Mom saw the tears in Vanessa's eyes. "Come on," she said, "I'll walk over to the Martins' with you."

"Here, Mrs. Martin. Your little black kitten followed us home this morning. We've had such fun today."

"That's not our kitten," Mrs. Martin said. "But I have no doubt about whose it is, or was." On our way out of town this morning we stopped by the market. There, in a box, were four furry little kittens exactly like this one. Mrs. Reeves was trying to give them away."

Vanessa looked up at her Mom with eyes that begged, "Please, let's keep the little black kitten."

Mom said, "The kitten is in your care. You have a responsibility to take care of it."

Source

Anthony V. Manzo. (1969). The ReQuest procedure. *Journal of Reading, 13,* 123–126.

Related Reading

Joseph L. Vaughan and Thomas H. Estes. (1986). *Reading and reasoning beyond the primary grades* (pp. 148–149). Boston: Allyn and Bacon.

4

Reciprocal Teaching

Reciprocal Teaching is a strategy for fostering students' skill at monitoring their comprehension of texts. Students develop competence in the areas of making predictions, asking questions, summarizing texts, and clarifying difficult or novel concepts.

As the strategy name suggests, the teacher and students take turns leading the instructional activity. Having observed the teacher overtly model teacher behaviors that simulate effective study behaviors, students assume an instructional role that similarly exhibits these behaviors. It is acting as teacher that students develop effective comprehension monitoring skills. As students make the kinds of predictions a teacher would make, they activate relevant background knowledge and make hypotheses that become purposes for reading.

Generating teacher-like questions increases students' engagement with a text and has them actively seek information that makes for a good question. Summarizing a text like a teacher leads students to identify its most important information. This also serves to integrate the text's information. Attempting to clarify the content of a difficult text increases students' awareness of impediments to comprehension. Reciprocal Teaching may be employed with individuals or with groups whose size allows active interaction among all participants. It is a strategy appropriate for students of all ages and in all academic subject areas.

Procedure

At the outset of instruction, the teacher explains that the purpose of the activities to follow is to enhance comprehension monitoring ability. The teacher describes how the students will take turns leading the instruction. Students are told that text activities will stress making predictions, asking questions, summarizing, and clarifying texts. In the early phase of Reciprocal Teaching, the teacher models these behaviors and encourages students to comment on each. During this early phase, students are routinely called on to make predictions, ask questions, summarize, and clarify the material being read. As students gain experience engaging in these behaviors, responsibility is transferred to them for initiating and sustaining the classroom interaction.

Gradually they move into the role of teacher. Playing the teacher's part, students monitor other students' success in understanding the material. The teacher's role becomes one of resource and back-up person. When students are unable to make predictions or ask questions, the teacher mentions clues provided in the text and lets students pick up the discussion from there.

Discussion

Reciprocal Teaching is a long-term strategy that may span several weeks. The procedure is described here in truncated form in order to present the strategy's essential features. With this strategy, students are given time, instruction, and opportunity to become independent users of texts. As students learn to monitor their own comprehension, they are more likely to check with themselves about the main ideas, to remember more of what they read, and to identify incongruities in the material they study.

EXAMPLE

A high school mathematics class is reviewing concepts underlying elementary arithmetic.

Renee: You know this material so well. I've had this material before, but most of it I don't remember and some of it I never really understood.

Teacher: You flatter me, but I must admit that I know this material because I teach it. Teaching it gives me little choice but to know it. As I teach it, I get to know it even better.

Isaac: How does teaching math help you to understand it? Some of this stuff is pretty abstract.

Teacher: When I teach math to others, I do much the same thing that learners have to do. I probably do it with greater deliberation.

Alice: What do you mean that you, as a teacher, do much the same as learners do?

Teacher: Reflect for a moment on the class and what I routinely do with the material.

Karla: You present math so we can make sense of it.

Teacher: But when I present it, I do four things. These are essentially the same four things that efficient learners do: I predict what I think we'll find in the material; I ask questions before we read and as we go over the material; I summarize the material at junctures in the lesson at which we have covered a point or set of points; and I try to clarify anything that might be hazy.

Gottfried: So, as learners, we should be doing these four things—predicting, questioning, summarizing, and clarifying?

Teacher: Yes, and also as mathematicians, should you decide to take up this line of work as your occupation.

Blaise:　What do you mean?

Teacher:　Teachers, learners, mathematicians all do these four things: They forecast, hypothesize, estimate; they inquire with specific questions in mind; they reflect and take stock of what they know about the matters they're dealing with; and they strive to remove undesirable ambiguity and static.

Archie:　How can we take the role of teacher? As the teacher, you control the situation and have the attitude that your superior knowledge of the subject gives you the authority to remain in control.

Teacher:　Yes, I suppose I do. But I would like to transfer that control and that attitude to you as much as possible. You can begin to acquire the kind of authority you mention by paying deliberate attention to my performance as predictor, questioner, summarizer, and clarifier. I invite you to critique my teacher behaviors in these areas.

The teacher goes on to say that, in the future, students themselves will be encouraged to practice the four teaching/studying behaviors. Eventually, students will be given opportunities to lead the classroom interaction. The class now turns attention to the topic of the *multiplicative inverse*. The teacher models the four teacher behaviors, encouraging students to critique his use of them and to engage in these behaviors themselves.

Teacher:　Now we open our text to the topic of the multiplicative inverse. Given that we've been studying common fractions, I expect that this will have to do with denominators and numerators, and more specifically, that it will have to do with inverting denominators and numerators. Please tell us, Renee, what you expect this to be about.

Renee:　It will involve multiplication.

Teacher:　Blaise?

Blaise:　It will say something about division, which is the inverse of multiplication.

Teacher:　I like that. You see in these somewhat technical words clues to a concept that is familiar to you. Isaac, what do you think this is about?

Isaac:　It will explain why the denominator and the numerator are inversely related.

Teacher:　Karla?

Karla:　It will explain what reciprocals are.

Isaac:　That's what I said.

Archie:　What are reciprocals?

Teacher:　Good question. I'm wondering if a multiplicative inverse is the same thing as a reciprocal. I'm also wondering why this is important to know. Alice, what questions do you have?

Alice:　I'd ask this: If it is possible to invert numerator and denominator, does the numerator become a denominator and does the denominator become a numerator? Or does the inverting amount to nothing more than a computational maneuver?

Teacher:　Gottfried?

Gottfried: Is this a principle that explains why the quotient of a fraction divided by another fraction remains the same when the numerator of one fraction and the denominator exchange places?

Archie: Huh? What are you talking about?

Teacher: Here's an example of what Gottfried is talking about:

$$2/3 \div 1/6 = 4$$
$$6/3 \div 1/2 = 4$$

Even though the 2 and 6 trade places, the quotient remains 4. And the quotient would remain 4 if the 1 and the 3 traded places.

Archie: Why?

Teacher: Good question. Let's read the text to find out if multiplicative inverse has anything to do with this and whether it can answer our questions.

Students silently read "Multiplicative Inverse."

Teacher: The text does deal with the things we predicted. And it does address the questions we raised. To summarize generally, the text defines multiplicative inverse, gives examples, and explains its application in computational procedures. Blaise, please summarize for us, more specifically, the text's definition of multiplicative inverse and its examples.

Blaise: Well, a multiplicative inverse is the same thing as a reciprocal, as Karla predicted it might be. Two numbers are called multiplicative inverses, or reciprocals, of each other if multiplying them times each other results in *one* as the product. Zero does not have an inverse, or reciprocal, number for multiplication, so it can't be a reciprocal itself. The text gave the example: $4/3 \times 3/4$ are reciprocals because their product is *one*.

Teacher: Renee, summarize for us the text's comment on division as the inverse of multiplication.

Renee: You can divide one number by a second number by multiplying the first number by the reciprocal of the second number. . . .

As the discussion proceeds, students complete summarizing the text. Predictions made prior to reading are recalled and questions posed at that time are addressed. This produces further questions, which are discussed. The teacher clarifies an area that remains murky for some students.

Teacher: All right, then, if you have no further questions, I'd like to return to one aspect of the lesson that we need to be clear about. It has to do with the use of reciprocals in division.

Renee: That's no problem. To divide a number by another number, we can multiply one of the numbers by its reciprocal.

Teacher: It is the *dividend* that is multiplied by the reciprocal of the *divisor*. Notice in this example how the reciprocal, or multiplicative inverse, and the multiplicative identity 1 are used to develop this principle:

$$2/3 \div 3/4 = \left.{}^{2/3}\middle/{}_{3/4}\right. = \frac{2/3}{3/4} \times 1 = \frac{2/3 \times 4/3}{3/4 \times 4/3} = \frac{2/3 \times 4/3}{1} = 2/3 \times 4/3 = 8/9$$

We multiply both the numerator and denominator by 4/3, which is the reciprocal of the denominator 3/4. This yields 1 as a denominator. . . . Students now critique the teacher's performance as director of the lesson. They comment on the teacher's predicting, questioning, summarizing, and clarifying behaviors. They also comment on other aspects of teaching.

Gottfried: One thing I noticed was that you always took the lead in initiating each of the four behaviors you want us to develop.

Alice: That was good because it prompted us to come up with similar predictions and questions.

Karla: But on the negative side, you preempted my asking a question I had.

Blaise: Maybe that's not all bad, Karla. You had a question worth asking, only someone else asked it first.

Karla: You have a point. I think we all would have asked why this concept is important to know.

Isaac: One thing I didn't like is that you could have elaborated on a prediction I made, but you didn't.

Renee: You also praised some of us, but not others.

Teacher: Let's take these criticisms one area at a time. First, let's talk about my predictions and my soliciting your predictions. . . .

The class discusses the teacher's predicting, questioning, summarizing, and clarifying actions, each in turn. A few lessons later, the teacher has begun to have students lead the class. The teacher stands by as a back-up and resource person.

Karla: Today's lesson is about opposites, negatives, and additive inverses. Whether this is analogous to reciprocals and multiplicative inverses we'll have to see. Gottfried, tell us what you think this is about.

Gottfried: I have no idea.

A long pause follows. Karla looks to the teacher.

Teacher: Gottfried, there's a number line in the text. You might take a clue from the number line to make a prediction.

Gottfried: Numbers on one side of zero have opposite numbers on the other side of zero.

Karla: Good. Alice, you must have some idea what this is about.

Alice: Well, I'd guess. . . .

Karla continues to lead the class. She initiates each aspect of the lesson. She makes predictions, asks questions, and so on, and then calls on other students to do the same. The teacher steps in only occasionally to keep the lesson on track and moving. Students take turns leading the lessons that follow.

Multiplicative Inverse

If the product of two numbers is one (1), then each factor is called the multiplicative inverse or reciprocal of the other. Zero has no inverse for multiplication.

6 and 1/6 are multiplicative inverses of each other because 6 × 1/6 = 1.

4/3 and 3/4 are multiplicative inverses of each other because 4/3 × 3/4 = 1.

Observe that when two numbers are multiplicative inverses of each other, the numerator of one fraction is the denominator of its reciprocal, and the denominator is the numerator of its reciprocal.

Division is the inverse operation of multiplication. When we divide 12 by 4, the quotient is 3. When we multiply 12 by 1/4, the product is 3. Dividing 12 by 4 gives the same answer as multiplying 12 by the reciprocal of 4 (which is 1/4). Thus to divide a number by another number, we may instead multiply the first number by the reciprocal of the second number (divisor).

Source: Edwin I. Stein. (1965). *Refresher mathematics with practical applications.* Boston: Allyn and Bacon.

Source

Annemarie Sullivan Palincsar and Ann L. Brown. (1986). Interactive teaching to promote independent learning from text. *The Reading Teacher, 29,* 771–777.

5

Guided Reading Procedure

The Guided Reading Procedure, or GRP, shows students how to deal with the explicit content of a reading selection. Specifically, it helps students recall the information given in a selection, formulate questions about it, correct misinterpretations, and organize their recollections of the material.

The premise of GRP is that acquiring information and comprehending the information accurately must precede higher-order comprehension and discussion. This is better achieved through students' own concentration than through response to questions posed by the teacher. With the GRP, expectancies are brought into sharp focus through students' efforts to reach agreement about the information they remember. Essential to these efforts are self-correction and the formulation of questions about the information recalled. As students attempt to organize the information they have recalled, they reflect on the ways the information may be tied together.

GRP is particularly useful in content areas that require careful reading and detailed recollection of factual information. The method is well suited to small-group instruction as well as to teaching entire classes (20 to 30 students). It may be used with students in the intermediate grade levels through college level. The length of the text varies with the maturity and reading proficiency of students (500 words for intermediate-grade students, 900 words for students in the upper-middle grades, 2,000 words for high school students, and 2,500 words for college students).

Procedure

Having introduced the subject matter, the teacher assigns students to read a selection for the purpose of remembering as much of its content as they can. The length of the selection varies from 500 words for intermediate-grade students to 2,500 words for college students. Once students have completed the reading, the teacher has them turn their texts face down and volunteer any information they can remember of the selection. The teacher records on the chalkboard (or overhead) all responses exactly as they are given. Initially, students may offer few recollections, but the responses will likely increase after a few minutes of reflecting on, associating with, and correcting one another's recollections.

Whenever there is a lull in the response, the teacher patiently waits while students think about the information already recalled. When it becomes apparent that students have given as much information as they can for one reading, the teacher asks students to read the selection again for purposes of correcting errors in their initial recollection and adding any significant information that may have been left out.

Following this rereading, the teacher calls on students to complete and correct their recollection of the selection. During this phase of the activity, the teacher may have students refer to the selection in order to resolve differences that might exist among individuals' recollections.

The teacher then leads students to organize the recorded information into an outline, sequence pattern, or concept map. To facilitate this process, the teacher asks nonspecific, guiding questions such as, "What is this selection mainly about?" "How does the information support this purpose?" During the discussion, the teacher solicits students' advice about which of the remembered information can serve as main headings or central notes, which would best serve as supporting details, and so on. Taking directions from students, the teacher develops an organized display of the recalled information on the chalkboard or overhead.

With the information pulled together in structured form, the teacher has students synthesize it and connect it with information they have previously learned. The teacher may wish to have students deepen their understanding of the material through further reading, writing assignments, or additional discussion. During a subsequent class meeting, the teacher may administer a test to check students' memory of the material.

Discussion

Even students who can remember little from an initial reading can benefit from the GRP. It is a method that provides an interesting approach to reviewing and rereading material not grasped in a first reading. If students' recall is poor due to lack of motivation, the game-like qualities of GRP may well increase motivation and thereby improve performance. With repeated use, the GRP may increase students' powers of concentration. It also may serve well those students who need instruction in organizing information. Not only does the teacher model techniques for organizing information, but students who are good organizers reveal to others their thinking processes during the organization phase of the lesson.

Although GRP is useful for fostering memory and organization skills, it is by itself inadequate for developing higher-level reasoning skills. And although its emphasis is on remembering and ordering factual information, its application should be distributed over several lessons in order to solidify students' acquisition of the subject matter.

EXAMPLE

A ninth-grade world geography class is learning about the cities of the United Kingdom. London is their current focus. The teacher has pointed it out on the classroom map and has given several reasons for knowing about London.

Teacher: Now that we know where London is and why it's one of the world's great cities, let's get better acquainted with it. I'd like you to read the textbook section entitled "Greater London." As you read, try to glean as much information as you can. When you've finished reading, I'll call on you to recite as many details as you can without looking back.

Meg: You mean we're suposed to read this and regurgitate it back to you?

Teacher: Read it and recite as much as possible. Our understanding of London or any place or, for that matter, practically anything is based on factual knowledge. So let's read. When you've finished reading, look up.

The class reads silently. When it appears they have completed reading the textbook section, the teacher moves to the end of the chalkboard and prepares to record students' recollections. Space will be needed for recording recollections from this reading and a subsequent reading, and for organizing the recollections into an outline afterwards.

Teacher: All right, turn your books face down on your desks. Now tell me everything you can remember of what you've just read.

Roseanne: There are flower boxes all over London.

Teacher: (recording "flower boxes" at the upper-left corner of the chalkboard) Good. Tell me as much as you can about London without looking back.

Mike: It's 37 miles south of the River Thames.

Teacher: You pronounce it "tims." Tell me more.

Amy: It's one mile wide.

Becky: The weather's cold and damp.

Beth: It's foggy.

Jack: Londoners like to build fires.

Alan: The fires cause pollution.

Carlos: The true Londoners are the Cockneys.

As the class recalls the information from the textbook, the teacher has to write fast to jot down all their remembrances. When students have exhausted their memory of the text, the teacher has them read it again.

Teacher: All right, now read the same section of your text again to see if there's any important information you did not remember, or you remembered incorrectly from your first reading.

Again, students read the text silently.

Teacher: Tell me, what did you read this time that you missed or misunderstood the first time you read?

Diane: Well, London is not 37 miles south of the River Thames. It's located 37 miles from the mouth of the River Thames.

Teacher: Excellent. What else?

Jim: It's the largest capital city in the world.

Meg: *Greater London,* he means. London is actually only one of the two cities and 28 boroughs that together make Greater London.

Amy: Combined, they're 722 square miles.

Ted: London itself is only one square mile. That's one mile *square,* not one mile wide.

Chris: A Londoner, a Greater Londoner really, knows all about his own borough— all its stories and songs and stuff.

Roseanne: It has more flowers than any other capital in the world.

John: It rains a lot.

Beth: So most people carry umbrellas there.

Roseanne: They love flowers. They like to make flower beds.

Dave: The temperature averages 38 degrees in the winter.

Jack: And 68 degrees in the summer.

Alan: Because of their love for fires, pollution has developed. Now there are strict antipollution laws.

John: It said they love the countryside.

Roseanne: The climate is ideal for growing flowers.

The class completes its recall of the text section on Greater London and this list of details has been recorded on the chalkboard:

flower boxes

37 miles from the mouth of River Thames

London 1 square mile wide

weather cold and damp

fog

Londoners like to build fires

pollution – strict laws

Cockneys are true Londoners

largest capital in the world

2 cities and 28 boroughs = Greater London

Greater London = 722 square miles

Londoners know own borough well

most flowers of any capital

rains frequently

most people carry umbrellas

38 degrees winter temperature

68 degrees summer temperature

climate ideal for flowers

Teacher: Good. You remembered quite a lot about Greater London. Now let's try to sort out what you remembered. What are all these details about?

Phil: About London and Greater London.

Meg: They give a description of London. Together they say London is an interesting place.

Teacher: OK. They're details about London, Greater London, and they describe an interesting place. In what ways is Greater London *interesting?*

Roseanne: It has flowers all over the place.

Teacher: Yes, that's an interesting detail and we'll want to remember that. I was wondering, though, how we might think of Greater London's interesting facts in three or four *general* ways. By general, I mean what the details add up to, like category headings under which the details could fit.

Becky: Seems to be there's quite a bit of information about the climate – I think enough to make a category heading.

Several: Right. There's information about fog and temperature and rain.

Teacher: OK. Good. That's what I mean by the *general* ways that Greater London is interesting.

Carlos: The people. The text has interesting things to say about the people of London, uh, Greater London.

Several: Yeah. The people. London has interesting people.

Teacher: Good. We have two *general* areas in which we may describe Greater London as interesting. Let's have one more general area.

Mike: How about the facts about the city. Its location, size, and stuff like that.

Teacher: (writing these headings horizontally across the right side of the chalkboard) I like your suggestion. It seems to cover the rest of the details we remembered. Let's try to group the details listed on the left side of the board under the appropriate heading.

The discussion continues and produces this display of the information on Greater London:

City	**Climate**	**People**
37 mi. up the R. Thames	av. summer temp. = 68°	flower lovers
London–1 sq. mi.	av. winter temp. = 38°	true Londoners–Cockneys
pollution laws	foggy	like to build fires
722 sq. mi.	rains frequently	carry umbrellas
world's largest capital	ideal for flowers	love countryside
capital w/most flowers	cold & damp	know boroughs well
28 boroughs & 2 cities		

Then, through discussion about subordinating the information, the class turns these groups of information into this outline:

Greater London
    37 mi. up the River Thames
    World's largest capital
        722 sq. mi.
        28 boroughs and 2 cities
        London 1 sq. mi.
    Capital with most flowers

Climate–cool and damp
    ideal for flowers
    rains frequently
    av. summer temp. = 68°
    av. winter temp. = 38°
    foggy

The People
    know their own boroughs well
    like flowers, fires, countryside
    carry umbrellas

Greater London

London is the capital of England. The city is located on the Thames River, 37 miles from the river's mouth. The city of London itself is only about one square mile in area. It is just one part of Greater London, which also includes Westminster and 28 boroughs. Covering an area of 722 square miles, Greater London is one of the largest cities in the world. Greater London's boroughs began as small villages, but over time they grew and eventually merged to form one large urban area. Citizens of Greater London are proud of their own borough. They know their own borough's folklore well and love to share its songs and stories. The people who live within the one square mile area of the city of London are called *Cockneys*. Among the people who reside in Greater London, only the Cockneys are considered city dwellers.

The climate of Greater London is damp and chilly. Temperature in the summer averages only 68°F, which is ideal for growing flowers. In the winter it averages a nippy 38°F. Understandably, Londoners are fond of open fires. Smoke from these fires combines with mist from nearby water to produce the famous London fog, which often becomes so thick that a person can see no more than an arm's length ahead. Enforcement of strict antipollution laws is reducing the fog problem, however. Because the weather may change suddenly from sunshine to rain, Londoners carry an umbrella everywhere they go.

Most of Greater London's people think of themselves as country people and, except for the Cockneys, do not consider themselves city dwellers. Londoners love nature and love the countryside. And they love to have gardens. If they lack space for a garden, they grow what they can in their backyard. People who have no yard cultivate flowers in flower boxes. Well known for its flowers, London is reputed to have more flowers than any other capital in the world.

Source

Anthony V. Manzo. (1975). Guided reading procedure. *Journal of Reading, 18,* 287–291.

6

Directed Inquiry Activity

The Directed Inquiry Activity helps students deal with a text that presents a multitude of facts. The activity develops students' ability to sort, categorize, and recover details.

The premise is twofold. First, the Directed Inquiry Activity gives students a purpose for reading. Students understand why they are reading and the goals they are trying to achieve. Second, it orients students to anticipate specific kinds of information in the upcoming reading. Because students become acquainted with the text before reading it closely, they attend to the text's important information and achieve a better understanding when close reading does take place.

The Directed Inquiry Activity may be used in many situations. It is adaptable to a variety of content areas, but it is especially well suited for texts and lessons in social studies. There is a need at all grade levels for students to assimilate facts. For this reason, the Directed Inquiry Activity would be useful at any grade level. The activity may be used with large groups of students. If groups are large, special attention should be made to include all the students present.

Procedure

The Directed Inquiry Activity begins by having the students skim a portion of the material about to be read. The students become familiar with the text by looking at titles and illustrations. In longer texts, the material may be surveyed by chapters and subheadings. The teacher directs students to the important information of the text by having them predict the text content according to six points of inquiry: Who? What? Where? When? Why? and How? At the chalkboard, the teacher records the predictions under headings for these points of inquiry.

During this time the teacher takes an active role in providing feedback to the students' predictions, encouraging students to trace connections among the predictions. It is through this feedback that the teacher encourages predictions about information students are to learn. After the predictions have been made and discussed, the students read the text to see if they can confirm hypothesized ideas and information. If the predictions cannot be verified, the students make corrections and add pertinent information from the text. In the discussion that follows, the material is analyzed and discussed in terms of the six points of inquiry.

Discussion

The Directed Inquiry Activity is an attractive method in several respects. It does not take a great deal of time to plan, if the teacher knows the material. It can be employed with moderately large groups of students and is suitable for virtually any content area. Its most attractive feature is that it encourages students to gather facts and come to basic understandings necessary for critical and creative thinking to take place.

As attractive as the Directed Inquiry Activity is, it has its limitations. Skillful questioning and responding to students' predictions depends heavily on the teacher's familiarity with the material. Unless the teacher has clear expectations for the students, the effectiveness of the activity is left to chance. Another limitation is that the method does not provide for teaching vocabulary. Although vocabulary could be taught while predictions are being made, there is no assurance that words warranting consideration will emerge naturally in the give and take. Nor can the teacher be assured that attention to vocabulary will not significantly distract students from the six points of inquiry.

EXAMPLE

The class is studying the Civil War. The teacher's objective is to have students learn the facts about the New York City draft riots and understand why the riots took place. The teacher begins the lesson by telling the students to skim the headings of the textbook section to be covered and to make predictions about the information that the text will offer for each of six questions that have been written across the top of the chalkboard:

Teacher: Looking at the title, what would you say this section is about?

Several: Draft riots in New York City.

Teacher: (turning to write under the *What?* column) Yes, it *is* about draft riots, and let me note here under *Where?* that they took place in New York City. When, might you think, did the riots take place?

Janice: Some time around the Civil War.

Teacher: Yes, but more exactly when? During the Civil War? Before? After?

Janice: I don't know. Maybe near the end of the war when most of the volunteers had been killed off.

Bob: Probably they happened after the people saw that a whole lot of draftees were getting killed, that it was *mostly* draftees who got killed.

Jetur: I think it was before the war. They did not want to have a war, so they started a riot.

The teacher records these possibilities under the *When?* column. Recognizing that students are already speculating about why the riots occurred, the teacher also records appropriate information under the *Why?* column. The teacher encourages students to continue connecting information across points of inquiry.

Teacher: These are plausible reasons for placing the New York City riots at these points in time. Let's also think about the particular people involved and why those people. Who were involved in these riots?

Johnny: Men who didn't want to get drafted.

Susie: Maybe they involved other people, too – people who just didn't like the idea of forcing anyone to join the army and kill people.

Teacher: Such as?

Susie: Well, mothers who didn't want to see their sons taken into the army.

Mary: And religious leaders who thought it wrong to force people to do violence to others.

Billy: Hey, but even businessmen, too. They would not have wanted to lose their workers to the army.

Erasmus: Look. It says right here, "A rich man's war, a poor man's fight." It must have happened that only the poor were getting drafted and they didn't like it.

The teacher records these possibilities under the *Who?* and *Why?* headings.

Teacher: Let's read to find out which, if any, of your guesses are right.

When it is apparent that students have finished, the teacher initiates a review of students' predictions.

Teacher: Well, obviously you were correct that this *is* about riots that took place in New York City. You were correct that they were a reaction to the National Conscription Act. But what about this, Jetur? Did they take place as a protest of a coming war?

Jetur: I guess not. By July 1863 the war had been going on for some time.

Teacher: July 1863. That means they didn't take place near the end of the war. Right, Janice?

Janice: Right, but they must've needed soldiers other than just volunteers.

Teacher: Good inference, Janice. But what was it about the way the National Conscription Act added to the volunteers that provoked rioting in New York City?

Erasmus: It's like I said the text would say. The poor thought it was a bum deal to have to fight for the rich.

Teacher: Where does the text say the National Conscription Act provided for drafting only the poor?

Erasmus: It doesn't say it straight out. What it says is that a person could pay $300 to get out of being drafted. The rich could afford it but the poor couldn't. This favored the rich, and the poor resented it.

Teacher: You're right. The poor were upset, and they got really upset once names were drawn from a wooden box to decide who would go to war. Which groups among the poor got really upset?

As the discussion continues, the teacher places a line through predicted information that the text does not support. Under appropriate headings, the teacher makes additions and corrections.

The New York City Draft Riots

Major riots in the history of the United States were the New York City draft riots of July 13–16, 1863. These riots were in reaction to the Civil War, which was considered "a rich man's war, a poor man's fight."

The National Conscription Act
On March 3, 1863, the United States Congress passed the National Conscription Act. This legislation sought to create a citizen army without the aid of state authorities. It was legislation that fixed the principle that every able-bodied male had an obligation to perform military service. Men between the ages of 20 and 45 were enrolled, and if their names were drawn they would serve for three years.

The National Conscription Act contained provision that anyone whose name was drawn from the box could pay $300 to the local draft board for a substitute or furnish his own replacement. This favored the rich because a laborer only made $20 a week.

Conscription in New York City
In New York City, under supervision of a provost marshall and a civilian draft board and doctor, names were written on slips of paper. The names were then placed in a revolving wooden box, from which the names would be drawn by a civilian. After the names had been drawn, opponents of the Act set into motion the longest, most widespread, and most destructive riot in American history.

A Rich Man's War, A Poor Man's Fight
The most strenuous opposition to the National Conscription Act was exerted by the poor of New York City. Particularly the Irish and foreign born were against the Act. The poor voiced their disapproval with the cry, "A rich man's war, a poor man's fight!"

Source

Keith G. Thomas. (1978). Directed inquiry activity. *Reading Improvement, 15,* 138–140.

7

Metacognitive Modeling

Metacognitive Modeling presents subject matter in a way that models for students a structured approach to learning the subject on their own. The teacher shows students how they can monitor their progress in learning novel subject matter. Through this monitoring, students see how they use and add new information to what they already know, and they identify what they yet need to learn about the material being studied.

Metacognitive Modeling teaches students to confront themselves constantly with the question: How do you know what you know, and how did you come to know it? It is a question that has students probe their own ways of knowing and examine the outcomes of those ways of knowing. It is a question that engages students in *metacognition* (i.e., thinking about thinking itself). Students are put in the position of having to explain why they understand or misunderstand. They must be aware of their purposes for studying and be able to say how they have gone about achieving those purposes. The teacher, through modeling the self-monitoring process, demonstrates to students how to articulate one's own thinking and learning processes. These processes include questioning, predicting, analyzing, clarifying, deducing, inducing, summarizing, and so on. Given a structure and opportunities to apply procedures of self-monitoring, students develop a routine for addressing the central metacognitive question: How do you know what you know?

Metacognitive Modeling is best suited to science and social studies classes at the upper-elementary, middle grades, and beyond. It works well in situations where previous instruction has established a base of knowledge upon which to build further understanding and knowledge. The method is intended to be used with textual presentations of subject matter. The textual presentations should be limited to two or three pages, and modeling comprehension of passages should be kept brief. Passages that have clear structural development, such as problem solution, comparison, time sequence, description by attributes, and the like, are best for modeling.

Initially, the procedure is used in whole-class instruction. As students become proficient with the procedure, modeling by the teacher gives way to modeling by students in small groups. Student modeling, in turn, gives way to independent individual activity. The procedure should be practiced frequently. Using the procedure once a week should pose no problems as long as the activity does not excessively consume time that can be profitably used in other ways for covering subject matter.

Procedure

Metacognitive Modeling begins with the teacher issuing students a worksheet to be completed during the lesson. Called a "What I Know Worksheet," it has sections for students to complete with information about the topic, purpose for reading/studying, and three aspects of their knowledge—what was previously known, what is currently known as a result of studying, and what still has to be learned. The worksheet looks like this:

What I Know Worksheet

Topic _____

_____

Purpose _____

_____

What I Already Know	*What I Now Know*	*What I Don't Know*

Answer to purpose question:

Before assigning any reading, the teacher has students write down the topic and previews the material with them. During the preview, the teacher attempts to summon students' knowledge of the topic. The teacher may ask questions about any illustrations or graphic aids in the material, elicit predictions about it, or otherwise discuss the topic with students. The teacher sets a thoughtful purpose for reading, one beyond simply having students search for an explicitly stated answer to a question.

In the space provided on the worksheet, students write down the purpose, and then in the *What I Already Know* column, they write down as much as they can remember about any knowledge they may already have about the topic. The teacher tells students that during reading they will encounter both old and new information. As they encounter old information not previously remembered and noted, students are to jot it down in the *What I Already Know* column. New information they think they understand should be recorded in the *What I Now Know* column. They are to write down any confusing information or gaps they sense in their knowledge in the *What I Don't Know* column. Students are told that they will check their worksheet against the teacher's, which will be shown with the overhead projector after reading.

After students have read the material and filled in as much of the worksheet as they can, the teacher asks students to write down an answer to the purpose question. Displaying a completed "What I Know Worksheet" with the overhead projector, the teacher describes the thinking processes used to complete it. The teacher describes the strategy used for constructing an answer to the purpose question, and points out difficulties that make it necessary either to reread or to ignore something temporarily.

As the teacher talks, students compare their "What I Know Worksheets" with the teacher's. The teacher's demonstration includes attention to a number of key points: awareness of what is to be learned, use of existing knowledge about the subject, recognition of text structure, consciousness of what is understood as well as what is not understood, and the use of writing to help organize and remember thoughts.

The teacher's demonstration is followed with small discussion groups in which students take turns describing what they did in order to accomplish the purpose for reading. The teacher circulates among the groups. The teacher then directs students to write a paragraph describing how their understanding of what they knew and did not know contributed to their learning the material. The activity ends with students sharing their paragraphs with classmates.

Discussion

The primary goal of Metacognitive Modeling is to increase students' awareness of how they can understand and misunderstand a particular concept. Several different angles are taken to achieve this goal. Students identify a specific purpose for reading. Teacher modeling contributes to students' awareness of their own comprehension processes. Students bring into play their knowledge held prior to the activity. They preview, predict, and question before reading. During reading, they analyze the material and connect it to related knowledge. Students reflect on the material and on their strategies for learning it during small-group discussions and as they write paragraphs.

The teacher has to be certain that the lesson's major information does not crowd out attention to relatively minor, yet significant, information. The time demanded by the method opens the possibility of this problem. Also, the teacher has to assure that each student participates actively. Some students may be tempted merely to copy what the teacher and other students have written on their worksheets. And, as in any small group situation, there is the risk that only the stronger students will carry the bulk of the task.

EXAMPLE

A sixth-grade science class has begun a unit on work and force. The teacher wants students to be clear about the difference between kinetic energy and potential energy and to be able to apply what they learn in this lesson to the remainder of the unit. The lesson begins with the teacher providing every student with a "What I Know Worksheet." Suddenly the teacher drops a textbook to the floor.

Teacher: When I dropped the book, did I work?

Mike: You did when you moved it.

Teacher: Did the book work when I let go of it?

Sally: No. It just fell.

Josh: A book can't do work.

Teacher: What if there had been a water balloon on the floor and I dropped the book on it?

Laura: It would've popped it.

Mark: It would've done work on the balloon.

Teacher: So a falling object *can* do work. Look at the title of this section of our textbook. What's it called?

Frieda: Potential and Kinetic Energy.

Teacher: Can everyone find that? Good. Now write the title of the section in the space on your worksheet that asks for the topic.

The teacher writes this title on a worksheet transparency on the overhead projector.

Teacher: What do you already know about kinetic and potential energy?

Matt: They are different.

Debbie: One involves movement, but I don't remember which one.

Teacher: What do you think this section of the text will have to say?

Ann: How to tell them apart.

Teacher: I bet you're right. But what kind of problem could we solve if we knew that? What if I asked whether two books falling would do more work than one book falling?

Mike: It will probably tell us why some objects have different energy than others.

Teacher: How could we say that in a question?

Josh: Why do some objects have more energy than others?

Teacher: That's great, Josh. On the worksheet, everyone write down the question in the space for purpose for reading.

The teacher writes the question on the worksheet transparency on the overhead projector.

Teacher: Now, to help you answer the question, write down everything you know about potential and kinetic energy in the column headed *What I Already Know*. The teacher turns off the overhead projector and also fills in the *What I Already Know* column.

Teacher: Now let's read the textbook section entitled "Potential and Kinetic Energy." As you read, if you come to things you knew but couldn't remember, go ahead and write them down in your worksheet's *What I Already Know* column. Whatever you come to understand as a result of reading, write down in the *What I Now Know* column. What you still need to find out, write down in the *What I Don't Know* column.

The class reads and works on the "What I Know Worksheet." The teacher also reads and fills out a worksheet, helping individual students who appear to be having difficulty.

Teacher: I see that all of you have finished reading and most of you are still working on your worksheet. Don't forget to write down your answer to the purpose question.

Debbie: It didn't say what the answer was.

Teacher: Not exactly, but it did give you enough information that you can figure it out. You just need to think about everything you wrote down in the first two columns—the *What I Already Know* and *What I Now Know* columns. Let me demonstrate by modeling for you my own metacognitive strategies for answering the question.

David: Your *what* strategies?

Teacher: My metacognitive strategies—what I was thinking as I was reading to figure out the answer. First, I was thinking about what I was supposed to learn—Why do some objects have more energy than others? So I wrote down everything I already knew about energy in the first column (it takes energy to do work, etc.). I thought about what kind of text this is. I knew it was expository because it is explaining information to me. Then, in the second column I wrote down everything it told me that I thought would help me answer the question (heavy objects have more potential energy, etc.). Next, I wrote down all the things I didn't understand in the third column (I reread the law of conservation of energy three times and I still don't quite know what it means). Then, I tried to answer the question. My answer may be different from yours, but I wrote that some objects have more energy than others because they have greater weight and speed.

Matt: That's what I got, too.

Teacher: Great! Now I want you to get into your work groups and take turns modeling what you were thinking as you worked through the activity.

The teacher floats during this time, walking around the room offering encouragement and support to students. The teacher closes the lesson by having each group explain the best strategy used in their group to answer the purpose question.

Teacher: T-birds, what was the best strategy used in your group?

Sally: Well, we decided that Josh's plan worked best. He only wrote down things that he thought he could use to answer the question and things that made him confused about answering the question.

Teacher: That's a good strategy. Do you see how knowing what you knew and understood helped you answer the question?

Frieda: Yes, it made it easier.

Teacher: In three or four sentences I want you to write how knowing what you knew and didn't know helped you to be a better reader. You can write on the back of your "What I Know Worksheets."

Potential and Kinetic Energy

You do work when you pour milk onto your cereal in the morning. Did you know that the milk jug can do work as well? It really can! Imagine that you have a milk jug suspended from a rope that is hanging on a pulley. On the other end of the rope you tie a one-pound weight. If you let go of the milk jug, what will happen? The weight will rise because the milk jug is working. While in your hand, the milk jug has stored energy that it can use to lift the weight once you let go of the jug.

Stored energy is called *potential energy.* Any object that can fall to a lower position has potential energy and the ability to do work. This energy is equal to the amount of work that the object can do when it falls. It takes about 2 newton-meters to lift the milk jug. The common milk jug therefore is capable of doing 2 newton-meters worth of work.

As an object loses height, it loses potential energy. Its potential energy is converted to kinetic energy. *Kinetic energy* is the energy of motion. All moving objects have kinetic energy. This means that all moving objects can do work. The kinetic energy that an object has depends on its mass and speed. An object with a large mass and speed has a greater kinetic energy than an object with less mass traveling at the same speed.

Energy can go back and forth from potential to kinetic energy and from kinetic to potential energy. When a ball is thrown upward, it has kinetic energy. At the moment it stops its climb and seems to stand still in the air, it has its greatest potential energy and its least kinetic energy. As it falls back to the ground, kinetic energy increases while potential energy decreases.

The form of energy of an object can change. The total amount of energy cannot. The *law of conservation of energy* is a natural law. It states that energy is not lost or made when it changes form. The total energy remains the same, no matter how often the energy changes form.

What I Know Worksheet

Topic <u>Potential and Kinetic Energy</u>

Purpose <u>Why do some objects have more energy than others?</u>

What I Already Know	*What I Now Know*	*What I Don't Know*
There is an energy of movement.	Potential energy is the stored energy of an object.	Law of conservation of energy.
It takes energy to do work.	Heavy objects have more potential energy.	Total energy does not change. Why not?
A falling book does work.	Kinetic energy is the energy of movement.	How the height of an object changes its energy level.
A book that is still has stored energy.	Two like objects with different masses have different kinetic energy when moving.	
	Two like objects with the same speed and mass can have the same energy.	

Answer to purpose question:

Some objects have more energy than others because they have greater weight and/or speed.

Sources

Mary F. Heller. (1986). How do you know what you know? Metacognitive modeling in the content areas. *Journal of Reading, 29,* 415–522.

Donna M. Ogle. (1986). K-W-L: A reading model that develops active reading of expository text. *The Reading Teacher, 39,* 564–570.

8

Analytical Reading: SQ3R

Analytical Reading provides the teacher with an algorithm by which to lead students through a systematic examination of subject matter presented in a text. One of these algorithms is the SQ3R method, which was originally conceived as a strategy for studying chapter-length material. SQ3R becomes a teaching method by translating its steps for studying texts into analogous steps for presenting the texts: Survey, Question, Read, Recite, Review. Students taught by these steps, or some variation of them, not only learn the subject matter but acquire a routine for dealing with the subject's literature on their own.

Analytical Reading cuts text study into subtasks and has students attend to each subtask in a fixed sequence of study acts: to preview in order to understand the gist of the text's presentation, to pose questions, to check the correctness of the answers obtained, and to review in order to pull the material together. This cycle of text study allows students to meet important conditions for learning. They understand the purpose for studying, break the material to be learned into manageable parts, and process the material until it becomes meaningful and memorable. Analytical Reading is appropriate for secondary and college-level classes that rely heavily on a textbook as a source of content. It is especially appropriate for science and social studies classes. Teachers of language arts and mathematics can also make effective use of this approach to teaching with texts.

Procedure

The teacher leads students repeatedly through a cycle of study acts. The teacher previews the material with students and has them formulate questions about it. Then students read to find answers to their questions. After finding answers to their questions, students are directed to recite the material or perhaps to rewrite it in different form. Finally, the teacher has students review the material studied.

During survey, the teacher prepares the way for students to set purposes for reading and studying. Then the teacher has students survey in order to find the underlying "hidden" outline of the selection. Finding the underlying outline is accomplished in two ways. The first is to read the introductory and concluding sections. The second is to skim headings and subheadings and observe how they signal the ways the text appears to advance its main idea.

Questions are then developed on the basis of the underlying outline found during survey. Questions are formulated by rewording headings and subheadings and by asking about the details of material either foreshadowed in the introduction or summarized in the conclusion. With these questions, students set their purposes for reading.

As students seek answers to these questions, they may find it useful to develop more in-depth questions.

Reading to find answers to questions, students look for specific details. As they do, the teacher may check their comprehension by asking them to cite information, make generalizations and predictions, and verify their interpretations. If graphic aids are present, the teacher directs students' attention to them. To answer questions, students may have to rephrase the text.

The teacher has students recite by having them answer the question: What did I just learn? Students are not to memorize or to restate information verbatim. Instead, they are to put the material in their own words, perhaps by writing notes, making outlines, or brainstorming their impressions.

To review the material, the teacher has students reexamine the main ideas hypothesized for the selection during the survey step. Questions developed during the questioning step are reconsidered and then answers are again noted. The teacher has students observe whether answers to questions make sense in relation to the selection's main idea.

Discussion

Analytical reading is an efficient, step-by-step procedure for presenting subject matter from texts. At the same time, it offers the teacher a way to model an efficient system of study. Although following the procedure takes more time than having students merely read the text, in the long run it actually saves time where students are expected to learn the material of the text. This is the case for studying as well as teaching. It reduces the material to manageable parts for teaching, and the structure and practice afforded by the procedure fosters remembering the material.

Poorly organized material may be difficult to teach with this method. It is important that the teacher begin with a text that is well organized and easily adapted to the procedure. Best are expository chapter sections whose parts are clearly marked with headings and subheadings. After students become familiar with the procedure, the teacher can work with more difficult texts.

EXAMPLE

A high school geography class is studying a unit on regions of the world designated according to natural vegetation. This lesson is on grasslands. The teacher covers the textbook material by an approach that both teaches the material and parallels an effective independent study strategy.

Teacher: Now we've come to "The World's Grasslands" in our textbook. Let's read the introductory paragraph and skim the headings in order to get an idea of what this section of the text has to say.

Vince: Just the first paragraph and the headings?

Teacher: Right. To begin this section, we'll just skim to find out what major points are presented. You'll only need about a half a minute.

Peggy: It's about grasslands.

Teacher: Right. What does the text have to say about grasslands?

Tony: That there are three kinds.

Rona: Savannas, steppes.

Russ: And prairies.

Teacher: Good. What do you think the text has to say about these three kinds of grasslands?

Frances: The introduction says grasslands are differentiated according to type of grass, terrain, and climate. So I'd guess that under each kind of grassland, there's information about type of grass, terrain, and climate.

Russ: There may be something about where these kinds of grasslands are located.

Teacher: So it appears that the text presents information about savannas, steppes, and plains. And you think that the information presented for each is about type of grass, terrain, and climate.

Russ: And location.

Teacher: And location. Let's note these things on the board. If the information is presented uniformly for each type of grassland, the text is likely to fit this outline (writing on the chalkboard):

Grasslands
  Savannas
    Types of grass
    Terrain
    Climate
    Location

  Steppes
    Types of grass
    Terrain
    Climate
    Location

  Prairies
    Types of grass
    Terrain
    Climate
    Location

Teacher: Now let's use this outline to ask ourselves questions that we can probably answer by reading the text.

Rona: What is a savanna?

Teacher: OK. The answer to that question will come with answering questions about the four points of information given for savannas.

Russ: The same thing would hold for asking What is a steppe? And for asking What is a prairie?

Frances: To answer these questions requires answering questions like What type of grass grows there? What's distinctive about the terrain? In what type climate is this grassland found? Where are these grasslands located?

Teacher: Right. We'll read each section to get answers to these questions. But there are other questions to ask.

Peggy: Like how is a savanna different from a steppe?

Vince: Or like how do all three types of grasslands differ?

Tony: Or in what ways are they alike?

Rona: Which two are most alike, and why?

Russ: Which two are most different, and why?

Teacher: Excellent questions. I'll write them here on the board. You write them in your notebook. Leave space for writing your answers when you find them.

Frances: Why can't we just read? Why do we need to have these questions?

Teacher: Questions set our purposes for reading. Here we have two kinds of questions. So we have two kinds of purposes.

Frances: Seems to me they're just questions that ask for information about grasslands.

Teacher: They do ask for information about grasslands. But one kind of question asks for information that describes each type of grassland. We can answer this kind of question *as* we read. The second kind of question asks about how different types of grasslands compare. These are questions we can answer only *after* we've read about all three types of grasslands.

Frances: So do we write down answers to the first kind of question as we find them?

Teacher: Yes, but as we read about each type of grassland. We go over the questions and answers in our mind just after reading about each grassland. Let's now read the section on savannas to get answers to our four questions for describing grasslands. Write down your answers when you've finished.

Students read and then write in their notebooks answers to questions about savannas.

Teacher: OK. Let's describe savannas by answering our questions. First, what kind of grass do they have?

Several: Tall grass. Twelve feet high. Elephant grass.

Teacher: Second question. What's the terrain like?

Several: A large plain.

Vince: It's soggy when it rains because the grass just grows in clumps.

Teacher: In what kind of climate do we find savannas?

Rona: One that has both wet and dry seasons. The text doesn't give a name for this kind of climate.

Teacher: OK. Where are savannas located?

Peggy: South America, Africa, and Asia.

Tony: I noticed that there was information for which we had not asked a question. What are the trees and shrubs like?

Teacher: Good. Let's add that question to our list of questions for each type of grassland. What *are* the trees and shrubs like?

Tony: They're low and flat-topped, and they have more trees and shrubs than other kind of grasslands.

Teacher: Good. Now let's go over our information about savannas again. Rona, describe savannas for us.

Rona: A savanna has tall grass that grows in clumps on a large plain that gets soggy when it rains. Savannas are found where there's both a wet and a dry season. Oh, and savannas have more trees and shrubs than other grasslands. They're low and flat-topped.

Teacher: Good. Now let's go over the section on steppes in the same way.

The teacher has students cover the textbook sections on steppes and prairies by the same procedure, by answering questions set in advance and then summing up their answers. The class then proceeds to compare the three types of grasslands.

Teacher: You seem to have a grip on the facts about savannas, steppes, and prairies. Now let's compare them. In what ways are they alike?

Frances: They all have grass.

Peggy: On both savannas and steppes the grass grows in clumps and there's soil erosion.

Vince: Both savannas and prairies have trees and shrubs.

Tony: Steppes and prairies have four seasons. In the spring it rains. In the summer it's hot. Autumns are cool. And winters are snowy cold.

Teacher: Now let's distinguish each type of grassland. What things are distinctive about each one?

Rona: Savannas have the tallest grass.

Peggy: Savannas have wet and dry seasons, but not the four-season cycle.

Vince: Savannas have the most trees and shrubs.

Frances: Steppes have short grass only.

Tony: Steppes have the fewest trees and shrubs.

Russ: There are steppes in Australia.

Teacher: What about the prairies?

Frances: The grass grows thick, not in clumps.

Russ: The terrain is rolling.

Vince: There are lots of colorful wild flowers.

Teacher: Now let's go over all of the grasslands one more time. Let's review them by filling in a chart together.

On the chalkboard the teacher draws a large 3 × 4 grid for filling in information about each type of grassland. The teacher heads the three columns with the names of the types of grasslands. On the left side of the rows, the teacher writes the questions formulated for finding out about the grasslands:

	Savannas	Steppes	Prairie
What type of grass grows there?			
What is the terrain like?			
What kind of climate does it have?			
Where is it located?			

Teacher: Let's take the first question and answer it for each of the three types of grasslands.

Rona: Savannas have tall grass that grows in clumps.

The teacher completes the lesson by leading students through a review that has students fill in the chart.

The World's Grasslands

Grasslands are flat to gently rolling stretches of land where the vegetation is predominantly grass. They are differentiated according to type of grass, terrain, and climate. Most grasslands are located in regions between deserts and forests. Grasslands are located on every continent except Antarctica.

Savannas
A savanna is a large plain of tall grasses, such as elephant grass. Savanna grass reaches as high as 12 feet. It grows in clumps, leaving much of the soil exposed to rain, sun, and wind.

Scattered among the grasses are low, flat-topped trees and shrubs. Savannas have more trees and shrubs than other types of grasslands.

Savannas have both dry and wet seasons. The dry season is the winter. The grass turns brown and often fires erupt and burn off extensive stretches of grass. The wet season is the summer. During summer, rain falls heavily and the plain turns soggy. South America, Africa, and Asia have the largest savannas.

Steppes
A steppe is a large plain covered with short grass. The grass grows in clumps, as it does on a savanna, leaving much of the ground bare. Erosion occurs as wind and moving water carry away the soil.

A steppe is virtually without trees. The few trees and shrubs that do grow on a steppe are small and widely scattered.

The climate of a steppe includes the four seasons—spring, summer, fall, and winter. It is during the spring that the steppe gets most of its rain. The summer is hot and dry. The fall is cool, and the winter is bitterly cold and snowy. Asia, Africa, and Australia have the largest steppes.

Prairies

A prairie is a large, gently rolling plain covered with both short and tall grasses. Growing together thickly, short and tall grasses leave little of the ground exposed. Prairie soil is rich and, left untilled, remains intact.

Scattered across a prairie are a few trees and shrubs. There are many wild flowers, which bloom in the spring and splash the prairie with rich, bright colors.

A prairie has four seasons. Most of the rainfall occurs in the spring. Summer is hot and dry. Fall is cool and dry. Winter is long, cold, and snowy. Prairies are found in Asia, North America, and South America.

Sources

Vince Orlando. (1980). Training students to use a modified version of SQ3R: An instructional strategy. *Reading World, 28,* 65–70.

Francis P. Robinson. (1946). Survey Q3R method of studying. In *Effective study* (pp. 13–41). New York: Harper and Row.

E. G. Stetson. (1981). Improving textbook learning with S4R: A strategy for teachers, not students. *Reading Horizons, 22,* 129–135.

Ellen Thomas and H. Alan Robinson. (1972). *Improving reading in every classroom* (pp. 115–150). Boston: Allyn and Bacon.

Related Readings

Kenneth G. Graham and Alan Robinson. (1984). *Study skills handbook: A guide for all teachers.* Newark, DE: International Reading Association.

Anthony C. Maffei. (1973). Reading analysis in mathematics. *Journal of Reading, 16,* 546–549.

Maxwell H. Norman and Enid S. Norman. (1968). *Successful reading.* New York: Holt, Rinehart and Winston.

Walter Pauk. (1974). *How to study in college.* Boston: Houghton Mifflin.

9

Analytical Reading: PQ4R

PQ4R is an analytical reading procedure for leading students through the study of texts systematically. A variation of SQ3R, the PQ4R method shows students how to deal with texts through a procedure of Preview, Question, Read, Reflect, Recite, and Review. Students actively process the text content by an approach that closely resembles study routines traditionally advocated for studying texts independently. Practicing this approach in class, students gain experience with a strategy they can apply when they study on their own.

As an analytical reading procedure, PQ4R has students approach the study of a text as a set of tasks to be undertaken in a set routine. These tasks account for essential conditions of learning and effective problem solving. Students gain an understanding of the material presented, raise questions, read for information, ponder the information, restate it in their own words, and review their thinking about the material. PQ4R is for high school and college classes that make substantial use of textual materials. It may be used with individual students, small groups, and whole classes.

Procedure

PQ4R is essentially the same procedure as SQ3R, but with an extra step that has students reflect on what they read. A modification of PQ4R suggested by Anthony Maffei makes the procedure uniquely suited for working out word problems in mathematics.

The teacher introduces PQ4R by describing its algorithm in general terms. For this introduction, the teacher provides every student with a "PQ4R Outline Sheet." PQ4R is then applied to specific mathematical word problems by following each of the method's six steps.

Step 1: Preview. The teacher directs students to read the problem in order to get its gist. In the space provided on the "PQ4R Outline Sheet," students write down any unfamiliar words or phrases. In class discussion an attempt is made to define the unfamiliar words and phrases in the context of the problem. A dictionary may be consulted.

Step 2: Question. Students reread the problem to determine what it specifically asks. Usually a math word problem asks its question explicitly. It may ask with a direct question, such as "How many . . . ?" or "What are . . . ?" Or it may pose an indirect question, such as "Find the maximum amount. . . ." Students write the question on the "PQ4R Outline Sheet" so that they keep their goal in mind.

Step 3: Read. The teacher has students read the problem again. This time, students are to read closely to find specific phrases and sentences related to the question in step 2. These include key phrases such as "more than," "is the same as," and "is as much as." The teacher advises students to think of these words and phrases in terms of mathematical operations and to write them down in some logical order.

Step 4: Reflect. The teacher asks students what type of problem they are facing. Is it a motion problem? A mixture problem? A geometry problem? Whatever the problem, the teacher has students label the unknown value on which the problem turns as *x*.

Step 4: Rewrite. The teacher turns students' attention to the word phrases of step 3 and leads the discussion toward transforming these word phrases into algebraic sentences. Here, the teacher has students write an equation and plug into it the numerical information of the problem. The class then solves the question.

Step 6: Review. The teacher has students check the solution. The entire process is reviewed to make sure everything makes sense in terms of the question in step 2.

Discussion

PQ4R is excellent for helping students approach the task of solving mathematical word problems. It provides an outline for attempting problems whose solution may appear impossible upon first reading. After repeated use of the PQ4R method and after students have developed confidence in their ability to work word problems, the outline may be discarded.

Although PQ4R shows students how to set up a word problem and build their confidence for working through such problems, it does not guarantee correct answers. Students have to be familiar with the concepts that are applied and know how to write equations. The method is of limited value for highly capable students who have their own way of working word problems. These students do not need the structure provided by the PQ4R method.

EXAMPLE

A high school mathematics class is solving word problems. The teacher's objective is to have students take a systematic approach to setting up the problems. To begin the lesson, the teacher writes the following problem on the chalkboard:

> Find 3 consecutive odd integers such that 5 times
> the first decreased by 15 is 4 times the second
> minus 2 times the third.

Teacher: Here's a problem to think about.

Darryl: The problem swamps me. There's too much there to deal with.

Teacher: The problem does look overwhelming, but it is manageable. You have to have a system for managing it. Let me propose the PQ4R system.

Lupe: Sounds like another math problem.

Teacher: It can help you solve your math problems. The letters of PQ4R stand for six routine steps you can take when you face a tough math problem: *P*—Preview.

First you preview the problem for its gist. *Q*–Question. Next, you find the question the problem is asking. *4R*–Read, Reflect, Rewrite, and Review. These are the steps you take to answer the question.

Matt: I find it hard to believe that these are six steps to math success.

Teacher: PQ4R gives you a starting place. There are things you have to do when you follow each of the steps. But you do pretty much the same thing with the steps every time you use PQ4R.

The teacher distributes the "PQ4R Outline Sheet."

PQ4R Outline Sheet

1. PREVIEW:
   a. First reading of problem
   b. List unknown words and phrases for possible discussion:
      1) _____
      2) _____
      3) _____
      4) _____

2. QUESTION:
   a. Second reading
   b. Write direct question of problem:

      _____

3. READ:
   a. Third reading
   b. List all word facts of problems in some logical order:
      1) _____
      2) _____
      3) _____
      4) _____
      5) _____

4. REFLECT:
   a. Fourth reading
   b. What is x, the unknown quantity, representing?

      _____

   c. Translate word facts into math facts with the use of x:
      1) _____
      2) _____

3) _____

4) _____

5) _____

5. REWRITE:

   a. Rewrite math facts in terms of a "balanced" equation and then solve.

6. REVIEW:

   a. Substitute value of x in equation to check for true sentence.
      CHECK:

   b. Does the problem make sense in terms of the question?

Teacher: This "PQ4R Outline Sheet" shows you what I mean. It reminds you of the things to do each step of the way in solving a math word problem.

Darryl: I don't see how this outline sheet can help with the problem on the board.

Teacher: Let's try to solve the problem by using this guide to PQ4R. Tell us, Tron, what's the first step?

Tron: Preview. The outline sheet says to read the problem and list unknown words and phrases.

Teacher: That's right. But the words or phrases don't have to be completely unknown. If they may have something to do with solving the problem and you want to be sure about their meaning, write them down. What words should we write down?

Denise: Integers.

Laurie: Odd.

Lupe: Consecutive.

Teacher: All right. Let's talk about these words. First, let's talk about integers. Who knows what *integers* are?

Denise: They're counting numbers, like 1, 2, 3, 4.

Teacher: Right. They're whole numbers, not fractions. What are *odd* integers?

Laurie: Odd numbers, like 1, 3, 5, 7.

Teacher: Good. They're every second number starting with 1. They alternate with the even numbers, which are 2, 4, 6, 8, and so on. What does the word *consecutive* mean?

Lupe: One following another in order.

Teacher: All right. Now, let's read the problem again to determine what question it asks.

The class reads the problem again.

Teacher: Matt, what are we to find?

Matt: The problem asks us to find 3 consecutive odd integers.

Darryl: So that means 3 whole numbers, odd, and one after another in a row.

Teacher: That's right. Now let's read the problem again. This time we'll read to note specific phrases that are related to the question.

The class reads the problem again.

Teacher: What phrases should we write down?

Laurie: Five times the first.

Teacher: Good. Others?

Denise: Decreased by 15.

Tron: Is 4 times the second.

Matt: Minus 2 times the third.

Teacher: I think you've got the essential phrases. Now, let's read the problem one more time. This time read in order to determine what kind of problem this is. What does the unknown value represent?

The class reads the problem a fourth time.

Teacher: Let's let x represent the unknown value that we're trying to find out.

Laurie: It's the first value we're trying to find. It's an odd integer. There are two other values we're trying to find. They are the next two odd integers that follow x.

Denise: So we could represent the first odd integer as x, the second as $x + 2$, and the third as $x + 4$, since consecutive odd integers would be every other number.

Teacher: Excellent. Looking back at step 3, we have other information we need to solve this problem. Let's write the phrase in algebraic form. Five times the first, meaning five times the first odd integer, which we represent as x.

The teacher shows that each phrase can be translated into an algebraic phrase and lists them on the chalkboard:

$$5\ (x)$$
$$-\ 15$$
$$=\ 4\ (x + 2)$$
$$-\ 2\ (x + 4)$$

Teacher: Be sure to write down these math facts in the spaces provided in step 4 of the "PQ4R Outline Sheet."

Darryl: I'm beginning to see how to tackle this problem. We have what we need to make a balanced equation.

Teacher: You're right on target. In step 4, you wrote the math facts as algebraic phrases. For step 5, you write out these algebraic phrases as a balanced equation.

The teacher writes this balanced equation on the chalkboard:

$$5 (x) - 15 = 4 (x + 2) - 2 (x + 4)$$

Tron: So now all we have to do is solve for x. Then we can know what the three integers are: x, x plus 2, and x plus 4.

Teacher: You do solve for x, and you do find the other two integers by adding 2 and 4 to x. But that's not quite all you have to do. You still have to check your answer. That's the fourth R in PQ4R.

Lupe: I think I've got it. It's 5, x equals 5. So the three consecutive odd integers are 5, 7, and 9.

Teacher: Let's check that solution. Let's substitute 5 for x in our equation and see if it works. Then we'll review the entire procedure to see if it all makes sense.

Sources

Anthony C. Maffei. (1973). Reading analysis in mathematics. *Journal of Reading, 16*, 546–549.

Ellen Thomas and H. Alan Robinson. (1972). *Improving reading in every class* (pp. 115–150). Boston: Allyn and Bacon.

10

RIDGES

RIDGES provides students with a systematic approach to the solution of word problems in mathematics. It is an approach that facilitates students' identifying relevant information and understanding of the problem through numeric, verbal, and pictorial means. RIDGES is an acronym for the method's six steps:

*R*ead the problem

I know statement

*D*raw a picture

*G*oal statement

*E*quation development

*S*olve the equation

The use of acronyms as mnemonic devices can be generally effective in teaching students to follow an algorithm. These devices are even more effective when they have students address problems on a concrete or visual level. With RIDGES, students sort out a problem's pertinent information and summon knowledge they have relevant to its solution. By drawing a picture, students focus on significant information. The visual aid stimulates thinking that leads to specific goal setting and equation solving. RIDGES may be used with students at the upper-elementary, high school, and college levels. It may be used with individual students or with whole classes. No special materials are required, but the teacher may want to make a poster or bulletin board display that lists the six steps.

Procedure

To heighten the mnemonic value of the acronym RIDGES, the teacher may introduce it by likening it to the ridge line of a rooftop. The structure undergirding the ridge line supports the solution to the problem. The teacher may illustrate this metaphor visually and explain that each rafter in the illustration depicts a step in the problem-solving structure.

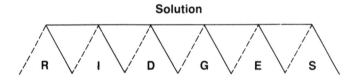

The teacher then presents the word problem and leads students through the six steps to its solution.

Read the problem. The teacher directs students to read the problem in order to understand the problem and identify the specific information it presents. Initially, the teacher helps point out this information. Students may need to read the problem several times.

I know statement. Once the information is identified, the teacher lists it in a statement written on the chalkboard. The statement begins, "I know that. . . ." Students list the information in an "I know" statement at their seats. All facts and figures are listed regardless of perceived importance. The teacher encourages students to add other knowledge they have that would help solve the problem.

Draw a picture. With the information listed in the "I know" statement, the teacher fashions a visual representation of the problem on the chalkboard. This may take the form of a chart, diagram, graph, or representational drawing. Students represent the problem in drawings of their own.

Goal statement. Once the problem has been sketched, the teacher leads students to formulate a statement that specifies the kind of solution to be obtained. The teacher writes a goal statement at the chalkboard while students write one in their own words. To formulate the statement, reference is made to the "I know" statement and the drawing.

Equation development. The teacher has students reflect on the process of drawing the picture and writing the goal statement. Students are asked what they deem the important information and where they think the information leads. Students are told to keep in mind the process of carrying out these earlier steps as they formulate a solution to the problems. The formulation may be written in words or framed as an algebraic equation. In class discussion, students share their formulations for solving the problem. Drawing on this discussion, the teacher writes a formula on the chalkboard. The formula is one that can be understood by students, if not already familiar to them.

Solve the equation. The teacher calls on students to take from their "I know" statements information that can be plugged into the equation. Together, the teacher and students perform the operations necessary to solve the equation.

Discussion

The usefulness of the steps represented by the acronym contributes to remembering this algorithm for solving math word problems, which can be overwhelming for many students. With this algorithm, students can develop confidence as they take on math word problems one step at a time. Students know to begin by getting the gist of the problem, then to sort out its information, and then to draw it. Students who have difficulty with abstractions find visual representations extremely helpful. Drafting the goal statement stimulates insight that works for students when they decide on a formula for solving the problem.

Like most methods, RIDGES is not for all students or all math problems. Nor is it a complete method. Able students do not need to be given an explicit step-by-step model for solving math problems. And students who *are* given this model need to understand that its application is limited to problems that can be drawn. Not all mathematics problems lend themselves to visual representation. Students should also be aware that RIDGES does not include a step for checking the solution, which is important to solving any math problem.

EXAMPLE

A high school mathematics class is solving word problems. Toward the solution of the problems, students are applying concepts that the class has recently been studying.

Teacher: Here's a problem whose solution is bound to result in a passionate response. It's about offering and denying jobs to people.

Brian: Those who get a job will be happy, and those who don't will be disappointed.

Teacher: Those who don't get jobs may be more than disappointed. They may get angry. Read the problem and see what I mean.

Students silently read the following word problem:

> The personnel manager at Acme Development Company has been authorized to hire as many new workers as possible within the restrictions imposed by its contracts with labor unions. The contract with the United Brotherhood of Electrical Workers limits the company to 75 electricians. The contract with the International Federation of Plumbers permits no more than 50 plumbers on the payroll. Currently working for the company are 52 persons who are electricians, 25 persons who are plumbers, and 15 persons who qualify as both electricians and plumbers. The company has taken applications from 23 job seekers. Of these job seekers, 7 are electricians, 3 are plumbers, and 4 are electrician-plumbers. How many of the job applicants may be hired?

Rosalie: I see what you mean. The company would like to hire all job seekers, but the unions may not allow all the applicants to get a job there.

Elliot: What's the big deal? Everybody can get hired. The electricians' union allows 75 electricians, but the company only has 52. The plumbers' union will allow 40 plumbers, but the company only has 25.

Shannon: What about the 15 plumber-electricians who are already on the payroll?

Elliot: What about them? The union contracts allow up to 125 electricians and plumbers, but the company only has 92 electricians and plumbers. Subtract 92 from 125 and that leaves 33 jobs. There are 23 job applicants. Even if all the job applicants were plumbers or electricians, which they are not, they would all still get a job.

Teacher: We had better take a closer look at this problem. It may be one we can solve with RIDGES. You know: Read–I know–Draw–Goal statement–Equation–Solve.

Elliot: Seems like a lot of bother for such a simple problem.

Teacher: Let's try it anyway. And remember, we should not be reluctant to reread a word problem several times if that's what it takes to get the information straight. Now, let's carefully reread the problem.

Students silently read the word problem again.

Rachel: As I read this, I'd guess that each union is concerned with its own interests. The electricians' union doesn't give a hoot if some electricians are also plumbers. Likewise, the plumbers' union doesn't give a hoot about how many plumbers happen also to be electricians.

Keith: That means that the maximum number of employees who are electricians is limited to 75. The maximum number of employees who are plumbers is limited to 40.

Teacher: OK. We're on the right track stating what we know about the problem. As we talk about the information given, I'll list it here on the board under this sentence stem "I know that. . . ." You should each do the same on a sheet of paper.

Rosalie: I think we should list the details about there already being 52 electricians, 25 plumbers, and 15 plumber-electricians on the payroll.

Shannon: We should say that the company is limited to 75 electricians and 40 plumbers.

Keith: We need to include information about the job applicants.

Elliot: There are 23 altogether.

Rachel: Among the job applicants there are seven electricians, three plumbers, and four plumber-electricians.

Teacher: We have the information explicitly stated in the problem. Now what?

Brian: Now we need to find out what those union contracts mean for the job applicants.

Teacher: Let's draw a picture of the situation. You draw a picture of the problem on a sheet of paper while I draw a picture on the board.

The teacher draws a Venn diagram showing two pairs of overlapping circles.

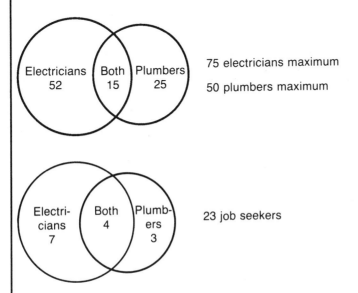

Electricians 52 Both 15 Plumbers 25

75 electricians maximum

50 plumbers maximum

Electricians 7 Both 4 Plumbers 3

23 job seekers

Teacher: My picture is a Venn diagram. It shows two pairs of overlapping circles. In the top pair, one circle represents the electricians and the other circle represents the plumbers. The shared area in which the two circles overlap represents the employees who are both electricians and plumbers.

Rosalie: Your bottom pair of overlapping circles shows occupational designation in the same way for the job applicants.

Elliot: The picture is starting to make some things clear. The top picture shows that the dual occupational status of some employees might keep some job applicants from getting hired. There might be openings for electricians, but an electrician who is also a plumber may be out of luck.

Rachel: The bottom pair of overlapping circles tells us that a lot of the job applicants are neither electricians nor plumbers.

Teacher: What are we trying to find out?

Brian: How many of the 23 job applicants may the personnel manager hire?

Teacher: All right. Let's write that down as our goal statement. Now let's think about how we're going to reach that goal.

Shannon: Well we've got some information listed in the "I know" statement.

Teacher: Good. What else?

Keith: And we've got the picture of the two pairs of overlapping circles.

Teacher: Think about what the overlapping of the circles means.

Rachel: It means that some employees and job applicants are included in both job categories.

Keith: But that some job applicants are excluded from both categories.

Rosalie: So what we have here is an inclusion-exclusion problem. Let's first determine how many of the applicants can be hired since there is no union restriction on them.

Shannon: They are the applicants left after you subtract the electricians and plumbers.

Teacher: Right. We can write what you're saying as a formula.

The teacher writes the following formula on the chalkboard:

$$N = A - E - P - B$$

Teacher: N stands for the applicants not restricted by union contracts. A represents all the applicants, and E, P, and B are applicants who are electricians, plumbers, and electrician-plumbers respectively. To find N, we substitute the numerical information for the letters and do some subtraction.

The teacher writes down these values:

$$N = 23 - 7 - 3 - 4$$
$$N = 9$$

Teacher: Now we add to the number of nonrestricted applicants the number of plumbers and electricians allowable. By subtracting 9 from the total applicant pool of 23, we find that there are 14 applicants who are subject to restriction.

Brian: The limit on electricians is 75 and there are already 67 at the company, counting both electricians and plumber-electricians. So that leaves 8 vacancies for electricians.

Rachel: The limit on plumbers is 50. Counting both plumbers and plumber-electricians, I get 40 plumbers on the job. There are 10 vacancies for plumbers.

Teacher: Would the personnel manager exceed the restriction on electricians if he hires every applicant who qualifies as electrician?

Shannon: Yes. Eleven applicants qualify as electrician.

Teacher: How about plumbers? Would the plumbers' contract be violated by hiring all who qualify as plumbers?

Keith: No. Only seven applicants qualify as plumbers.

Rosalie: So the personnel manager has only to worry about the restriction on electricians, right?

Teacher: Right. So what does that suggest for solving the personnel manager's problem?

Keith: He only has to subtract from the applicant pool the number of job seekers who qualify as electricians or plumber-electricians over the maximum allowed.

Teacher: That suggests a formula for finding out how many applicants the personnel manager can hire.

The teacher writes the following formula on the chalkboard:

$$H = A - (E + B - Ve)$$

Teacher: In the formula, H is the number of applicants who can be hired. A stands for all applicants. E and B are applicants who qualify as electricians and as both plumbers and electricians. Ve represents the vacancies for electricians allowed by the contract with the electricians' union.

Rosalie: Now all we have to do is plug in the numbers.

The teacher has students say the numbers to write on the chalkboard:

$$H = 23 - (7 + 4 - 8)$$
$$H = 20$$

The class reviews the procedure to check the reasonableness of steps taken and the accuracy of computations.

Source

Kathleen Snyder. (1988). RIDGES: A problem solving math strategy. *Academic Therapy*, 23, 261–263.

11

Predict-Test-Conclude

The purpose of Predict-Test-Concludes (P-T-C) is to build students' problem-solving skills. These include skills needed for formulating and testing hypotheses and for drawing logical conclusions.

P-T-C has students actively use their existing knowledge in order to make sense of newly introduced information and to add new information to their fund of knowledge. The lesson is structured so that students apply their knowledge in three distinct ways. They make predictions, test hypotheses, and draw conclusions. P-T-C may be used in a wide range of instructional situations. It is not limited to a particular grade level or age range. It can be used with individuals or groups, but the student or students must have some background knowledge of the subject if the lesson is to be effective.

Procedure

The lesson comprises three parts—one each for predicting, testing hypotheses, and drawing conclusions. These parts of the lesson correspond with the three conventional phases of text-based instruction: prereading, text-engagement, and postreading follow-up.

During the prereading phase, the teacher induces students to make predictions about the material to be read. It is helpful if the teacher has prepared several questions for this purpose in advance. These are conditional questions such as cause-effect and if-then questions. Since the reasoning required for responding to this kind of question may be difficult for some students, the teacher can expect to have to rephrase questions and to offer comments that lead students' thinking in the desired direction. The teacher may try other approaches to encourage students' predictions. Students may be divided into pairs or small groups for topical discussions, or students may be provided a written overview or outline of the text. On the basis of questioning, small-group discussions, or text overview or outline, students write down what they would predict the text's content to be. In the discussion preceding reading, students explain the reasoning behind their predictions.

Students then read in order to test their predictions and possibly to alter them or to generate new ones. The teacher may assign students to complete a worksheet designed to foster their confirming, disconfirming, and modifying predictions as they read. Students may read silently or aloud, depending on what the teacher judges to be appropriate for the material.

After reading, the teacher leads a discussion linked to questions and predictions posed in the prereading phase of the lesson. In the discussion, the teacher asks probing questions that help students make appropriate connections and inferences.

Discussion

P-T-C has several positive features. It encourages students to speculate and to reason about their speculations. It can be used with individuals or groups of students, and it can be applied to any type of text. A word of caution is in order, however. If students are not sufficiently prepared and well guided, they may become lost in the details of the task. The teacher has to anticipate this kind of problem and try to avoid it. The teacher should be prepared to bring students back on track if they become derailed by details of the lesson.

EXAMPLE

A business class is studying the role of entrepreneurship in free enterprise. The teacher's objective is to acquaint students with the characteristics of successful entrepreneurs. The teacher has prepared for the lesson by developing a handout for students to fill in and by formulating three questions that will encourage students to hypothesize about the nature of entrepreneurship:

1. When entrepreneurs take risks, what is it they hope to gain?
2. If there were no entrepreneurs, how would our economy be different?
3. If a person studied entrepreneurship, would that person automatically become a successful entrepreneur?

The term *entrepreneur* has been introduced and a discussion of *entrepreneurship* is in progress.

Teacher: These are interesting observations that you make. They provide background for exploring this concept, entrepreneurship. Let's think now about what entrepreneurs are like and how the qualities they possess are essential to free enterprise.

Susie: Do you mean like that entrepreneurs believe it's important to be their own boss?

Teacher: Yes. That's an important characteristic of entrepreneurs. But there's more to that characteristic than not liking to take orders from a boss. Why is the desire to be one's own boss important in our economy?

Mary: Everyone can't be the boss. There wouldn't be any workers.

Teacher: Even a boss works. But let's consider your point, Mary. What if nobody had a boss? What if everyone were self-employed?

Billy: That's pretty much the way it was in olden times. If your thing was soap, you made soap and sold it to others. If you were a farmer, you just raised everything you needed for your family to live.

Bob: Yeah, that's fine for producing simple stuff. But there are some things that need teams of people to put together, and some of the tasks have to be controlled so they all fit together right.

Teacher: Hmm. So you seem to be saying, Bob, that if everyone were an autonomous member of the economy, production would be restricted to what could be accomplished by individuals. Let's think about the other side of the question. What if there were no entrepreneurs? What would our economy be like?

The teacher has interjected one of the three key questions prepared for the lesson. As the discussion proceeds, the teacher will work the other two questions into the class discussion. The teacher concludes this introductory discussion on entrepreneurship by bringing students back to the central concern about how the characteristics of entrepreneurship are necessary to sustain free enterprise. The teacher states, rhetorically, the three questions prepared for addressing that concern. To give further emphasis to the lesson's focal concern, as well as to take students through routine steps of problem solving, the teacher asks students to respond in writing to items on the handout that has been prepared for the lesson.

Teacher: Before we read what our textbook has to say about these matters, let's be clear about our purpose in discussing and reading about entrepreneurship. Then we can try to anticipate what the text might have to say relative to our purpose. This handout is for solidifying the things we've been talking about and for guiding us when we read. OK, take a few minutes to answer the first three items on the handout.

After it appears that students have reacted to those items on the handout, the discussion resumes.

Teacher: What are we dealing with here, Ted? What did you write down for number one?

Ted: Entrepreneurs.

Teacher: Entrepreneurs. Just entrepreneurs?

Ted: Well, how they figure in our economy.

Teacher: Good. There are questions we might ask to get at that. Beth, share with us one of the questions you wrote down for number two.

Beth: It's like we talked about. I wrote this: "What are entrepreneurs like?"

Sharon: I have a question like that, too, but mine has more in it. I wrote, "How are the traits of entrepreneurs essential for our economy?" Is that like what you want us to ask?

Teacher: Couldn't have asked it better. How about some possible answers to that question? How about entrepreneurs' risk taking? What do they get out of it? What do we all get out of it?

Larry: They are people with a drive to get rich.

Mike: Yes, but they also need to prove that they don't need to depend on other companies.

Shirley: Or to see if their ideas are as good as they think they are. If they have good ideas, sure they make money and stuff, but the rest of us benefit from their good ideas, too.

Teacher: We're sharing possible answers to a question like Sharon's: "What is it about entrepreneurs that's essential for our economy?" You *have* written down those answers you gave, haven't you?

The teacher leads the ensuing discussion to deal with all three of the lesson's guiding questions. Once students have addressed these questions with hypotheses about the contributions of entrepreneurial qualities to free enterprise, the teacher asks students to read for the purpose of confirming or rejecting their hypotheses. On the handout, students are to jot down things that support or disprove their hypotheses. Following the reading of the text, the teacher poses questions that look back to those posited by students during prereading (and to the three questions that the teacher prepared for the lesson).

Teacher: Shirley, you said earlier that one of the reasons entrepreneurs take risks is to see if their ideas are as good as they think they are. Now that you've read the text, would you still say that?

Shirley: The way the text describes entrepreneurs, trying out their ideas is as important as making money—even more important, according to the text.

Teacher: What did you write on your handout as evidence for your hunch about this motive of entrepreneurs?

Shirley: I just said this: "Ray Kroc was real impressed with the cleanliness and efficiency of a hamburger stand in Illinois. He thought people everywhere would also be impressed, so he started the McDonald's chain, which was modeled after the Illinois hamburger stand he liked." I also said: "Mary Kay Ash had an idea that a lot of customers would rather buy cosmetics directly at home. So she started up her direct-sales makeup company."

The teacher solicits other responses that students made on the handout and probes to help students make causal connections and draw inferences.

Teacher: Let's go back to Shirley's statement that one of the chief motives of entrepreneurship is to test an idea. She supported that notion with information from the text, about Ray Kroc and Mary Kay Ash, who got rich testing their ideas. What made them so sure their ideas would succeed?

Billy: They knew what people wanted badly enough to pay for, so they gave it to them. They knew people would pay for fast hamburgers and makeup sold door to door.

Teacher: They *knew* that?

Billy: They got rich, didn't they.

Teacher: How could they *know* it?

Billy: You got an idea people will pay for, you provide it, you get rich. That's how they knew it.

Teacher: You make it seem self-evident that acting on good ideas is rewarded. Look at the last paragraph of the text, the second sentence.

Erasmus: Risk taking is what entrepreneurship is all about. That means there are winners *and* losers. Sure, you hear mostly about the success stories. But there's no law that says good ideas necessarily pay off.

Entrepreneurs in Free Enterprise

Entrepreneurs are people who take monetary and personal risks in order to make an idea or dream into a reality. They are an important part of American economy. They represent the American belief that every person has the right to succeed at whatever one wants to do. An entrepreneur has several basic qualities.

A successful entrepreneur must have an idea about what product or service will sell well to the public. Ray Kroc recognized the friendly service given in a hamburger stand in Illinois that was clean, prepared food assembly-line style, and involved no dishes to clutter the place. He understood the public's need for fast, friendly service and good food. So, turning the hamburger stand into a franchise, he created the McDonald's food chain to meet these needs. Mary Kay Ash recognized that women wanted a beauty treatment they could trust and buy at home, so she relied on her experience in direct sales to build an organization that personalized the sale of cosmetics.

An entrepreneur must find a way to provide the product or service that will satisfy the consumer. This can be accomplished by creating a good original idea or by putting together several unoriginal ideas to create a new, hopefully better, product or service.

The entrepreneur must organize a business in a way that brings about profit. This can be a complicated process and can involve several aspects of a business. Important aspects of business that affect profit are pricing, cost of business space, employee cost, and advertising, to name a few.

An entrepreneur must create an efficient organization. This is important because it is the organization that determines positive consumer response, positive employee response, and time efficiently spent. Some qualities of an efficient organization are clear guidelines, uniform rules, and a clear chain of command.

> Finally, an entrepreneur must take a monetary risk. There is no guarantee at the beginning that any business will succeed. An entrepreneur must believe strongly enough in an idea to invest a substantial amount of money in it. In addition, the entrepreneur may have to wait a long period of time before the business makes any profit.

Source

Marvin L. Klein. (1988). *Teaching reading comprehension and vocabulary* (pp. 39–46). Englewood Cliffs, NJ: Prentice-Hall.

12

Vocabulary Translations

The Vocabulary Translations method promotes higher-level interpretation skills necessary for problem solving. It is particularly effective for interpreting word problems in mathematics. The teacher guides students through a process that requires students to translate across three levels of vocabulary–general, technical, and symbolic levels. Vocabulary Translations has students visualize and form a general idea from the words given in a problem, interpret them in mathematical terms to solve the problem, and then turn the interpretation back into its general meaning.

As students begin to read a mathematical word problem, they first decode the words and recognize how the words are related in a particular context. Then they integrate the specific definitions of separate words into the general meaning of the problem. Students encode this meaning into symbolic vocabulary and perform the computations. The teacher guides students through each step, asking questions that require thinking about the problem. The process leads students to realize that there is a logical solution to the problem and that they have the knowledge to solve it.

Vocabulary Translations can be used with entire classes or small groups. This method is teacher directed, but every student can become personally involved. Students are encouraged to interpret problems as they see and understand them. Students are provided a thought-provoking and nonthreatening learning environment, which is important for developing the academic skills of students.

Procedure

The teacher selects a word problem that involves mathematical computations that are already familiar to the students. The students read the problem silently and the teacher guides them in decoding and integrating the words by asking for the information presented in the problem. The teacher makes sure students understand the general meaning of the word problem and the question they are asked to answer. Students translate this message into a technical message. The teacher asks which information is useful in solving the word problem, restricting the students' replies to include only information needed to solve the problem. To have students translate this into a symbolic sentence or equation, the teacher encourages students to create a mental image of the information. The teacher leads students to formulate this image by drawing pictures or diagrams on the board. Then students are directed to solve the problem individually and to relate this solution to the general question being asked.

Discussion

Vocabulary Translations can be helpful to students who have difficulty with word problems. Perhaps its main strength is that it takes students step by step through three levels of understanding the vocabulary of a problem. Students are encouraged to refine their interpretation skills and to apply higher levels of thinking. Teachers can identify students who need further development of these skills.

There are few limitations with the Vocabulary Translations method. It does require substantial time, which is devoted entirely to dealing with the terms and procedures of individual word problems. Students may become proficient in working word problems like the ones being studied, but students are unlikely to gain versatility in working word problems of various kinds since mathematics instruction and textbooks tend to focus exclusively on one skill area at a time. For the method to be effective, the word problems have to be written at the students' level of comprehension, and students have to be able to perform the computations required.

EXAMPLE

A sixth-grade class has just completed a lesson on the process of multiplying whole numbers and fractions. The teacher's objective is to have the students solve a mathematical word problem by writing a number sentence and applying this multiplication process. The teacher begins the lesson by asking the students to read the following word problem silently:

> While Susan was at work, she decided that she would surprise her family with a special dessert. Her husband's favorite dessert was chocolate cake, but her children's favorite was chocolate chip cookies. She planned to buy both, but when she arrived at the bakery, all the chocolate cakes had been sold. So she bought a box of twenty-four chocolate chip cookies. When she left the bakery, she saw that the traffic had gotten worse. She decided to cross the park in order to avoid the traffic. As she walked across the park, she ate one-fourth of the cookies. Remembering that she had bought the cookies as a surprise for her family, Susan closed the package and ate no more. She had eaten some of the cookies, but she still had cookies when she arrived home. How many cookies did she still have?

Next, the teacher guides students in decoding and integrating the words into a general message.

Teacher: After reading through this problem, what kind of information are we being given?

Cathy: It's about a woman named Susan.

Mike: She went to the bakery and bought some cookies.

Kyle: She bought twenty-four cookies.

Teacher: What other information are we being told?

Janet: She walked through the park from Broad Street to Park Avenue.

Wendy: She ate some of the cookies while she was walking home.

Teacher: What questions are we being asked to answer?

Scott: How many cookies she had left when she got home.

At this point, students understand the general meaning of the problem. The next step is for the students to translate this general message into a technical message.

Teacher: How many cookies did Susan have to begin with?

Kyle: Twenty-four.

Teacher: What happened to the cookies?

Cathy: She ate one-fourth of them.

Teacher: OK, so how many cookies did she have left?

Janet: We don't know. That is what we are supposed to find out.

During this discussion, the teacher has written on the chalkboard:

> Had twenty-four cookies.
>
> Ate one-fourth of the cookies.
>
> Number left.

Now the teacher leads students to translate these statements into a symbolic sentence or equation.

Teacher: How do we express twenty-four in numerals? Write it for us here on the board.

Amy writes 24 on the chalkboard.

Teacher: Amy, what does the 2 stand for?

Amy: It means we have two groups of ten cookies.

Teacher: John, what does the 4 represent?

John: It means four cookies.

Teacher: So we have . . . ?

Kyle: Twenty-four cookies.

Teacher: How many cookies did she eat?

Cathy: One-fourth.

Teacher: How do we express one-fourth?

Mike: Draw a line and put a 1 on top and a 4 on the bottom.

The teacher writes ¼ on the board.

Teacher: How would we draw a model of one-fourth?

Wendy: Draw a circle and divide it into four equal parts.

Teacher: Like this?

The teacher draws a circle on the board.

Wendy: Yes. Now shade in one of the parts.

The teacher shades in one part of the circle.

Tim: The shaded part is one-fourth.

Teacher: Good. Can anyone think of another way of drawing a model of one-fourth?

Amy: Draw four cookies and shade in one cookie.

The teacher draws four cookies and shades one in.

Teacher: This is also correct. But we have twenty-four cookies in our problem. How do we represent one-fourth of these cookies?

Mike: Divide the cookies into four equal rows or groups.

Teacher: OK. How many cookies will be in each row?

Scott: If we divide twenty-four by four we get six.

The teacher draws four rows of six cookies.

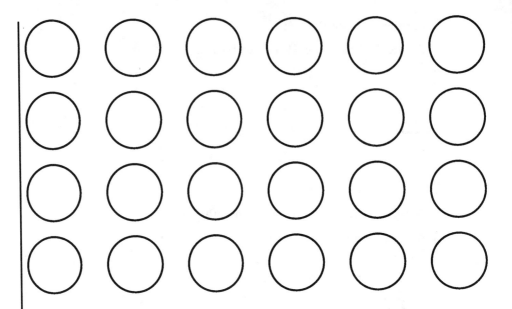

Teacher: Now that we have divided the cookies into four equal parts, how do we show one-fourth of them?

John: Shade in one of the four rows.

The teacher shades in the second row from the top.

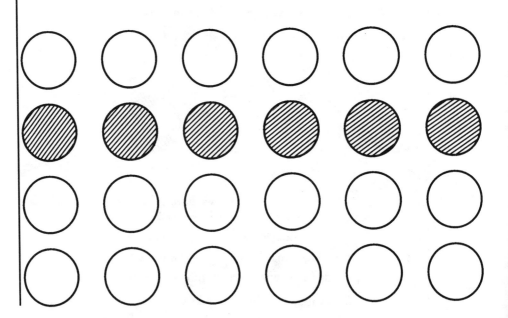

Teacher: What do we do with the six shaded cookies?

Scott: Cross them out.

Teacher: Why?

Scott: Because that is how many Susan ate.

Teacher: This row represents what fraction of the cookies?

Amy: One-fourth.

Teacher: One-fourth of how many?

Kyle: Twenty-four.

Teacher: *Of* means *multiply,* so I write one-fourth of twenty-four this way: 1/4 × 24.

The teacher crosses out six cookies.

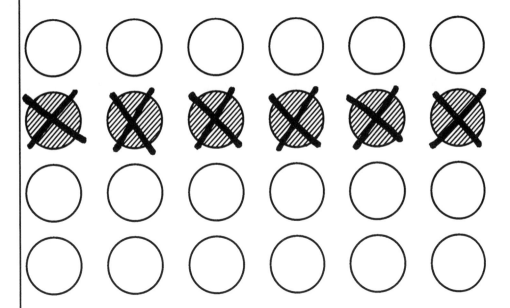

Teacher: What do we show by crossing out these cookies?

Mike: That we're subtracting them.

Teacher: OK, so we're subtracting this row, which is one-fourth of twenty-four, from what number?

Cathy: Twenty-four.

Teacher: Let's write this out as a mathematical sentence: twenty-four minus one-fourth of twenty-four.

The teacher writes out the equation on the chalkboard:

$$24 - (1/4 \times 24) = ?$$

Teacher: We have the numeral twenty-four, followed by a minus sign, followed by what we're subtracting, followed by an equal sign and question mark. What we're subtracting, one-fourth of twenty-four, we enclose in parentheses to show that what we're subtracting has first to be determined within the parentheses.

Scott: So, what's in parentheses stands for a number you get by doing the arithmetic you're shown to do inside the parentheses.

Teacher: Right. *Of* means *multiply*, so one-fourth of twenty-four means one-fourth times twenty-four. The number you get is the number you subtract from twenty-four. Go ahead, now, and do the computations.

The teacher allows time for the students to perform the computations. The next step for the students is to translate the results of these calculations back into the technical message.

Teacher: How many cookies did Susan eat?

John: Six.

Teacher: How many cookies did she have left?

Cathy: Eighteen.

The final step is the translation from the technical vocabulary into the general vocabulary in order to answer the original question.

Teacher: How many cookies did Susan have when she arrived home?

Janet: Susan had eighteen cookies left when she got home.

Source

William P. Dunlap and Martha Brown McKnight. (1978). Vocabulary translations for conceptualiziang word problems. *The Reading Teacher, 32,* 183–189.

Related Readings

James D. Riley and Andrew B. Pachtman. (1978). Reading mathematical word problems: Telling them what to do is not telling them how to do it. *Journal of Reading, 21,* 531–533.

Carol Thornton and Nancy Bly. (1982). Problem solving: Help in the right direction for LD students. *Arithmetic Teacher, 29,* 38–39.

SECTION TWO

Expanding Understanding

The first objective in teaching is to render the subject comprehensible. After that, the objective is to enable students to use the subject's material flexibly and appropriately. Obviously, subject matter can be of little use to students unless they can understand it. Equally obvious, the more students understand it, the better they can apply it and transfer it to situations beyond the instructional situation itself.

To open the way to an initial understanding of a subject, the teacher arranges instructional activity so that students can make connections in its information. The teacher has students attend to regularities amid a flux of varying information. As students pull the material together, they establish a mental framework for organizing and placing related information that they will encounter in future experience.

As instruction goes forward, the teacher introduces additional subject matter, which students understand, largely by placing it within the pattern of knowledge they have formed. By connecting new material to students' established pattern of subject matter knowledge, the teacher attempts to build connections within the information. In this way, the teacher organizes the material so that students find it accessible at a later time. Students have, then, a ready fund of knowledge that they can use for further understanding the subject and things related to it.

Students understand new subject matter by drawing on the knowledge they have previously acquired. From this knowledge they add to information that is given. These additions are inferences. They are the judgments, comparisons, correlations, causes, effects, and predictions that students make of subject matter. It is by making such inferences that students come to understand and make use of subject matter. Making inferences is the process by which students refine their thinking about a subject. The methods in this section have students make inferences that can ultimately become useful knowledge. Described are methods for having students reflect on and evaluate things they see, hear, and read. Presented are methods for having students:

- *Liken new information to familiar experience*
- *Take stock of their own feelings and beliefs*
- *Respond to conflicting ideas*
- *Sort facts from opinions*
- *Engage in internal dialogue as a way of evaluating their own thinking*
- *Discriminate between supportable and unsupportable inferences*
- *Respond overtly to material they read*
- *Maximize participation in activities in which students interact about subject matter*

The methods of this section are for expanding students' understanding.

13

Analogize-Fit-Infer

Analogize-Fit-Infer (AFI) is useful for introducing subject matter that students may find difficult due to its novelty or abstraction. It is also useful for introducing students to metaphor and other forms of symbolic expression.

Through discussion, the teacher establishes a frame of reference for understanding unfamiliar material. The frame of reference is a comparison model that encourages students to draw parallels between familiar experience and the material to be learned. It allows students to think, "This known thing is put together in about the same way as the new material is put together." As students observe the similarity, they may reason analogically, "Features A and B of this known thing seem to be related to each other in about the same way that features C and D are related in the thing to be learned." Or they may reason, also analogically, "This known thing and the material to be learned share feature A, and the feature A is related to feature B in the known thing approximately as it is related to feature C in the material to be learned." Thinking that follows the pattern of an analogy (A:B::C:D or A:B::A:C) lets students become acquainted with the new subject matter and gain confidence in its application.

Because analogic teaching simulates natural processes of thinking and learning, AFI is appropriate in most instructional situations. It can be used effectively with students of all ages and in all academic subjects. It is a productive technique for both large and small groups. If a highly personalized comparison model can be provided, AFI is most effect with individual students. An AFI lesson should take no longer than a single class period of 40 to 50 minutes.

Procedure

The teacher engages students in discussion about a familiar topic with which they may compare the subject matter to be introduced. The topic may include actual or vicarious experience or some aspect of the subject matter previously learned, and it should resemble the new material in its important features. In the discussion, the teacher draws attention to these features and fills in any gaps that may exist in students' knowledge. Once it is certain that students are clear about the familiar topic, the teacher introduces the new subject matter by making a general comparison between the two. As the new material is presented, the teacher refers to similar features of the familiar topic. The teacher uses expressions such as "Notice that this is like . . . ," "See how this resembles . . . . ," or "This is similar to. . . ." Several likenesses are pointed out before the teacher makes explicit contrasts between the new material and the comparison model.

Throughout the introduction of the new material, the teacher makes sure to present substantially more likenesses than differences. If reading is assigned, the teacher directs students to keep the familiar topic in mind and, as they read, to look for likenesses and differences to it. Following the initial presentation and reading, if any, the teacher leads discussion so as to elicit from students inferences that involve analogies between the new material and the familiar topic. Usually the discussion remains closely connected to the established analogy, except when the teacher may encourage students to think of other analogies. The teacher may help students make more effective use of the comparison model by assigning worksheets with analogies that gradually become more complex.

Discussion

Teachers and students alike find AFI a comfortable way to deal with new, abstract subject matter. The comparison model gives teachers an effective device for explaining new material. And by observing students' references to the comparison model, teachers can know whether students are catching on to the new material. Students have an analogy to something familiar that lets them know approximately how the material is supposed to fit together. When the fit is made, students experience a sense of mastery over the newly presented subject matter.

Analogies can be highly productive instructional devices, but they are not appropriate for every situation. Some material can be taught best through a straightforward presentation, especially if students cannot see how familiar experience approximates the new subject matter. If students' grasp of material in the familiar domain is rigid, they may be unable to vary their understanding enough to apply it to anything different. The teacher also has to take care that conclusions about analogous material are not erroneously made about new subject matter.

EXAMPLE

A seventh-grade science class has just begun to study animal cells. In order to introduce the basic structure of animal cells, the teacher establishes a comparison model by having students visualize a raw egg.

Randy: OK, I think I understand what you're saying about all animal tissue being made up of cells. But what do cells look like?

Teacher: Most cells are so small they can only be seen by a microscope, but not all. An egg is a cell you can see.

Randy: So cells look like eggs, only most are smaller?

Teacher: Cells have many different shapes and sizes, as well as functions. But in a very basic way, all cells have features in common. So cells in some ways do look like eggs.

Patty: Like in what ways?

Teacher: Let me have you tell me. You've cracked an egg before. Think for a moment. What's it look like on the inside?

Tony: Inside it's got runny stuff. Most of it's clear, but there's a yellow yolk.

Paula: Sometimes you can see tiny specks.

Stella: And there's some white gunk, too.

Tony: I meant the egg white when I said there's runny stuff.

Stella: I know. But I'm talking about the really white gunk.

Teacher: The white gunk is the chaleza that keeps the yolk suspended near the center of the egg.

Tom: There's something I notice when I crack a really cold egg. Just under the shell there's a skin.

Paula: You can see that skin on a boiled egg, too.

Teacher: Good. You've noticed that an egg has distinct parts. Other cells have parts like those, too.

Tom: You mean cells have a shell, yolk, chaleza, and stuff?

Teacher: These are names that apply to the parts of eggs. There are more general names that apply to all animal cells. The outside part of an animal cell is called the *cell membrane*.

Paula: The shell is the cell membrane?

Teacher: The shell is the cell membrane's protective covering. Actually, the cell membrane is that thin skin just under the shell.

Tony: If there weren't a hard shell, the membrane could break and the runny stuff would run everywhere.

Teacher: Right. And all cells do have runny stuff. In an egg, it's called the egg white or *albumen,* which is just a Latin word that means white. The general name for it in all animal cells is *cytoplasm.*

Stella: Cytoplasm. That's a strange word.

Teacher: It's a word made from two Greek words for what cytoplasm literally means. *Cyto* means a hollow place, like a room or a cell. *Plasm* means fluid–you know, something that takes the shape of its surrounding form. Plastic is called *plas*tic because it's shape is molded in a form.

Randy: So cytoplasm in Greek just means cell fluid?

Teacher: That's right. In the cell fluid, the cytoplasm, float the other parts. The main part is the cell nucleus.

Patty: That's like the egg yolk, right?

Teacher: Right. It's the main part of the cell. It's the core, the central lump. In it are still other parts that control what the cell does–like how it grows and reproduces.

Stella: Is one of the other parts in the cytoplasm like the chaleza.

Teacher: Yes, sort of. But in other cells it serves a different purpose. It's called the *endoplasmic reticulum.*

Stella: Also a strange word.

Teacher: *Endoplasmic* just means "in the fluid," and *reticulum* is a Latin word for a net or web. It's a web-like structure in the cytoplasm.

Paula: And the specks found in the egg white?

Teacher: Actually, in an egg those are particles of blood. But, similarly, there are floating particles in the cytoplasm, too. These are called *mitochondria*.

Stella: Another science word.

Teacher: Again, we have a word made of two Greek words—*mito,* meaning thread, and *chondros,* meaning grain.

Randy: Thread-like grains.

Teacher: That's the literal meaning. Now, turn to the textbook section "The Structure of Animal Cells." As you read it, think about the egg and about how its parts correspond to the parts of other animal cells.

Students silently read the passage.

Teacher: In what ways did the textbook description of cells resemble the discussion we held before reading?

Randy: It's like you said, the parts of cells are like the parts of eggs.

Paula: The cell membrane is like the outer skin and shell of an egg.

Tony: The cytoplasm is like the egg white.

Patty: The cell nucleus is like the egg yolk.

Tom: And the membrane surrounds the cytoplasm the way the shell surrounds cytoplasm.

Paula: And the cytoplasm contains the nucleus and endoplasmic reticulum and mitochondria, sort of like egg white has a yolk and a chaleza and specks in it.

Teacher: You said "sort of like."

Paula: They're not exactly alike. The endoplasmic reticulum surrounds the nucleus and provides a network of channels to move stuff between the nucleus and cell membrane.

Teacher: Good. The chaleza doesn't surround the yolk. It just connects at the ends of the egg membrane.

In the discussion, the teacher explores the analogy between eggs and animal cells. As a closing activity, students are divided into groups and assigned to formulate other comparison models for describing animal cells by analogy.

The Structure of Animal Cells

The basic unit of living things is the cell. Every cell has structures or parts. An animal cell has three basic parts, within which are still other parts. The outer covering is called the *cell membrane.* Filling most of the cell is a jelly-like substance called *cytoplasm.* The innermost part of the cell is the *cell nucleus..*

The cell membrane is very thin. It has tiny holes through which nutrients enter the cell. Waste products also leave the cell through these holes.

In the cytoplasm float the *mitochondria.* The mitochondria store energy taken from nutrients. Also in the cytoplasm is a network of canals called the *endoplasmic reticulum.* These canals connect the cell membrane and the cell nucleus. Substances pass through and are stored in the endoplasmic reticulum.

The cell nucleus regulates the activities of the cell. The cell nucleus is itself covered with a membrane. The *nuclear membrane* controls the entry and exit of materials in and out of the cell nucleus. Within the cell nucleus are structures called *chromosomes.* The chromosomes store the code that regulates the cell's activities.

Source

Marvin L. Klein. (1988). *Teaching reading comprehension and vocabulary: A guide for teachers* (pp. 46–52). Englewood Cliffs, NJ: Prentice-Hall.

14

Intra-Act Procedure

The Intra-Act Procedure develops skills of critical reading and evaluative thinking. Toward developing these skills, students become consistent and active in their valuing the thoughts and opinions of others. This kind of valuing results from internal dialogue, *intra*personal dialogue, in response to *inter*personal discussion with others.

Through active listening and personal reflection, individuals grow and apply knowledge in everyday living. By listening to the thoughts and opinions of others, students reflect on and refine their own thoughts and opinions. This produces evaluative thinking, which over time becomes incorporated into one's personal philosophy or way of life. Intra-Act provides a small group exercise that fosters this kind of thinking.

Almost any content area can make use of this method. And students at any grade level can derive benefit from it, though some modifications would be needed for very young students. It is especially suitable for social studies, current events, values clarification, and literature classes. The method's format, a 40-minute small-group exercise, fits well into the daily class schedule of most schools.

Procedure

The teacher divides the class into discussion groups of four students each. The purpose for this is to encourage all students to speak and interact with others. Each group chooses a leader. The teacher assigns the group to read a selection on the topic currently being studied. Once students have read the selection, the group leader briefly summarizes the selection and initiates a discussion. Within each group of four, students exchange comments and reactions for approximately 10 minutes. Then the teacher issues a list of value statements derived from the selection. The teacher may, alternatively, choose to write these statements on the chalkboard. Students individually indicate whether they agree or disagree with the statements by marking an answer sheet.

Following this, students indicate on the same answer sheet how they think each other group member would respond to the statements. Then, students check their answer sheets. They quickly note whether they had correctly guessed the responses of their group-mates. The teacher makes clear that there are no "correct" answers, that individuals reflect their own opinions and values in choosing to agree or to disagree with the statements. Finally, the groups engage in free discussion for the purpose of exchanging ideas and exploring reasons for responding to the value statements. Students should complete the activity with the feeling that they have thought about the topic and expressed opinions to which their peers listened.

Discussion

Teachers want students to think, to express opinions, and to know the difference between right and wrong. Yet quite understandably many teachers are reluctant to impose their own beliefs on students. The Intra-Act Procedure offers a way for students to develop their own belief systems without the teacher supplying one. It is a method that can be adjusted and used comfortably in a variety of instructional situations.

The method does presume verbal competence and at least a minimal level of sophistication about the material studied. It works well with high school students. With close guidance, it can also work well with middle-school students. Students at any age love to argue, so the teacher should take care that they stay on task.

▌ EXAMPLE

High school history students discuss the expansion of women's political rights during the nineteenth century. The teacher aims for students to develop rational beliefs through interactions with classmates. Students have been divided into discussion groups of four and assigned to read a textbook section entitled "Women Get the Vote."

Teacher: Now that you've read the passage, group leaders should initiate discussion by briefly summarizing what you read.

The teacher circulates among the groups as they talk. One group is questioning the fairness with which the text treats the topic and is disputing the goals of the women's movement.

Bubba: The way the text tells it, you'd think women were badly abused back then.

Susan: They were, and we still are.

Bubba and Sonny: Haw Haw.

Beth: Really, the text just skims over women's problems. But it's what you'd expect of a text written by a male.

Sonny: Skims over? It tells facts about women getting the right to vote.

Beth: Yes, ever so blandly.

Susan: And ever so few are the facts given.

Bubba: The facts are that things were different back in the 1800s. It's not right to ignore the way things were and to look back as if things were like they are today.

Susan: Things would still be the same as then if you had your way.

Bubba: It's not *my* way. It was the way of the culture. And in our culture, then and now, men and women take different roles.

Beth: That's so much history. There's nothing inevitable about the roles for men and women.

Sonny: So, OK. The text said women needed the vote in order to have power. So they got the vote and the power. Women haven't used their power to have the same things as men.

Beth: Women don't want all the *same* things. They want fair treatment and equal rights in the political system.

After about 10 minutes, the teacher hands out a sheet that contains value statements related to the topic. Students are assigned first to agree or disagree with each statement and then to guess how each other group member would respond to the statements, as seen here:

	Group Members			
Value Statements	*Bubba*	*Sonny*	*Susan*	*Beth*
1. Women lack judgment for choosing candidates for public office.	A D	A D	A D	A D
2. Women should not have had to struggle for so long for the right to vote.	A D	A D	A D	A D
3. We should all remember the hard-won struggle for democracy and vote at election time.	A D	A D	A D	A D
4. The writer of the text is correct in asserting that women should have the same rights as men have.	A D	A D	A D	A D

Teacher: Now, in your group, talk over why you responded to each statement as you did. The statements are not universal truths. They are value statements. So responses to them are personal opinions, not answers that are right or wrong.

Susan: They seem clearly right or wrong to me.

Sonny: To me, too.

Teacher: Have reasons for your responses. And listen to your group-mates' reasons.

The teacher circulates among the groups as they discuss their responses to the value statements.

Bubba: Women just don't think about politics the way men do, so I agreed with the first statement.

Beth: I knew you would.

Bubba: But I know women think they should have a say, so I figured you girls would disagree with the first statement.

Susan: You're darn right I disagree. I figured you'd think that way, so I circled that you'd agree with the first statement.

Sonny: Given what we said before about cultural roles, it's not anything in nature that keeps women from having political judgment. It's the culture. I had to agree with the first statement.

Beth: And you circled that I'd disagree, and so would Susan. Well about the culture, it increases women's sensitivity to political issues.

The group discussion continues until all students have expressed their opinions about each statement. Finally, the teacher brings the activity to a close.

Teacher: Expressing opinions and listening to the opinions of others is a healthy experience. If you predicted accurately what your group members would agree and disagree with, that means you listened well. You heard what they were thinking and got to know them better. Listening to the thoughts and opinions of others helps us clarify and develop our own values.

Women Get the Vote

By the end of the nineteenth century, women were aggressively seeking to have a greater say in the management of community affairs. This meant seeking a political voice. With no vote, they were powerless. Women had to struggle to overcome the enormous opposition to granting them equal status with men in determining political policies and electing public officials.

A major step had already been taken in 1869 when Wyoming granted women the right to vote. When it was admitted to the union in 1890, however, it was the only state that allowed women full political equality. Colorado, Idaho, and Utah followed suit by 1896, and Washington did so in 1910. With the ratification of the Nineteenth Amendment to the Constitution in 1920, women were granted political equality throughout America. Women won the right to vote, but they soon realized that the struggle for equality was far from over.

Source

James V. Hoffman. (1979). The Intra-Act Procedure for critical reading." *Journal of Reading, 22,* 605–608.

15

Planned Inferential Reading Lesson

The Planned Inferential Reading Lesson (PIRL) is a technique for improving students' ability to make inferences as they read. Students learn to verify whether information is actually present in the text and to use that information to support their interpretations.

An inference is information a person adds to information that is given. The information given provides premises on which added inferential information stands. Inferences cannot usually be correct if their premises are not present or are not correct. Nor can an inference be correct if it is not logically consistent with the explicitly given information, its premises. In this activity students increase their awareness about inference making. They determine whether information is or is not explicitly given in a text. And they check the fit between the given information and other information that it may imply. The activity provides for sharpening students' ability to discriminate between supportable and unsupportable inferences.

PIRL can be adapted to many subjects and instructional situations. It can be readily used in language arts (English, literature, reading), science, and social studies. It can be used effectively with classes of up to 20 students. Larger classes can be divided into groups small enough to encourage all students to participate significantly.

Procedure

The teacher presents students with a list of true statements from a text they are studying. Some of the statements are explicitly given in the text, and some are implied. Students first read the list of statements and then the text from which they have been derived. The teacher asks students to say which statements are explicitly stated in the text and which ones are implied. Once students have sorted the literal statements from the implied statements, the teacher has students point out the exact language in the text that leads to the implied statements. The teacher makes note of references students make to knowledge they had prior to reading.

When students are competent with the first phase of the activity, the teacher moves them to making discriminations between true (supportable) and untrue (unsupportable) inferences. This is accomplished with another list of statements derived from the text. None of the statements on the list is explicitly given in the text. Some of the statements are supportable inferences and some are unsupportable. Again, students first read the list of statements and then read the text. Finally, they identify which of the statements are supportable and which are not.

Discussion

The ability to make valid inferences is an important skill not only for reading in school but in everyday reading as well. Magazines, newspapers, procedural instructions, and various types of documents require readers to make appropriate inferences. In school, the demands for inferential reading comprehension increase as students progress through the grades. Teaching students to make valid inferences is an obviously justifiable endeavor. PIRL offers a practical approach to developing inferential comprehension. It can be adapted to use with small or large groups. It can easily be completed within the typical 50-minute class period. And only a moderate amount of teacher preparation is required.

There are limitations on the use of PIRL. Obviously it is not a spontaneous or impromptu method; the teacher has to prepare for the activity. Another related limitation is that the method does not provide for teaching difficult words that may appear in a passage. Preteaching vocabulary may be necessary to prepare students for the activity. The most serious limitation is that readers may not understand the passage, and thus not understand the process for discerning the correctness of an inference.

EXAMPLE

High school students in a social issues class have taken up the topic of women's problems. The teacher engages students in an activity designed to teach them to recognize the difference between literal and inferred interpretations and to examine the correctness of inferences.

Teacher: Take a look at this list of statements about women's problems in the 1800's.

Anthony: Is this a preview of today's lesson?

Teacher: It's a list of statements based on a short text we're going to read. As soon as we read this list, we'll read the text.

The teacher reads the statements aloud as students follow along reading silently:

> In the early 1800s, women had special problems to endure.
>
> Women earned less money than they should have.
>
> A married woman's personal property belonged to her husband.
>
> College was primarily for rich men.
>
> Opening colleges to women eventually led to raised expectations among women.
>
> Educated women gathered to discuss literature and culture.
>
> Women struggled for the vote so they could manage things.
>
> In the nineteenth century, a few states recognized that women deserved the right to vote.

Teacher: Now let's read the text entitled "Women's Problems in the Nineteenth Century."

The class reads the text.

Teacher: Let's look again at the list of statements we went over before reading the text. Which ones of the statements are actually given in the text?

Lucy: All of them.

Teacher: They're all statements that can be verified by the text. But the text does not say everyone of them outright.

Lucy: In so many words, it does.

Teacher: Right. Some statements the text makes outright. But some, only in so many words.

Hugo: What's the difference?

Teacher: The difference is that the reader has to read some things between the lines. In fact, most things.

Beth: The text says the first statement outright.

Clarence: But not the second. The text only says women worked alongside men but were paid less. It doesn't say directly that they should've been paid more.

The class sorts the explicit statements from the implied. The teacher then directs students to identify statements in the text that lead to the implied statements on the list.

Teacher: So, what is given in the text to imply that raised expectations among women resulted from opening colleges to them?

Lucy: First, they went to college, then . . .

Teacher: (interrupting) It is not stated in the text that women went to college.

Lucy: It says there were coeducational colleges and women's colleges, and it says women became educated.

Teacher: Yes, it does. But it does not say straight out that women went to college. You *inferred* that. And quite correctly. But you inferred it nonetheless. So, what *does* the text say that warrants inferring that going to college raised women's expectations?

Anthony: That there were coeducational and women's colleges and that women became educated. Educated women discussed social problems. They sought to have a say in the management of things.

Beth: It seems correct to *infer* that higher education enabled women to discuss social problems, that discussing problems is more than just having them, and that seeking to manage things in order to fix the problems shows that women had come to believe they deserved the right to vote.

Teacher: Anthony's information from the text justifies Beth's sequence of inferences, information that she added from her own knowledge.

As students point out explicit text statements that prompt their inferences, the teacher continues to emphasize that readers can arrive at these inferences only by adding their own knowledge to the text's literal message.

Teacher: So, the thoughts you have when you read are largely the products of your putting what the text says together with what you already know. The way you comprehend this text about women's problems depends on what you know–about your language and things in general, as well as about women and their problems.

Hugo: What if you don't know enough to put anything with the text?

Teacher: Then you can't understand it, or if your knowledge is sketchy or incorrect, you risk *mis*understanding it.

Clarence: Or if you are careless about the way you add your knowledge to the text.

Teacher: That's right. Your inferences should be supportable by what the text actually says. Here is another list of statements about "Women's Problems in the Nineteenth Century." They're all inferences.

The teacher reads the list of statements aloud:

> In the 1800s, women deserved to earn as much pay as men.
>
> Women worked in the company of men outside the home.
>
> Married women themselves did not own property.
>
> Giving a woman access to higher education was the sure way to change her subordinate social status.
>
> If a woman could go to college, she could hope to change her social status.
>
> Poor men could not attend college.
>
> Slowly opening higher education to women allowed women to adapt to their educated status properly.
>
> Women's goal of political equality included the right to vote.

Clarence: Some of those statements don't seem right.

Teacher: Because they can't be supported by what the text actually says. Let's read the text again, this time to see which of these inferences can be supported by what the text states explicitly.

Students again read the text silently.

Clarence: Now I know what's wrong with that first statement. The text did not say women *deserved* as much pay as men. It says, "They toiled side by side with men, but earned less pay."

Susan: That's the author's way of saying they deserved as much pay.

Clarence: Maybe. Certainly that's an inference you *want* to make, and the author wants you to make. From the way we see things today, we'd say women deserved as much pay as men. But the information is not there in the text to *support* that inference.

Susan: What more information could there be?

Clarence: Plenty–mainly that women were as productive as men.

Susan: But they were.

Clarence: Says you, not the text.

Teacher: Our contemporary sense of fairness *would* justify the inference. But to make it, a reader has to rely on that contemporary sense of fairness and knowledge associated with it. In the 1800s, people sensed fairness differently. Circumstances were different. There may be information the author has left out, perhaps even deliberately. *Deserve* is a word that entails a value judgment.

Beth: So, you're saying we may be right to make the inference that women deserved as much pay as men got, but the text itself doesn't support such an inference.

Teacher: Seems that way to me.

Women's Problems In the Nineteenth Century

The early 1800s saw many changes in American life, and with them the emergence of many problems. Women had their own special problems to endure. In addition to taking care of household chores—cooking, cleaning, and childrearing—women were expected to work outside the home. They toiled side by side with men, but earned less pay. If they were married, their earnings and personal property belonged to the husband.

Without access to higher education, women could have little hope of doing anything about their subordinate status. College was primarily a rich man's arena. This did change, but very slowly. In the midwest and west, colleges became coeducational, and in the east, colleges for women were established. As women became educated, they gathered to discuss literature and culture. More and more, they took up social problems—health care inequities, poverty, and political corruption.

And more and more, women sought to have some say in the management of things. But without the right to vote, they were without power. Women struggled for political equality. By the end of the nineteenth century, a few states did give women the right to vote. But full political equality for women had to wait until the twentieth century.

Source

James E. Cunningham, Patricia M. Cunningham, and Sharon V. Arthur. (1981). *Middle and secondary school reading* (pp. 230–232). New York: Longman.

16

RADAR

RADAR is an analogy-based technique for reinforcing and exploring subject matter concepts. It encourages students to take an inquiring, creative approach to subject matter learning. RADAR is an acronym for the method's five steps: *R*ead, *A*nalogize, *D*iscuss, *A*pply, *R*eview.

Students are challenged to create analogies between the subject matter and familiar concepts. In the analogies, relatedness between aspects of the subject matter is compared to the way aspects of familiar concepts are related. As students explore the analogies, they go over the subject matter's significant details and reflect on the processes by which it works. Inquisitiveness and creativity are fostered by applying diverse analogies to the subject matter.

Because analogy is a generally useful ploy for teaching, RADAR can be used effectively in teaching most academic subjects. It is especially effective in teaching science and social studies. Because young children may have difficulty exploring relatedness across diverse topics, the method is best used with older students (i.e., students beyond the intermediate grades). This is a discussion method for groups ranging in size between 6 and 15 students.

Procedure

Read. The lesson begins with a reading assignment. If a specific analogy is to be explored, the teacher tells students to read with that analogy in mind. If students are to generate their own analogies, the teacher asks students to read with a general question in mind. In the event that students have trouble with the analogy, or are likely not to understand how to formulate analogies later in the lesson, the teacher prepares students with warm-up exercises. These exercises help students compare dissimilar concepts and free them from stereotypical thinking, which could hinder discovering common features across concepts. Warm-up exercises may be spread over several days previous to reading.

Analogize. Once reading is completed, the teacher asks students either to explain the analogy presented previous to reading or to make up analogies that help clarify the topic. The teacher records students' responses on the chalkboard for discussion later. The teacher may then divide the class into groups for developing further analogies.

Discuss. The teacher leads students to point out the major elements of the subject matter to be learned. Here, students point out parts of their analogies that clarify important aspects of the subject matter. Students comment on the parts of their classmates' analogies that make the most sense and that best highlight the important facts about the material being studied. The teacher sees that the discussion gives attention to three areas: generating numerous analogical approaches to the subject matter, maintaining consistency in developing the analogies, and noting how details of the analogies add to understanding the subject matter. This is accomplished by prompting students to discuss or to answer questions about areas being ignored.

Apply. Students are now led to use the ideas from the discussion to approach the solution of problems. The teacher has students think about the analogies they have proposed and encourages them to see possibilities for dealing with a variety of problems.

Review. Finally, the points discussed are reviewed. This may involve the use of charts, graphs, and so on to illustrate related features of the analogous concepts discussed. The teacher may wish to use the review step to introduce follow-up lessons.

Discussion

Teaching methods that involve analogy making hold great potential for teaching new concepts, as well as for taking a fresh look at old ones. As students apply what they already know to explore subject matter, they engage in creative thinking. And they tend to become more active readers as they integrate new material with analogous knowledge. In RADAR, there are two major objectives: to establish a basis for concept learning by relating subject matter to familiar experience and to free students from stereotypical thinking. It is not essential, or even important, that the analogies draw exact parallels between subject matter and familiar experience. Approximate parallels are more likely to reveal new ways of looking at subject matter and its related problems.

EXAMPLE

A ninth-grade general science class is learning about electromagnetic wave energy and its applications (radio, television, x-ray, radar). Throughout the unit, the teacher has been suggesting comparisons with concepts previously taught as well as with students' personal experiences. The teacher stays with this approach as students learn about radar.

Teacher: Another device that makes use of electromagnetic wave energy is radar. As we'll see, radar locates things by detecting a kind of echo produced by electromagnetic waves, specifically a kind of radio wave. Before reading about radar, let's think about other things that make use of echoes.

Paige: Bats.

Rudy: Dolphins and whales.

Dick: Sonar.

Teacher: All good examples. How do they use echoes?

Paige: Bats can't see very well, but their hearing is keen. They send out a sound, and by the way it echoes back to them, they know where to fly to catch insects.

Rudy: Dolphins and whales do a similar thing, but they do it in water.

Dick: Like where sonar is used. It sends out a sound and listens for an echo to locate submarines.

Nick: And it's used by fishermen to find fish and to know how deep a river or lake is.

Teacher: So they work by detecting echoes of sounds they send out. Radar works something like that. We learned about sonar in the fall. Because sonar is a human-made device whose working principle is like that of radar, let's think about how sonar works as we read our textbook section "Radar." Afterward, we'll formulate some analogies between the two.

The class silently reads "Radar."

Teacher: Now, give me some analogies between radar and sonar. Feel free to use different forms analogy, like *A* is to *B* as *C* is to *D,* or *A* is to *B* as *B* is to *C.* I'll record your analogies here on the board.

Chris: Sonar is to sound navigation and ranging as radar is to radio detecting and ranging.

Teacher: Your memory is good, Chris.

Valerie: Sonar is to sound waves as radar is to radio waves.

Louise: Sonar is to underwater as radar is to atmosphere.

Henry: Sonar is to submarines as radar is to aircraft.

Nick: Sonar is to fish as radar is to weather systems.

Teacher: OK. Let's talk about these analogies. How about Chris's analogy?

Valerie: They've both got the word *ranging.*

Teacher: They do, but the important thing is they're both acronyms.

Henry: And the acronyms tell the purpose of each.

Louise: The purposes are analogous. Sonar does its thing underwater, but radar does its thing in the atmosphere.

Dick: So you would expect sonar to find submarines underwater and radar to find aircraft flying in the air.

Nick: They both find other things, too.

Teacher: Yes they do. Several applications of radar are well known: to guide aircraft, to track weather systems, to catch drivers who violate speed laws. Now let's divide into groups and come up with some other ways that radar can be used. Let's think of some problems it might help solve.

The teacher circulates among the groups as they discuss possible applications of radar for solving problems.

Teacher: Rudy, what did your group come up with?

Rudy: We think we know a problem that radar could solve. Automobiles could be equipped with radar devices that keep them from crashing into things–other cars and even stationary objects.

Teacher: Go on.

Rudy: The radar would detect objects that are too close to the car for the speed it's traveling. The radar would be coupled with another device. The radar would signal the other device and that device would adjust the speed and direction of the car so it wouldn't hit the detected object. The whole thing would be automatic.

Teacher: A wreck-avoidance system. That would certainly be a welcome application of radar.

Paige: Our group thought of a similar but simpler application of radar. Put it on train locomotives to prevent collisions with cars at railroad crossings. Trains can't change directions or slow down fast, so have a big broom at the crossings that the radar signals. The big broom would gently but swiftly sweep the track clear.

Teacher: Interesting thought. It might be cheaper and simpler to install more automatic gates at railroad crossings. We already use radar to control traffic signals, you know.

Nick: Our group thought of applying radar to duck hunting. Hunters go out during the night to wait for ducks to fly in during the early light of morning. They *hope* the ducks come, but they can't be sure that after waiting out there in the wet and cold there'll be any duck action. With radar, hunters could know if there are any ducks coming in. And they could know how many, the path they're flying, and what time to expect them.

Teacher: Give the hunters a sporting chance, huh?

Nick: Well, give them a better chance for some sporting action. There's no need suffering out there if there are no ducks coming. Radar could let hunters know what to expect.

Teacher: Three possible applications of radar have been suggested. Now let's review the main points about radar. The term *radar* is an acronym for the words that tell its function. It works by sending radio waves and picking up the echoes of those waves. The location of blips on a CRT screen corresponds to a target object in the atmosphere.

The review continues with the teacher elaborating on each point. Following the review, the teacher assigns students to complete a worksheet that has students develop the analogy between radar and a flashlight.

RADAR

Radar is a device for detecting distant objects by the use of reflected radio waves. The word *radar* is an acronym formed from the words *radio detecting and ranging*, which indicates its function. It is used principally to locate and guide aircraft, to monitor weather systems, and to detect speeding automobiles.

The principle underlying radar is simple. The radar sends out radio waves. When the radio waves hit an object, they are deflected. Some bounce back to the radar source. The radar's antenna picks up the returning radio waves and determines the direction from which they came. The radar's timer measures the interval between the time the original wave was sent and its return. The speed of radar waves is 299,993 km per second. Information about the direction

of returning waves is combined with information about the time interval between their emission and return. Together, this information is used to locate
the object exactly.

Radar reception is shown on the screen of a cathode ray tube (CRT). From
inside the tube, an electron beam sweeps across the screen. Returning radio
beams show the deflecting object as a spot of light on the screen. The object's
direction and distance are indicated by their location on the screen.

Source

Charles E. Martin. (1981). Using *RADAR* to zero-in on content area concepts. *Reading Horizons, 21,* 139–142.

17

REAP

REAP is an acronym for *Read, Encode, Annotate, Ponder*—the four steps of a strategy designed to refine students' subject matter knowledge through overt, thoughtful responses to reading. It also serves to enhance students' analytical thinking and communication skills.

The premise of REAP is that it is in the communication of ideas that ideas come to be understood well. When combined with reading, writing and speaking foster the identification of significant information in a text and encourage reflection on that information. And motivation is heightened. As students share their reactions to reading in writing and speaking activity, they experience an increased sense of intellectual vigor. They take pleasure in witnessing their personal deliberations contribute to the learning of others. The result is that their own knowledge becomes clearer and more durable.

REAP may be used productively in instructional situations that take the subject matter largely from textual materials. It is especially well suited for use in literature and social studies classes where texts provide the focus for class discussions. REAP is easily adapted to a variety of grouping possibilities. It may be used with whole classes, small groups, or individual students. The activity assumes that students are able to read and write, at least at a basic level.

Procedure

The teacher leads students through a four-step cycle of text study that has students read, encode, annotate, and ponder the content. The teacher assigns students to read a selection or text segment (read), privately translate it into their own way of thinking and saying it (encode), and react to the material by writing a brief comment or explanation (annotate), which the teacher then uses to elicit discussion about the subject matter (ponder). At the core of the procedure is having students write annotations (i.e., their own notes that explain or comment on the text).

Different types of annotations provide for deliberating on different aspects of the material and for reflecting on it at different levels. The *heuristic* annotation is simply a quotation from the text that gives the essence of the author's message. The *summary* annotation condenses the content of the text. The *thesis* annotation states the gist or main idea. The *question* annotation formulates a question that can be answered by reading the text. The *critical* annotation comprises three sentences: one that states the text's thesis, one that states the student's position, and one (at least) that defends the student's position. The *intention* annotation clarifies the author's intentions (to be persuasive, satirical, etc.). And the *motivation* annotation comments on the author's perceptions or personal beliefs that appear to have driven the writing of the text.

The teacher assigns students to read a selection or textbook segment and react to it by jotting down their thoughts about it. The teacher specifies how students are to react by selecting from among the annotation types. By selecting carefully among them, the teacher can orient students' thinking about the material. When students have read and annotated the text, the teacher initiates discussion by calling on some of the students to read their annotations. The teacher may ask other students questions, such as "How does your annotation compare with Marilyn's?" "Does your annotation agree with Tony's?" "Does Ron's annotation seem to capture what the author is saying?"

The cycle of reading, thinking, writing, and discussing continues as the teacher directs it. The teacher may have students proceed to a subsequent selection or text section, or students may be asked to reconsider the same material by reacting to it with a different type of annotation. The class may be divided into groups, or students may be assigned to annotate and ponder the text on an individual basis.

Discussion

The primary utility of REAP is that it provides a thorough approach to text analysis that can be conveniently applied under most circumstances. It emphasizes to students that thinking about a selection does not stop after it is read, but instead only begins if its content is to be learned. Discussion of assigned reading with REAP gives students a chance to gather their thoughts before speaking. And it gives every student an opportunity to contribute to the discussion, even if the contribution is limited to reading one's annotation. For the teacher, REAP provides a device for exercising control over the discussion. It allows eliciting response to reading, but at the same time discourages domination of the discussion by very assertive students. Most importantly, it allows the teacher to direct and adjust the level of thinking through careful selection of annotation types.

For most students, learning to write annotations can be incidental to learning subject matter; annotation writing can simply be a task they undertake as part of considering assigned material. However, some students may require explicit instruction in annotation writing itself. These students may need instruction in recognizing and defining material to be included in an annotation and in discriminating appropriateness of certain annotations; they may need to see the teacher model the process of annotation writing, and they will surely need practice at annotating texts.

EXAMPLE

A high school American literature class reads Robert Frost's "Fire and Ice." The teacher's objective is to have students interpret the poem on multiple levels. This objective includes having students share evidence for their interpretations. First, students demonstrate their comprehension of the poem's literal content.

Teacher: (concluding an introduction to the poem) . . . burn and freeze, hot and cold, FIRE AND ICE—words that speak to our senses in the extreme. There's an intriguing title for you, certainly. Let's go ahead now and read the poem. As is our practice, we'll read the poem several times.

Merve: First to get the literal meaning.

Cassandra: Then to interpret beyond the literal meaning.

Art: And to examine the poet's method.

Teacher: Right. You know that to appreciate a poem is to read it again and again. Now let's read the poem. Think about what the words are saying literally, explicitly. Then, in your own words, write down what the poem plainly says.

The teacher reads the poem aloud:

> FIRE AND ICE*
>
> Some say the world will end in fire,
>
> Some say in ice,
>
> From what I've tasted of desire
>
> I hold with those who favor fire.
>
> But if it had to perish twice,
>
> I think I know enough of hate
>
> To say that for destruction ice
>
> Is also great
>
> And would suffice.

Then, as students write down their *summary annotations,* the teacher writes one on an overhead transparency to be shown after students have presented theirs.

Teacher: OK. Merve, let's hear what you wrote down.

Source: From *The Poetry of Robert Frost* edited by Edward Connery Lathem. Copyright 1923, © 1969 by Holt, Rinehart and Winston. Copyright 1951 by Robert Frost. Reprinted by permission of Henry Holt and Company, Inc.

Merve: (reading from his paper) People disagree about how the world will end. Some people believe it will end by fire, and some people believe it will end by ice.

Teacher: Gwen, how does your annotation compare with Merve's?

Gwen: Merve is right about what people believe about the way the world will end. But I think the poem says more. Here's what I wrote down: "The world could end either by fire or ice, but probably by fire."

Teacher: That does seem to include more of the message. Art, what do you think?

Art: I think so, too. Here's mine: "Fire or ice could destroy the world. Although it will probably end by fire, ice would destroy it just as much."

Teacher: You observe that the poet gives importance to the destructive power of ice, too. But does he say fire and ice are equally destructive?

Students continue reading and commenting on one another's annotations. The teacher's annotation is shown and discussed. When it is apparent that the students understand the poem's literal message, the teacher encourages them to think further as they write a *thesis annotation*.

Teacher: Let's read the poem again. This time, let's read to discover the poem's controlling idea. After reading the poem silently, write down in your own words the point Frost tries to make in the poem.

As the students read the poem and write annotations, the teacher writes a thesis annotation on an overhead transparency.

Teacher: Lance, what did you write down?

Lance: I think it's obvious. There's no hidden meaning here: "The world will surely end. Fire is enough to end it, but there's also ice to end it as well."

Cassandra: Really, Lance. What you call obvious sounds shallow to me.

Merve: Not to me. That's sorta what I wrote.

Cassandra: Little minds think alike.

Teacher: What Lance and Merve probably mean by "obvious" is that they can suport their statement of thesis with the poem's language. Do you see something more subtle here, Cassandra?

Cassandra: Shall I explain my thesis annotation before reading it, or read it and then explain?

Teacher: Read it, but see if it will stand the test of others explaining it to your satisfaction.

Cassandra: "Excessive passions destroy you, whether they're passions of desire or of hate."

Gwen: I think I know what your getting at, Cassandra. Fire and ice are symbols for our emotions in the extreme. The world represents whatever there may be. Life itself. Life within you.

Emily: Wanting something too much can be destructive. Like we already said, everybody wanting what everybody can't have leads to fighting and wars.

Richard: Or it's like the all-consuming passion Romeo and Juliet had for each other. It destroyed both of them.

Sarah: On the other hand, cold indifference can be just as destructive. You might blackball a person or a whole group of people. You know, freeze them out. You may hurt them, but you may also destroy yourself cutting yourself off from what you need to thrive.

The discussion proceeds to consideration of other students' thesis annotations and finally the teacher's. The teacher then directs students to write *question annotations* in order to have them focus sharply on the poet's devices for achieving the poem's effect.

Teacher: Keeping in mind what you've said about the poem's theme, now write two or three questions about the devices used to advance that theme. In other words, think about the poem's essential idea and write two or three questions whose answers require examining the poem for evidence that indicates the poet's intended message. What might some of these devices be?

Emily: Choice of words.

Lance: The poem's form. Maybe its appearance on the page.

Art: Its sound, its rhythm, its rhyme.

Sarah: Its appeal to universal feelings and experiences, like what you said about T. S. Eliot's "objective correlative."

Teacher: Good. Go ahead, examine the poem closely and write your questions. Let's hear one of your questions first, Art.

Art: How does the poem's rhyme scheme tie together the emotions of anger?

Emily: Fire rhymes with desire. Fire and desire are both symbols for heated feelings, like anger and, maybe, envy–which is a kind of destructive anger.

Richard: And, hey, check this: Both words, *fire* and *desire,* contain the word *ire.*

Teacher: Astute observation, Richard. *Ire* is more than a poetic word for anger. Ire is intense rage.

Merve: Well, I have a question that asks how the rhyme says something about these emotions, too.

Teacher: Let's hear it.

Merve: How does the rhyme suggest that hate is more powerful than desire?

Sarah: Twice rhymes with ice. Could that hint that ice is twice as powerful as fire?

Merve: You're with me on this, I think. But there's more to it.

Sarah: Ice also rhymes with suffice.

Merve: Right. Ice has twice as many rhyming words as desire. Consider that with the fact that six of the poem's lines are about ice and only three are about fire.

Gwen: The hate-great lines aren't necessarily about ice.

Merve: Not necessarily. But they are tied with the twice–ice–suffice lines.

Emily: Which all contain the word *ice*.

In the discussion that follows, students continue to react to one another's question annotations about the poet's method.

Source

Marilyn Eanet and Anthony V. Manzo. (1976). REAP–A strategy for improving reading/writing/discussion skills. *Journal of Reading, 19,* 647–652.

18

Polar Opposites

The Polar Opposites method is useful for guiding critical reading and stimulating discussion about a topic under study. It can also be used as a prewriting activity for composition assignments that call for developing an opinion or judgment.

Polar Opposites is an instructional adaptation of a psychometric method that makes use of contrasting adjectives to determine a person's attitudes about a given topic. Students are asked to express judgments about the subject matter in terms provided by the teacher. Specifically, students are asked to indicate where along a continuum between contrasting adjectives (e.g., good–bad, happy–sad, hot–cold) aspects of the material best fit. In order to respond, students have to think about the material carefully, take account of what they already know about it, and perhaps sort out their feelings and beliefs about it. They nearly always have to refer to the text. Differing responses among students provide the basis for discussion that leads to refined thinking about the material.

Polar Opposites may be used effectively in any academic subject, especially if the material lends itself to the expression of opinions or judgments. Its effectiveness may be somewhat limited if the instructional purpose is to present factual material about which there can be little or no disagreement. Polar Opposites may be used with expository, narrative, or persuasive selections. The method is ideal for groups of 10 to 20 students. Fewer than 10 students may not provide adequate discussion, and more than 20 may prove inhibitive for reticent students and possibly disruptive of the classroom order. As with any other method, care should be taken that it is not used excessively.

Procedure

For the subject matter under study, the teacher develops a set of four or five pairs of contrasting adjectives. These adjective pairs are placed either on the chalkboard or on a worksheet with five spaces separating them. The spaces are for indicating gradients of meaning between the extremes of the contrasting discriptors. For example:

As the story unfolds, Francisco becomes _____ about his situation.

certain _____ _____ _____ _____ _____ bewildered

After presenting the material in a lecture or text, the teacher has students mark the space between each pair of polar opposites to indicate how they believe the information is represented. The teacher then has students defend their ratings with specific examples or references to the text.

Discussion

Developing students' critical thinking abilities is one of the most difficult and important challenges that the teacher faces. Developing these abilities in students calls for providing them with opportunities to clarify their own perceptions and values as well as to sort out facts and contrasting ideas. Polar Opposites has obvious utility for developing critical thinking, especially when it is used in instruction designed to have students distinguish fact from opinion, detect propaganda, and weigh variant perspectives. In most lessons, the teacher, having prepared the Polar Opposite items, can more or less predict the direction that discussion will take, but without prescribing particular right or wrong responses for students.

Initially, students may become frustrated in an activity that calls for them to respond to material for which absolutely correct responses are not possible. And they may become further frustrated when they believe they are correct yet cannot find clear support for their beliefs in the material presented. Once students become accustomed to this kind of activity, however, they tend to enjoy the freedom to express and defend individual responses.

EXAMPLE

An eighth-grade geography class, involved in a unit on the Arctic, is taking up the topic of polar bears. The teacher has introduced this topic and assigned students to read a brief textbook segment that is to be discussed as students respond to a "Polar Opposites Worksheet" (prepared in advance of the lesson).

Teacher: Now that you've read the textbook section on polar bears, let's complete the sentences on the worksheet by placing a check on the blank that you think best fits what you've read. Let's do them together, item by item.

The teacher reads the following:

Polar Opposites Worksheet

1. The color of polar bears' coats is _____ snow white.

   always _____ _____ _____ _____ _____ never

2. Polar bear liver is _____ by hunters.

   prized _____ _____ _____ _____ _____ shunned

3. According to the text, polar bears have _____ heads.

   large _____ _____ _____ _____ _____ small

4. A man _____ lift a polar bear easily.

   could _____ _____ _____ _____ _____ could not

5. Polar bears are _____ .

   aggressive _____ _____ _____ _____ _____ shy

Bobby: What do we do if we don't favor either one of the words?

Teacher: Good question. If you don't favor either term, place a check in the middle space.

Billy: Is this a test? Is it OK to look back?

Teacher: This is not a test. And it is OK—in fact you *should*—refer to the text. How about the first one? Who would check the first space? The second? The third? The fourth? The last one? Betty, please explain why you chose the first blank.

Betty: The text says the color of their coat is a good camouflage against the snow and ice. Snow and ice are white. Therefore they are always snow-white.

Sue: Look at the sentence before that one, Betty. It says their fur ranges from white to yellowish-tan.

Teacher: So how did you mark your worksheet, Sue?

Sue: I put a mark on the second space. Although polar bears' fur may *range* from white to yellow-tan, it's mostly white.

Bobby: It doesn't say that in the text.

Sue: True. But, as Betty says, their fur serves as camouflage and it changes with the season. In the Arctic, it's mostly snowy. So most of the time, they would have white fur, but not always.

Teacher: Good inference, Sue. Explain how you marked yours, Bobby.

Bobby: Well, I really didn't think their fur was ever truly *snow* white. But I didn't mark the space all the way next to "never." I marked the next to the last space, just in case I was wrong.

Teacher: (laughing) OK, Bobby. Please, Mary Lou, tell us how you marked the first one.

Mary Lou: I marked the second space.

Teacher: Why?

Mary Lou: I don't know. I just did.

Teacher: Class, let me remind you that if you can't find support for your response, perhaps you should reconsider it. Billy, would you like to give us the reason you marked the first item as you did?

Billy: I changed mine because I agree with Sue.

Teacher: All right. How about yours, Carol?

Carol: I marked the middle space. I didn't see the words *never* or *always*, so I checked the middle space like you told us to do if we didn't favor either.

Teacher: OK. Sometimes, students, you will not find exact words. You need to make inferences on your own.

The discussion continues for the other items on the worksheet.

Polar Bears

Polar bears inhabit the Arctic Circle. They are also known as white bears, sea bears, and ice bears. The bears are hunted by humans for their hide, fur, and fat. Their livers, however, are inedible because of their high concentration of Vitamin A. The fur, which ranges from white to yellow-tan (depending on age, season, and other factors), is a distinctive characteristic of polar bears. The color of their coat is a good camouflage against the snow and ice, thus protecting them from their enemies. The coat also protects the animal against the cold. The polar bears' feet are protected by their hairy soles. The average weight and length of these bears is 900 pounds and 8 feet long respectively.

Polar bears have other distinguishing characteristics. They exhibit an excellent swimming ability, which use when searching for food (seal, walrus, and fish) in the winter. Their eating habits change during the summer as they begin to feed on things closer to shore (seaweed, marine grass, birds, and an occasional beached whale).

Weighing an average of two pounds at birth, polar bears usually remain with the mother from 10 months to 2 years. The gestation period of the mother ranges from 240 to 270 days. The animals grow to be shy, but dangerous when attacked.

Source

Thomas W. Bean and Ashley L. Bishop. (1986). Polar opposites: A strategy for guiding students' critical reading and discussion. In E. K. Dishner, T. W. Bean, J. E. Readence, and D. W. Moore (Eds.), *Reading in the content areas: Improving classroom instruction* (2nd ed.) (pp. 246–251). Dubuque, IA: Kendall/Hunt.

19

Controversy

Controversy is an activity in which students assert arguments for and against controversial propositions. Students evaluate arguments, synthesize evidence, and draw reasoned conclusions. The activity promotes students' interest in the subject matter and stimulates reading and thinking about it critically.

Long recognized as an effective ploy in teaching, controversy motivates students to relieve dissonance that is created by conflicting ideas. Such dissonance gives impetus to close examination of positions taken either in textual materials or by individuals. By examining arguments closely, students seek to sort facts from opinions and to distinguish reasoned explanations from rhetorical manipulations. Students listen and read with the clear purpose of determining truth.

Controversy is well suited for school subjects that, by their nature, involve controversial issues. These include subjects chiefly in the areas of literature and social studies. Since controversy is principally an activity of debate and exchange of ideas, it is necessarily a group activity. Group size has to be limited so that all students can contribute to the give and take exchange. Controversy is appropriate for students in high school and college.

Procedure

The teacher's task is to bring students' attention to controversial questions posed by the subject matter and to have students explore those questions. Part of the teacher's preparation is to determine whether additional literature should be provided. In the lesson itself, the teacher introduces the dimensions of the controversy. Students discuss the question, read material related to it, and then reconsider their thoughts about the controversy in light of what they have read.

How the teacher handles controversy depends to a large extent on the class literature. If there is a textbook that points out controversial matters but remains neutral, the teacher may provide additional materials that argue opposing points of view. If the class literature presents one perspective, the teacher may provide literature that presents an alternate perspective. Providing additional material is not always needed or appropriate, however. Works of fiction often present dilemmas for readers to deal with according to their own values.

Before students read, the teacher raises the issue to be argued in the lesson. The issue is broached through discussion and questioning: How do you feel about . . . ? What would you do if . . . ? To guide the discussion and have students consider key aspects of the controversy, the teacher presents a list of statements expressing principles for governing one's actions or decisions relative to the matter at issue. Students react to each statement, explaining their agreement or disagreement. Throughout the discussion, the teacher maintains a neutral stance.

Having considered the dimensions of the controversy, students read a selection or selections that raise the issue. Following the reading, students are asked to say whether the author would agree or disagree with the statements on the list of statements they discussed prior to reading. If the selection is a story or other narrative account, students are called on to indicate how the characters would stand on each statement. When there are two or more selections read, students react to each one immediately after reading it (before reading the next selection). After all selections are read, they are compared as to their agreement or disagreement with each statement on the list discussed before reading.

Finally students reconsider their earlier positions of agreement or disagreement with each of these statements. For some statements they may wish to modify their position as undecided pending further reading. The teacher should be prepared to suggest other sources of information on the topic.

Discussion

Where it is possible to inject controversy into a lesson, there is an opportunity to increase students' interest and participation. There is also an opportunity to develop students' research skills and to encourage outside reading. As it is typically presented in textbooks, however, the content of school subjects generates little excitement. Often the content is potentially exciting, but the teacher misses opportunities to make it so. With the Controversy method, it is possible to introduce controversial material and enliven the class atmosphere. Care should be taken to introduce controversy as it fits the content and meets overall instructional goals.

The teacher does not have to look hard to find opportunities to bring controversy into instruction. The teacher has only to remain alert for information the textbook omits. School textbooks tend to avoid controversy, even at the cost of covering the subject inadequately. As the teacher augments the textbook presentation, conflicts and contradictions on the material become apparent. When this occurs, students see that knowledge is often relative, and that the significance of facts may change when presented with certain other facts or when presented from a different perspective. Some students find this disconcerting, especially students who view all knowledge as absolute and unswerving, and who look to the teacher to cover the "right" material and to pose questions that have "right" answers.

To head off untoward reactions from students, and possibly students' parents who sense a challenge to their wisdom or authority, the teacher needs to exercise judgment in presenting controversial material. The material should be appropriate to the school subject and to the analytical skills that students have developed or are developing. The teacher should allow different points of view to be expressed without letting vocal students dominate the discussion. And the teacher's own biases should be held in check. By supporting a particular point of view the teacher risks loss of standing as a fair-minded observer. The teacher's role in this procedure is to encourage students to advance as many arguments and cite as much evidence as they can for different sides of the issue under consideration.

EXAMPLE

A high school English class is beginning a unit on the theme *truth* as it has been treated by major writers. To introduce the unit, the teacher has students examine their own beliefs about truth and truthfulness.

Teacher: So, John, what does truth mean to you?

John: It means just that, truth. It is what is so, what is actually the case.

Teacher: And what does it mean to you, Shirley?

Shirley: I agree with John. But it means even more to me personally.

Teacher: Oh?

Shirley: Truth is what I live by. I count on it. And, really, so does everybody. Truth makes everything we do possible. It is because we can trust one another to be truthful that we can do things together cooperatively.

Teacher: You're saying that reliability in human affairs is predicated upon truthfulness.

Shirley: Right.

Mike: That may be so, but not everyone sees truth in the same way.

Teacher: What do you mean?

Mike: Well, some people think truth is the way *they* think things actually are.

Denise: Right. We have all kinds of opinions about political stuff and people believe their own opinions are the truth.

Clai: And then there's the matter of holding only *some* things to be absolutely truthful about but other things it's OK to fib about.

Melissa: Yeah, like a white lie you tell to save hurting someone's feelings.

Teacher: Excellent. You're bringing up some important issues surrounding the matter of truth. Issues like these make it a theme rich in possibilities for writers.

John: But the truth is the truth, plain and simple.

Shirley: The importance of remaining always truthful is certainly rich in possibilities for writers.

Teacher: That is an important angle for writers to pursue. There are others, as well. Let me ask you to reflect on some different thoughts about truth and truthfulness. Take a minute or so to think about the statements listed on this handout.

The teacher distributes this handout:

HANDOUT: "Keep Thy Tongue"

This list of statements represents a range of values regarding truth telling. Read each statement thoughtfully. In the space provided, indicate either your agreement (by writing *yes*) or your disagreement (by writing *no*).

1. _____ It is always wrong to lie, under any circumstance.

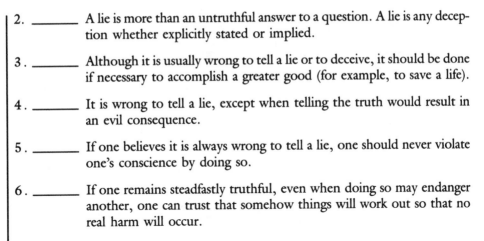

2. _____ A lie is more than an untruthful answer to a question. A lie is any deception whether explicitly stated or implied.

3. _____ Although it is usually wrong to tell a lie or to deceive, it should be done if necessary to accomplish a greater good (for example, to save a life).

4. _____ It is wrong to tell a lie, except when telling the truth would result in an evil consequence.

5. _____ If one believes it is always wrong to tell a lie, one should never violate one's conscience by doing so.

6. _____ If one remains steadfastly truthful, even when doing so may endanger another, one can trust that somehow things will work out so that no real harm will occur.

Teacher: To the left of each statement, indicate your agreement by writing "yes" or your disagreement by writing "no."

After giving students time to answer each statement, the teacher continues.

Teacher: John, I think I know how you answered number 1.

John: And number 2. Lying, deceiving, they're the same thing and they're both wrong.

Mike: Even if to do a greater good, as it says in number 3 – or to avoid something evil from happening, as it says in number 4?

John: A lie *is* evil. You would just be trading one evil for another. Liars are always using hypothetical situations to argue for moral relativism.

Teacher: What do you believe, Leigh Ann?

Leigh Ann: John is right. It is wrong to lie.

Shirley: Yes it is. I agree with John. Statements 3 and 4 are cop-outs that liars use.

Denise: Would you really call lying in order to save a life a cop-out?

Shirley: Of course it is. I also agree with number 6.

As the discussion continues, students share their reactions to the statements on the handout and debate the moral issues of lying or deceiving in order to prevent an evil from being perpetrated.

Clai: Well, I don't care what you say, number 5 is true. You should stick to what your conscience tells you is right and never lie. The truth is "a lamp unto our feet and a light unto our paths."

Teacher: Think about these statements and what you've said about truthfulness as you read "Keep Thy Tongue from Evil and Thy Lips from Speaking Guile." Try to figure out how each character would react to each of the statements we have discussed. And try to figure out the position that the author would take on them.

The class silently reads the short story.

Teacher: Tell us, Melissa, how does this story treat the question we've been talking about? What is truth?

Melissa: There's this scripture-quoting girl, Esther, whose boyfriend is visiting. But he's not supposed to be there because he's an Israeli soldier. So when the Druzes come looking for Israeli soldiers, he has to hide. When they ask where's any Israeli soldiers, she cannot tell a lie. So she tells them, but only sort of.

Teacher: How would the characters, say Esther, respond to the statements on the handout?

Clai: Obviously she would agree with numbers 1, 2, 5, and 6. She would disagree with the others.

Denise: Yeah, she even risked her boyfriend's skin, and everyone's, in order not to violate her conscience.

John: The story promotes the view of moral relativism. It presents a fictional situation that exaggerates the ordinary negative consequences that sometimes threaten when we stick to the truth.

Shirley: Right. And besides, the story was written from the perspective of Esther's family. From the Druzes' perspective it would have shown them harboring a dangerous enemy. Their not cooperating with the search is like our not cooperating with the police when they ask us to help them find criminals.

Mike: But what you're saying only proves what I said earlier, that not everyone sees truth in the same way.

Clai: But Esther remained steadfastly truthful. She knew that if she did, no harm would come to any of them.

Denise: But she hid Moise from the Druzes. That in itself was a deception.

John: No, it was David and Abe who hid Moise.

Shirley: Right. And Abe scolded Esther for sticking to the truth. He and David were the ones who would have been responsible for everyone's getting shot had the Druzes found Moise. *They* were the ones who hid him.

John: Abe and David are like you, Mike, and you, Denise and Melissa. They're moral relativists.

Teacher: Leigh Ann, you haven't said anything. Are you sticking by the position you took before reading the story?

Leigh Ann: Well, I have to say it's one thing to say you wouldn't ever lie or deceive someone, even if it meant saving your life or the life of someone else. But I have to admit this story puts lying in a situation that, if I were in it, I'd have to lie. The situation justifies it.

Shirley: Oh, Leigh Ann, this is a story, fiction.

Leigh Ann: Yes, but it does pose a situation that could happen. If I were in that situation, to be honest, I'd lie. I'd lie to save my skin or yours.

Shirley: No thank you.

Discussion of the story continues until students' opinions about truthfulness and deception have been thoroughly aired. Then the teacher suggests further reading on the issue.

Teacher: Now that we've broached the subject of truth, we'll next consider whether political leaders are ever justified in deceiving others. Tomorrow we'll read Jonathan Swift's "The Art of Political Lying."

Keep Thy Tongue from Evil and Thy Lips from Speaking Guile

We were sitting around the kitchen table lamenting the great calamity that had befallen our beloved Beirut. The city had become a battlefield, a rubbled heap of terror, where it was all but impossible to tell friends from enemies. Moslems were fighting Christians; Jews were fighting Moslems; Moslem factions were fighting among themselves. Commiserating with us was an accomplice to the calamity, a young Israeli soldier, Moise, who had come courting our sister, Esther.

Suddenly David burst into the room, his face white with fear. "They're coming!" our eldest brother cried, "Druze militia! They're searching house to house for Israeli soldiers."

"Quickly, Moise, you have to get out of here," said Esther. "Go! Now, or they'll shoot us all."

"Wait," said David. "They're already outside. We'll have to hide you."

Abe knew the place: "In the hole. It's the only place we have to put him."

In an instant, Abe dragged the table aside, yanked the rug from the floor, and pulled open the trap door to the small root cellar. Without a word, Moise scrambled in. We closed the door, pulled the rug over it, and dragged the table back into place. Over the table Esther whipped a large tablecloth and began to set dishes as if for the evening meal.

The front door flew open with a loud crash. Three Druze militiamen rushed into the kitched, pointing their rifles at us. "Your hands in the air!" a tall soldier shouted. The noise of his comrades knocking over chairs and scooting furniture came from the other rooms.

"Where are they?" the tall soldier demanded. We stood there trembling and silent. "There are Israeli soldiers about. Where are they? Where are you hiding them?"

The tall soldier stared at us one by one. He fixed his stare upon Esther and she began to cry. Her tears were streaming. He would not unlock his stare from her. "Enough," she said regaining her composure. "Look under the table. My faith does not allow me to veer from the truth. Look under the table."

Our hearts sank as all guns turned downward under the table. The tall soldier grasped a corner of the tablecloth and snatched it off. Suddenly Esther burst into shrieks of laughter. Then, in a moment of awareness, the rest of us joined her in hysterical laughter.

The tall soldier swung his rifle toward us. Angrily he growled, "Do not mock us."

Looking down the barrel of his rifle, we became quiet again. The tall soldier stared at us menacingly, then turned and stormed out of the kitchen. The other soldiers followed him, and just as suddenly as they had come, they were gone.

That evening we celebrated our having successfully hidden Moise right under the noses of the Druzes, and our deliverance from sure death had he been discovered. Pouring another round of drinks, Abe began to scold Esther. "You and your reverence for the truth nearly got us all killed."

"Keep thy tongue from evil and thy lips from speaking guile," Esther smiled piously, "Psalm 34."

"You carry your faith too far," Abe lectured her. "Had they found Moise, they would have executed us all right then and there."

"Ah, but they didn't find me," said Moise coming to the defense of his lover and savior.

"And I knew in my heart they wouldn't," preached Esther. "'The righteous cry, and the Lord heareth, and delivereth them out of all their troubles.' Same Psalm, verse 17."

Sources

Alan M. Frager and Loren C. Thompson. (1985). Conflict: The key to critical reading instruction. *Journal of Reading, 28,* 676–683.

John P. Lunstrum. (1981). Building motivation through the use of controversy. *Journal of Reading, 24,* 687–691.

20

Cooperative Conflict Resolution

Cooperative Conflict Resolution is a discussion/debate procedure that strengthens students' advocacy skills. It discourages hostility and narrowmindedness when arguing a position on a controversial issue. Students learn to criticize ideas, not people.

Controversy stimulates interest in a subject and motivates students to probe deeply for information. As students become informed, they take a position on controversial issues. To persuade others to agree with that position, students have to know more than the facts about the issue. They have to know how to frame the issue, how to evaluate evidence, and how to summarize information. They have to listen carefully and be able to take different perspectives. Cooperative Conflict Resolution gives practice in developing these skills in a sequence of small-group activities. The activities may take up to three one-hour class periods. The procedure is appropriate for high school and college classes in social studies, philosophy, and literature.

Procedure

The teacher divides the class into groups of four, which are then subdivided into pairs. Students are told that one pair will take the *pro* side and the other pair will take the *con* side of a controversial issue in the subject. The teacher presents the controversy and describes the activities to follow.

Procedure and Rules Handout*
PROCEDURE

1. Meet with your partner and plan how to argue effectively for your position. Make sure you and your partner have mastered as much of the material suporting your position as possible.

2. Each pair presents their position. Be forceful and persuasive in presenting your position. Take notes and clarify anything you do not fully understand when the opposing pair present their position.

3. Open Discussion. Argue forcefully and persuasively for your position, presenting as many facts as you can to support your point of view. Critically listen to the opposing pair's position, asking them for the facts that support their point of view. Remember, this is a complex issue and you need to know both sides to write a good report. Work together as a total group to get all the facts out. Make sure you understand the facts that support both points of view.

4. Reverse the perspectives in the group by each pair arguing the opposing pair's position. In arguing for the opposing pair's position be as forceful and persuasive as you can. See if you can think of any new facts that the opposing pair did not think to present.

5. Come to a group decision that all four of you can agree with. Summarize the best arguments for both points of view. Detail what you know (facts) about the topic. When you have consensus in your group, organize your arguments to present to the entire class. Other groups may make the opposite decision and you may need to defend the validity of your decision to the entire class.

RULES

1. I am critical of ideas, not people. I challenge and refute the ideas of the opposing pair, but I do not indicate that I reject them personally.

2. Remember, we are all in this together, sink or swim. I focus on coming to the best decision possible, not on *winning*.

3. I encourage everyone to participate and to master all the relevant information.

4. I listen to everyone's ideas, even if I do not agree.

5. I restate what someone has said if it is not clear.

6. I first bring out *all* the ideas and facts supporting both sides, and then I try to put them together in a way that makes sense.

7. I try to understand both sides of the issue.

8. I change my mind when the evidence clearly indicates that I should do so.

The teacher goes over the handout and emphasizes that each group is expected to reach consensus and at the end of the lesson submit a written report. The pro and con pairs are given the same material to read and are directed to read and prepare their arguments. After about 20 or 30 minutes, the pairs meet with other pairs taking the

Source: Tom Morton. (1986). Decision on Dieppe: A co-operative lesson on conflict resolution. *History and Social Science Teacher, 21,* 39.

same position for the purpose of exchanging arguments and information. Now debate begins within the groups. The pairs meet with the other half of the group and follow a structured procedure, which is outlined on the handout issued by the teacher. The teacher moves from group to group, observing students' debate skills. The teacher's observations of these skills are recorded on a chart, as follows:

Observation Sheet for Conflict Resolution*

Names

S K I L L S	Criticizing ideas, not people			
	Restating or paraphrasing			
	Encouraging			

Instructions to Observer: You are not to participate in the discussion, only observe and record. Put the initials or names of the group members along the top row. Each time one of the group members uses one of the skills listed in the left-hand column, put a mark in the column under the person's name across from that skill.

If it appears that some groups will not be able to reach consensus, the teacher may allow those groups to submit reports that reflect the disagreement. Toward the end of the lesson, the teacher may take a poll of students' individual positions on the issue and have some students explain their positions. The teacher gives each group its observation sheet and asks the group to respond with comments about what went well and what could be done better in the future. The teacher collects the written reports.

Discussion

This is a lesson procedure that engages students' skills in an integrated way. Students read, listen, speak, and write in an activity that maximizes individual participation. Students become immersed in a controversy, and as they do, the material comes alive for them. Students are motivated to master the material and think about it constructively in order first to try to prevail in the debate and then to contribute their part to consensus building and report writing. As students participate in debate, consensus building, and writing, they learn that to be taken seriously they have to participate

---

*Tom Morton. (1986). Decision on Dieppe: A co-operative lesson on conflict resolution. *History and Social Science Teacher, 21,* 41.

responsibly. This means understanding and thinking rationally about the subject matter from different perspectives. And it means comporting themselves with civility when disagreeing with others.

The activity does include verbal confrontation as an essential feature. This introduces the risk that socially immature students might resort to personal insults and that feelings might be hurt. It is those students, however, who have much to gain from the activity. Arguing both sides of an issue teaches students that people have reasons for holding opinions different from their own. Contributing to consensus building helps students see that most controversial issues cannot be resolved simply. Writing the group report requires cooperation and compromise.

EXAMPLE

High school students in a United States history class have been reading and talking about the organized labor movement during the 1930s and 1940s. In this lesson, the teacher emphasizes the issues that divided public opinion about President Truman's role in dealing with the struggle between labor and management.

Teacher: This was how President Truman attempted to remove restrictions that the Congress had placed on organized labor during the economic setback following the second world war.

Joel: Why did labor let Congress get away with taking the rights they had won with the Wagner Act of 1935?

Tony: Haven't you been listening, dimwit? Labor unions were threatening to destroy the economy if they didn't get their way.

Michele: You are such a twerp. The Taft-Hartley Act was just a reactionary reaction to labor having a greater voice in the economy.

Teacher: The country was divided on Taft-Hartley and President Truman's attempt to veto it and, failing that, to turn it around legislatively. Many of the basic issues surrounding the controversy remain with us even today, but reasonable people can discuss these issues without calling each other names. Let's air the dispute with civility in our own debate.

Lee: Debate is fun if you get to say all you want. But there are so many of us in the class that a lot of us will get crowded out of the discussion.

Teacher: You're quite right. Each of you should participate fully. That means listening patiently to others as well as having your say. So let's debate in groups of four. Within each group, one pair of you will argue one side of the controversy and the other pair will take the other side.

The teacher divides the class into groups of four and then subdivides each group into two pairs.

Teacher: Let's sum up our discussion and clarify the question to be debated. We've been discussing the labor movement of the 1930s and 1940s. The Wagner Act of 1935 gave labor unions new powers to organize and bargain with employers, but the Taft-Hartley Act of 1947 restricted those powers. Part of President Truman's "Fair Deal" legislative package of 1949 was to repeal Taft-Hartley. The question you are to debate is this: Was President Truman's attempt to repeal the Taft-Hartley Act in the best interest of the country?

Lee: So we decide which pair is to debate which side and start debating?

Teacher: Go ahead and decide which side you will debate, but before you begin, let me describe what you're expected to do in this activity.

The teacher allows the student pairs to choose the side of the issue they will debate. While students are deciding which side of the controversy to argue, the teacher hands out a sheet that states the procedure and rules to be followed.

Teacher: The sheet I've handed each of you spells out what you're expected to do and the rules you are to observe. In general, here is what you do. With your partner, prepare your arguments and then exchange ideas with other pairs of students who are arguing the same side. Your group then comes together and each pair presents its side. Following this, you argue your position in open discussion. Next, you reverse your perspective and argue the opposite position. Finally, the group comes to consensus and writes a report to present to the entire class. Now, let's go over each step in greater detail.

The teacher refers to the handout while clarifying the procedure. Students begin preparing their arguments by studying the textbook section "Returning to a Peacetime Economy" and identifying facts in support of their respective positions. The teacher moves among the pairs of students, observing them prepare their arguments.

Joel: Here's something we should stress. Taft-Hartley was passed in "an atmosphere of anti-labor feeling."

Michele: Right. And we should also specify restrictions on labor that show that the intent of Taft-Hartley was to destroy labor. Letting employers hold collective bargaining elections that keep striking workers from voting was obviously aimed at stripping unions of their power.

Joel: And the government sanctioned all this. It's the kind of thing police states do.

Michele: Let's say that. It will show that Truman was thinking of the best interest of the country.

After about 20 minutes, the teacher tells students to exchange ideas with other pairs of students who are preparing to argue the same position. Following this exchange of ideas, students come together in their groups of four to begin the debate.

Teacher: To begin the debate in your group, each side makes an initial presentation of its case. First to be presented is the case that President Truman was correct in trying to repeal Taft-Hartley.

Joel: That's us. Truman was correct in trying to repeal Taft-Hartley, which had been forced through Congress in a highly emotional and reactionary climate. Under the pretext of protecting workers from labor bosses, Taft-Hartley was simply an unjust law that required a police state mentality to enforce. As an amendment to the Wagner Act, Taft-Hartley posed as pro-labor legislation. Actually, however, its intent was not to protect organized labor but to destroy it. It provided for restraining picketing. Employers could hold collective bargaining elections. Strikers could be disallowed from voting in these elections and, if the outcome were nonunion, the government would enforce it. It was in the best interest of America for Truman to try to reverse Taft-Hartley.

Teacher: Now, the *no* side makes its opening presentation.

Lee: Truman was dead wrong to try and kill Taft-Hartley. Labor and management were not the only ones involved. When there's a strike, the wider community, even the whole country, is affected. Truman was thinking of the support given him by organized labor, not the general public and its welfare. Truman's bill would have allowed injunctions against strikes and secondary boycotts only in the case of unions disputing with each other over jurisdictional claims. But strikes in one area of the economy affect other areas of the economy. The consequences of strikes in the coal and steel industries are obvious examples. The time of crisis when the Wagner Act was passed, the great depression, was over. No longer was it necessary to worry about crushing labor. So Truman was wrong, dead wrong, to try to repeal Taft-Hartley.

Teacher: Now that you've made your opening statements, continue arguing your positions as persuasively as you can. Remember, you're arguing ideas and opinions about an event in history, not attacking one another personally.

The teacher moves among the groups, observing students' discussion skills and making notes on the Observation Sheet.

Joel: Lee, in your opening statement, you said that Truman was acting on behalf of his political supporters in labor and not on behalf of the American people.

Lee: You heard me correctly.

Joel: Taft-Hartley was passed in 1946 by a reactionary Congress that was voted out of office in 1948.

Tony: The people voted for the eightieth Congress, which passed Taft-Hartley, and the subsequent Congress did not in fact repeal Taft-Hartley.

Michele: The people were fed up with the eightieth Congress. It restricted social security, killed housing legislation, and passed Taft-Hartley. And so the people voted them out and reelected Harry Truman.

Tony: You are such a numbskull. Truman was taking care of special interests and ignoring the public and ordinary workers.

Joel: Taft-Hartley had gone beyond labor-management relations. It outlawed unions from supporting pro-labor political candidates.

Tony: Look, creep, are you brain dead or what? The unions were run by racketeers. Without Taft-Hartley, the racketeers would have been out of control.

Lee: It's true. The Truman bill would have allowed a closed shop, leaving the unions to do the hiring. Those who could afford high initiation fees could get jobs.

Joel: Obviously the purpose of Taft-Hartley was to weaken labor unions, and that put America at the mercy of big business.

Michele: The elections of 1948 clearly reflected the American people's disgust with Taft-Hartley.

Tony: No, bean-brain, the American people were disgusted with the racketeering and featherbedding. You're so dense you can't see that, can you? Unions were encouraging workers to loaf so as to create jobs. The more jobs, the more union dues paid in.

Teacher: Now, reverse your position. Argue against the side you previously argued for.

Tony: This is going to be tough. I mean to argue what you dodo birds have been saying.

Lee: From Truman's point of view, American workers had a right to keep their wages in line with soaring prices, which had resulted from the post-war frenzy of lifting war-time price controls.

Michele: Business had been fettered too long. It had a right to make profits in a free-market atmosphere.

Tony: It wasn't that way at all, Simple Simon. All the people, not just business, wanted free of government controls. It was too soon to let up controls on prices on goods that were in short supply.

Joel: Business decisions should be made by management, not the workers.

Michele: And especially not by workers who reduce competitiveness by their demands for security and ever more money.

Tony: Is your brain running in neutral? That's the stupidest thing you've said yet. Productive workers are the backbone of prosperity.

Student pairs continue debating from perspectives opposite their original views. After about ten minutes, the teacher instructs students to begin trying to reach consensus.

Teacher: Now that you've argued both sides of the question, you are in a position to reach some agreement about what to make of the controversy. Maybe all of you in your group are persuaded to take one side over the other. Maybe you see merit in arguments for both sides. Try now to determine your group's collective feelings and arrive at a way of looking at the controversy that is more or less ageeable to all of you.

For the next 10 minutes, students talk over the controversy with the aim of reaching consensus.

Joel: My personal biases are in favor of the underdog. Truman was always an underdog and so is labor, so I'm leaning toward the position that Truman did try to act in the best interest of the country.

Tony: Who's the underdog depends on how you look at things. Since Roosevelt and the New Deal, business had been the underdog. During the war they had profits limited by price controls. Business had not really been free to manage their own affairs.

Michele: There are good arguments for both sides of this question.

Lee: Well, let's begin with that idea. Let's agree that Taft-Hartley was controversial and there are good arguments on both sides of the controversy.

Michele: OK. Let's go with that. We can take the points, argue on both sides, and present the controversy as objectively as we can.

The final phase of the group activity has students cooperatively writing a report that presents the group's collective position on the controversy. While students are writing this report, the teacher gives each group an Observation Sheet that shows the frequency of desirable behaviors observed of each group member. On this sheet, the teacher has added evaluative remarks.

Teacher: We're nearing the end of the class period. Before we adjourn, I'd like to know how you personally feel about the controversy we've been debating. Let's see a show of hands of all who believe President Truman was acting in the best interest of the country to try to repeal Taft-Hartley. Joel, why do you think so?

Joel: Labor had made a lot of progress that Taft-Hartley undid. Business just didn't want to recognize the important contribution that labor makes to the economy.

Teacher: Now let's see a show of hands of all who believe that President Truman was not acting in the best interest of the country. Lee, why do you think so?

Lee: Because the unions were being run by racketeers. Strikes were hurting the country. Besides, closed shops kept out workers who wanted to make up their own mind about union membership. And there was featherbedding.

Teacher: Take a look at the Observation Sheet I've completed for each group and reflect on your group's activity. What did you do well and what could you do better next time?

Lee: In our group, I think we all argued forcefully, on both sides of the question.

Michele: And we worked cooperatively to reach consensus and write our report.

Teacher: Tony, what would you do better next time?

Tony: On the Observation Sheet, you said that I make unkind personal criticisms. So I guess I should watch that sort of thing in the future.

Teacher: Hand in your group reports and we'll share them next meeting.

Returning to a Peacetime Economy

Following the second world war, the greatest single domestic problem for the United States was returning to a peacetime economy. People had money to spend, but goods were scarce. Prices soared. To curb inflation, government economists advised continuing wartime price and wage controls. Businessmen argued that increased production would stabilize prices. Weary of wartime restrictions, Americans wanted an end to all controls.

In 1946, the people expressed their dissatisfaction with economic controls by electing a large majority of pro-business politicians to Congress. The eightieth Congress went to work dismantling the government's economic programs, most of which had been put in place during the prewar depression years. It killed housing legislation, restricted social security, and removed much of the leverage that could be used by labor unions. Congressmen avoided the wrath of rank and file workers by focusing criticism on labor bosses, whom they accused of racketeering and featherbedding. In an atmosphere of anti-labor feeling that followed nationwide strikes by railroad unions and mine workers, the Congress passed the Taft-Hartley Labor-Management Relations Act.

The Taft-Hartley Act was an amendment to the National Labor Relations Act of 1935, also known as the Wagner Act. It continued the Wagner Act's recognition of labor's right to organize, but it outlawed certain union practices. It banned the closed shop (i.e., restrictions on employers to hire only union members). It disallowed excessively high fees to join labor unions. Unions could no longer engage in featherbedding by demanding that a certain number of workers be hired when they are not needed. Taft-Hartley provided for delaying strikes up to 80 days if a national emergency might result. Striking unions were not allowed to bring pressure on uninvolved parties not to do business with the employer. Striking in sympathy with other unions was prohibited. Unions could not strike over disputes with each other about which union has the right to work on a job. Employers could bring labor disputes to resolution by holding collective bargaining elections in which striking workers were not allowed to vote. Unions were prohibited from barring union membership on the basis of race. The law required unions to publish financial statements. No longer could unions contribute money to political campaigns.

President Truman tried unsuccessfully to veto the Taft-Hartley amendment to the Wagner Act. Failing with the veto, Truman took his case to the people in the presidential campaign of 1948. Truman won the election and brought a majority of Democrats to the Congress. Feeling confident about his base of Congressional support, Truman set about to reverse the work of the eightieth Congress with a set of legislative proposals he called the "Fair Deal." It was a legislative package that called for increased public housing, full employment, higher minimum wages, farm subsidies, and regional development projects. The package included a labor bill to repeal the Taft-Hartley Act. The bill's restrictions on labor were limited mainly to prohibiting secondary boycotts and jurisdictional strikes. The labor bill failed to become law, though some of the other features of the Fair Deal proposal were enacted.

Source

Tom Morton. (1986). Decision on Dieppe: A co-operative lesson on conflict resolution. *History and Social Science Teacher, 21,* 238–241.

21

Be the Focus

Be the Focus is a motivational technique for increasing the confidence of students who are reluctant to contribute to class discussions. It gives all students a period of time to express their ideas in a small group. The activity encourages maximum student participation, which in turn can increase academic achievement.

Unmotivated students will participate in class activity if they can be made to feel comfortable about doing so. This technique structures class activity so that a few students cannot take over. This provides an environment that allows individual students to gain recognition. Recognition increases self-confidence and self-confidence leads to increased learning.

The technique may be used in any academic subject and with students through high school age. It is designed to be used with students who have difficulty learning or who have low self-confidence. Nearly every class has these students. The technique calls for dividing the class into groups of three, though the size of the groups need not be limited to this number. For variety, students can work in large groups, as long as time permits focusing equally on each student.

Procedure

The teacher presents an issue, fact, or concept to students, who are divided into groups of three. Within the groups, students have two minutes each to agree, disagree, or react in some way to the teacher's presentation. Other group members listen without interrupting. The group chooses a spokesperson to present to the class a summary of the reactions. Students come together as a class, and as each spokesperson relates group members' comments, the teacher discusses and organizes the comments on the chalkboard.

The teacher directs students to read to see if their initial reactions are addressed by the text. Students take notes as they read in order to validate or extend these reactions.

After reading, students are guided by the teacher to recall information in the selection that substantiates or refutes the reactions written on the chalkboard. The teacher encourages students to discuss information not addressed by the author or by the class before reading. Students may read aloud portions of the text that substantiate their earlier reactions. The teacher notes on the chalkboard any significant information not previously mentioned. The teacher then guides students to summarize major facts and concepts and to ask questions left unanswered. The teacher makes a list of the questions and from them offers students a choice for further study.

Discussion

In many classes there are unmotivated, passive students who decline to participate. This technique encourages participation by every student present, in an activity that concentrates on the subject matter. Every student is given at least two minutes to be heard by classmates, as well as the opportunity to cooperate with them. Three students working cooperatively can often produce better results than students working individually. Students learn from one another when they listen attentively, and when others listen to them. Be the Focus has the obvious advantages of any well-prepared lesson. With its discussion before and after reading, it incorporates the essential features of instruction that involves a text. It gives students the opportunity to organize information, make inferences, and verify interpretations. But what is special about this technique is that it provides every student time to be heard.

The time is provided, but there is no guarantee that students will listen to one another. This is the technique's chief limitation. Recognizing that classmates are not listening, students may become discouraged. To counter this possibility, students can be taught techniques of listening and responding to peers. Teachers can provide activities that demonstrate positive behaviors in small-group discussions.

EXAMPLE

A high school English class grapples with problems surrounding the virtue of truthfulness. The teacher intends that every student consider issues attendant to questions about truthfulness and formulate a personal ethic about truthfulness. The teacher has divided the class into discussion groups of three students each.

Teacher: Truth is a virtue. We all agree on that. Where we disagree is whether it is a virtue to be accepted absolutely. Can one ever be less than truthful and remain virtuous? Or put another way, can lying ever be justified? That's the question you are to take up in your groups.

Kathy: You mean like, is it OK to tell white lies, or just not say certain things to certain people?

Teacher: Deciding on what constitutes a breach of the truth is something your group may like to talk about. So that everyone can have a say, you are to take two-minute turns to tell your thoughts about the question. When you're not talking, please listen and don't interrupt the person who is.

Sheila: This is not a give-and-take, right? You want us to talk for two minutes.

Teacher: Right. And listen without interrupting when it's not your turn to talk. We'll have give-and-take later.

Dudley: What if you don't say anything?

Pat: Or don't use up two minutes?

Teacher: Then there will be some silent time at your group. But I expect everyone in here has opinions about this question. Now, choose a group leader and decide the order of your turns. I'll time your two-minute turns.

Group activity begins, and the teacher circulates among the groups. At one of the groups, in the corner of the room, Kathy has launched into an account of a neighbor's lying.

Kathy: This guy who lives next door, he wouldn't tell the truth even if it was better than a lie. Once when he came home from fishing , . . .

Kathy relates a rambling series of lies told by her neighbor. After two minutes, the teacher calls time and directs the next speakers to be the focus. In the corner group, Sheila explains why she never lies.

Sheila: I'm a member of Young Scientists, an organization dedicated to knowing the truth about, well, about everything. Where the truth stops, science stops. That's our motto.

Sheila tells examples of setbacks to science caused by various forms of dishonesty— falsifying experimental data, drawing conclusions not justified by facts, and so on. After two minutes, the teacher calls for the third speakers to be the focus. In the corner, Pat admits to being less than perfectly truthful and points to instances when remaining absolutely truthful may not be best.

Pat: I know that I am not 100 percent truthful all of the time. And a lot of other people, too. There are times when no harm is done not to be *completely* truthful. In fact, it may be best not to be.

At the end of this two-minute segment, the teacher tells the groups they have two minutes to summarize the group members' comments. When the time elapses, the teacher calls students back together as a class.

Teacher: Now let's hear from the group leaders. The corner group first.

Pat: Members of our group had different views. Sheila thinks it's never OK to lie. Kathy told about her neighbor's lying. We disagree about the harmlessness of his lying. My own view is that complete honesty is not always best.

Teacher: Let me make two columns here on the board, one for comments that defend absolute truthfulness and one for justifying nontruths.

Pat: Sheila believes that dishonesty compromises science. We rely on science too much in our everyday living to let it be compromised. Things could just fall apart.

Teacher: Like if a drug company faked its research on a product, consumers could get hurt. They can't know what to trust at all. And more broadly, if there were no ethic of honesty in science, scientists couldn't trust one another. And no progress could ever be made.

Pat: Something like that. Kathy seemed to be saying a similar thing about her neighbor. She knows he lies, so she doesn't trust him at all.

The teacher records the comments summarized by Pat and other group spokespersons, responding to them orally as well.

Teacher: Now let's find out how your thoughts square with our text. Read "Is Lying Ever Justified?" See what the text says about your personal position.

Dudley: Do we get back in our groups to read?

Teacher: Just read this individually.

Students read silently.

Teacher: Sheila, how does the text deal with your position on truthfulness?

Sheila: My position on truthfulness is scientific. The text's is moralistic. It does point out, however, that lying is deception. I agree whole-heartedly with one sentence of the text: "If one sticks to the truth, things work out for the best."

Teacher: Kathy, to what extent does the text reflect your beliefs?

Kathy: It's like I said about my neighbor. He embellishes facts. But he does it for no high-minded reason. He's a liar, plain and simple.

Teacher: Embellishing the facts, your neighbor intends no harm? And does no real harm?

Kathy: Not really, except to himself. You can't believe anything he says.

Pat: You could make the effort to sort his fantasies from facts. He may be protecting himself from your harsh appraisal. He may even be sparing you from pitying him.

Kathy: Ha!

Teacher: What does the text say about your view, Pat?

Pat: That there are times when it's necessary to be untruthful. And even when it's not *necessary,* it can accomplish something good.

As the discussion proceeds, the teacher adds arguments to the columns for defending and for compromising absolute truthfulness. Also listed on the chalkboard are questions raised about truthfulness in a number of areas: advertising, religion, and politics. The activity closes with the teacher's assigning students to choose one of these questions for further study.

Is Lying Ever Justified?

A lie is a falsehood. It is more than speaking falsely or answering a question untruthfully. It is any deception. It may be withholding information so as not to let the truth be known. It may be embellishing facts, or twisting them outright. Whether lying can ever be justified is a question that tries our ethics.

For some, lying can never be justified. For these, it is always wrong to lie—under any circumstance. Even when the truth would endanger others, the truth must prevail. A person who believes it is always wrong to lie believes that it is a bald violation of conscience to do so. If one sticks to the truth, things work out for the best. Some even trust that by remaining steadfastly truthful, one may expect divine/supernatural intervention to prevent harm from occurring.

For others, lying may be justified. Although for these lying is generally wrong, there are occasions when it is necessary. One such occasion would be when it accomplishes a good thing, such as saving a life. Another occasion would be when it prevents the perpetration of evil, such as misleading a would-be-rapist. Some can justify lying, even when the consequences of lying are not dire. Lying may be acceptable in order to save someone from embarrassment, disappointment, or hurt feelings, or, on the other hand, even to make someone feel good. Some feel no twinge of guilt about lying in order to gain something for family or loyal friends.

Source

Patricia Cohen Gold and David Yellin. (1982). Be the Focus: A psychoeducational technique for use with unmotivated learners. *Journal of Reading, 25,* 550–552.

22

Guided Imagery

Guided Imagery is an image-evoking activity used to enhance reading comprehension and appreciation of imaginative literature. It is an excellent exercise for initiating creative writing projects, and it may also be used to help students visualize historical events and faraway places.

Students individually generate images in a group process that suggests the images to be conjured and that provides a structure within which to fit them. Through the process, students explore, clarify, and fill out their images. Combining memories of familiar experience with images they invent, students create the imaginary material they need for writing descriptive compositions or for understanding strange and different situations. The method can serve well as a catalyst for classroom discussion, group inquiry, and classroom projects. It may be used effectively with an entire class or with small groups of students. Given the nature and simplicity of the activity, it is suitable for children in the elementary grades. If not overused, the method is also apropriate for high school students.

Procedure

To prepare for Guided Imagery, the teacher assembles materials prior to class and provides for a lesson free of disruptions. If the lesson is to focus on a particular selection, the teacher may wish to write an image-evoking script to get students ready for creating images from the selection itself. The teacher creates a relaxed atmosphere and minimizes the possibility of interruptions during the exercise. This may call for preparing an alternate activity for students who do not wish to participate.

The lesson consists of three phases: teacher modeling, guided practice, and independent practice. In the first two phases, the teacher plays an active role, showing students how to generate productive images and directly engaging students in interactions that will accomplish that end. The third phase is devoted to students' applying image making to a practical task.

Teacher Modeling. The primary aim of teacher modeling is to show students how to create a structured daydream. The activity may make use of a textbook selection or a script the teacher has written for this phase of the lesson. Students are directed to imagine that they are experiencing what the teacher reads. The teacher has students close their eyes and, if circumstances permit, lie down. They are to visualize what is being said and to try to make details come to life in their mind. The teacher tells students to open themselves to images of color, sound, and smell; to sense location; to let their feelings and emotions flow with the images.

The teacher reads a brief portion of the script or the selection and pauses to describe and model the kind of imaging that students are expected to do. The teacher's own images are described and an attitude of openness to seeing further images is conveyed. The teacher may anticipate upcoming images by posing self-questions about where the selection is leading. The teacher begins the reading again, this time reading the script or selection in its entirety. The presentation is slow and clear, and it is punctuated with pauses that allow students time to produce images as vividly as possible. Following this presentation, the teacher has students explore the daydreams they have created. Students may write down their thoughts individually or share their daydreams in group discussion.

Guided Practice. The activity now advances to having students openly share the images they create as the selection is being read. If the teacher's own script was read during teacher modeling, in this phase students focus on the textbook selection to be studied. Again, the teacher reads a portion of the material and pauses to think aloud about the images evoked by the material. This time, students are encouraged to tell about the images they are experiencing. They are asked to describe how their images resemble and differ from the teacher's and their classmates' images.

Independent Practice. Once students learn to concentrate on generating images, they can form groups and lead one another through readings on their own. Students may apply image making to specific texts to be studied independently. A particularly apt activity for applying image making is a summary-writing assignment or a creative writing project.

Discussion

This is an activity that most students enjoy. It is a game-like activity that encourages students to think creatively about subject matter and to express their feelings about it. It also helps students get started on writing projects in a fun way. Teachers like the activity because they find it useful in a variety of ways. They can use it for such purposes as helping students build mental models for understanding difficult concepts, clarify and solve problems, enhance self-concept, and develop social and interpersonal skills.

The exercise does require full concentration and participation of students who wish to be included. Participation involves students' listening, being still and quiet, visualizing the material, and imagining that they are experiencing what they hear.

Students need to be open minded and relaxed. Sometimes all of this is difficult to achieve with children in the elementary grades.

EXAMPLE

A high school English class is reading and writing descriptive compositions. In this lesson, the teacher wants to stimulate students' imagery for the twofold purpose of enhancing their appreciation of a writer's use of images and preparing students to compose a description that relies heavily on images to achieve a desired effect.

Teacher: Daydreaming. I do a lot of it and I guess everyone does. In school, you're sometimes told not to waste time daydreaming. But, you know, daydreaming is not altogether a bad thing.

Andy: I hope not because I sure do a lot of it.

Teacher: Idle daydreaming can waste our time. But daydreaming for a constructive purpose is a different matter.

Patsy: What do you mean?

Teacher: When we read, we take mind trips, short side trips to make the reading meaningful and, if possible, relevant to our personal experience. And when we write, we daydream what we have to say.

Bob: So, in spite of teachers' faulting us for it, daydreaming can be all right.

Teacher: As I said, it's a necessary part of the things we do in school. The constructive daydreaming we do in school is active, not passive. We deliberately try to imagine things as if we see and hear and smell them. I'll show you what I mean by trying deliberately to create images by which to experience things vicariously. Pay close attention.

The teacher begins to read from the script prepared for the lesson:

> You are walking barefoot
>   alongside a shimmering, green lake.
> The sand feels warm and soft between your toes.

The teacher pauses to reflect aloud about the images presented and to encourage students to open themselves to the situation.

Teacher: I know this experience well. It's one I most love. I think of a familiar lake, and I can just see and smell that shimmering, green water inviting me to linger, . . . to bathe, to wade, to drink in its serenity. And, oh, the freedom of going barefoot. The sensation of soft, warm sand seeping between my toes is one of life's supreme pleasures. To enjoy it, I simply have to take off my shoes and put my feet next to the earth. What joy! It's as if my feet and the sand are kissing. You know what I'm talking about. You've had the experience. I wonder what else this text will have us see and hear and feel at the lake. Let's read to find out. Now, close your eyes and try to make what I'm reading to you come alive. See it in your mind. Feel it.

The teacher starts over and reads the entire script slowly, pausing to let students create images of the scene presented.

> You are walking barefoot
>   alongside a shimmering, green lake.
> The sand feels warm and soft between your toes.
> The sun sets red into the lake.
> Twilight casts a purple mist.
> You notice a flicker in the distance.
> On the edge of the lake, a campfire glows orange.
> As you approach the campfire, you see it larger and larger.
> You are welcomed by an old man.
> His beard is long and silky and white.
> Other faces around the campfire welcome you.
> You sit with them and smile with them.
> They serve you food and drink until you are full.
> Together, you get up and walk along the water's edge.
> A warm summer's breeze touches your back.
> Moonlight glimmers in the ripples across the lake.
> You feel strong hands on your back and shoulders.
> They nudge you into the water.
> They coax you into the canoe.
> Paddles are lapping in the water.
> Warm wind blows against your face.
> You and your friends in the canoe skim across the lake.
> You are the wind, the water, the moonlight.
> You are Ghost Lake.

Following the reading, the teacher invites students to share feelings and images.

Mary Jane: You already feel good because you're at the lake. As evening comes, things get better, and they keep getting even better. You meet friendly people who share their campfire and supper with you. Then you get into the lake together.

Teacher: Did you see colors?

Jim: A green lake and red setting sun.

Elinor: Purple twilight and an orange campfire.

Bob: Moonlight is white.

Patsy: The old man's beard is white.

Teacher: What about images of touch? We already mentioned bare feet on the warm sand.

Jim: There's a warm breeze touching your back.

Mary Jane: Strong hands nudge your back.

Bob: And wind in your face.

Teacher: How did you feel inside as you listened?

Mary Jane: As I said, you already feel good because you're at the lake, but things get better as you're invited to take in the lake more and more.

Andy: Right. You're already feeling good because of the colors, the smells, the serenity of the lake, and the calmness that comes over everything with twilight. And then you meet with friendly people who accept you and like you.

Patsy: They feed you and smile a lot. And then you all go into the lake together.

Elinor: It's like everything is so right that you become part of the scene, part of the lake. No, it's like more than becoming part of it. It's like you melt into it. You are the lake and all of it.

Teacher: I think you're getting the idea about going with the reading—making the images it describes come alive and experiencing the feelings it suggests.

Jim: The feelings I got were pleasant, but there at the end they were kinda eerie. I mean it ended with the words *Ghost Lake*.

Elinor: It's like I said, you become the lake and all. I mean like the spirit of it.

Teacher: Here's another selection about the lake, Ghost Lake.

The lesson moves into guided practice, in which students will share their feelings and images as the selection is being read. The teacher begins to read "Watching for the Skaters of Ghost Lake."

> Ghost Lake is dark and deep and cold. Around its edge and above, steep-standing firs guard the secrets of the lake.

The teacher stops and asks students to tell what they are feeling and seeing in their mind.

Bob: This may be Ghost Lake, but it's different from the last Ghost Lake. This one is shivery cold and dark.

Jim: It's eerie right from the beginning. It has secrets, probably creepy secrets.

Mary Jane: And they're guarded by steep-standing firs. It makes you feel little and like you ought not be there. I don't know what the secrets are, but they're probably awful, horribly awful.

Students continue to share their impressions and predict what follows. The teacher leads students through the selection, reading brief increments and pausing to let students describe their feelings and images. After the reading and discussion, the teacher has students recount the selection's images.

Teacher: Now let's go over the images again.

Andy: They're all dark. There are no colors.

Patsy: And no smells, except maybe the smell of snow and ice.

Jim: The ice is black, black as ebony.

Mary Jane: The lake is wide and surrounded by tall firs.

Andy: Whisps of ice-dust swirl on the lake.

Bob: You can hear a sound that resembles the scrape of skates on ice—a whir and a ring-tinkle-ring.

Patsy: The moonlight is cloudy and dim.

Jim: Something sweeps out and glides over the ice, dark and graceful.

Andy: Maybe, just maybe, it's the ghosts of the lost lovers, Jeremy and Cecily.

Bob: That's creepy.

Patsy: And yet romantic. The ghosts of lovers, long ago lost mysteriously to the lake, skate forever together.

Elinor: It's like there's a story, but it's a story that's not told.

Mary Jane: That's the mystery. That's the secret guarded by the sentinel firs.

Following the discussion of "Watching for the Skaters of Ghost Lake," the teacher moves students into an independent practice activity.

Teacher: Here's yet another selection about Ghost Lake. It's William Rose Benet's "The Skater of Ghost Lake." You'll immediately recognize the images of coldness, darkness, and mystery. Be open to these images and to your feelings as you read the poem. After you read, make a list of the images and feelings suggested by the poem. Then use your list to write a description of Ghost Lake.

Watching for the Skaters of Ghost Lake

Ghost Lake is dark and deep and cold. Around its edge and above, steep-standing firs guard the secrets of the lake.

On late winters' evenings, you may hear a faint ring-tinkle-ring and a whispering whir from the distant ice. Is it the skur of steel you hear out there on the ebony ice? Is it Jeremy Randall and Cecily Culver whose shadows you see in the darkness? In the dim moonlight, the wind whisps and the ice-dust swirls. That's when you may catch glimpse of the lost lovers skating, skating. Look hard and across the black lacquered expanse—you may discern something that glides. Is it Jeremy and Cecily veering out in wide sweeps across the ice? It is Jeremy and Cecily in the cloudy moonlight you hear flit-flittering, you see gliding out and rising up together as a large night bird winging darkly over the ice?

Black is the ice of Ghost Lake. Around the lake steep stand the sentinels in the night. Ghost Lake is dark and deep and cold.

Sources

Linda B. Gambrell, Barbara A. Kapinus, and Robert M. Wilson. (1987). Using mental imagery and summarization to achieve independence in comprehension. *Journal of Reading, 30,* 638–645.

Bob Samples, Cheryl L. Charles, and Dick Barnhart. (1977). *The Wholeschool book: Teaching and learning in the late 20th century.* Reading, MA: Addison-Wesley.

23

Information Intermix

Information Intermix increases students' knowledge of subject matter, develops their ability to communicate it, and improves their skills for interacting with others. In the activity, students become better acquainted with their classmates.

Information Intermix is an activity in which students learn in groups and in pairs. In these groups and pairs, students assume roles both as teacher and as learner. Students' understanding of the subject matter increases as they attempt to teach it to their classmates. Communication and interpersonal skills are applied as students hold subject-related interviews with classmates. The activity provides opportunities for students to have positive complementary experiences: learning and teaching, thinking and feeling, reflecting and acting, remembering and telling, moderating and emphasizing, and giving and taking.

Although the method is designed for use with college students, it can be used successfully with students in the secondary and middle grades. It can also be used in teaching any academic subject. It is especially well suited for subjects in which there is much factual material to be learned. The activity is best conducted in a large classroom where desks or chairs are movable.

Procedure

The teacher informs students that they will be teaching one another first in a small-group activity and then in pairs. The teacher tells students that they are to learn as much information as possible. Students are told to listen for the teacher's instructions about what to do and about when and where to move.

In a class with many students who do not know one another, the teacher may have students introduce themselves in a warm-up activity. For this, the teacher asks students to form a circle large enough that they can move around and talk with one another. The teacher directs students on one side of the circle to choose a person on the other side of the circle whom they do not know well and to go over and become acquainted. After about three minutes, the teacher has students resume their places and then asks students on the other side of the circle to become acquainted with another person across the circle from them. This warm-up procedure is repeated as time permits.

Attention to subject matter begins with the teacher asking students to form groups of four. This is the home group. Students must remember who the other members of the home group are and where the group meets. The teacher gives each group a "Concept Slip" or short passage whose content group members are to learn well enough that they can teach it. After allowing enough time for groups to make sure each member knows the material, the teacher directs students to pair up with a member of another group. In these pairs, students teach each other the material assigned to their respective home groups. After several minutes, the teacher directs students to pair up with a member of a different group and, again, to teach each other the material assigned to their respective home groups.

This is repeated until each student has met with one student from each of the other groups. To facilitate recognition of the different groups' members, students may be given name tags whose color indicates group membership. Finally, students return to their home groups and discuss the material they have learned from members of the other groups.

Discussion

Information Intermix is ideal for use early in a course. It establishes a comfortable atmosphere for students to get acquainted as well as to learn subject matter. Students are afforded an opportunity to become familiar, but in the business-like context of studying the subject. Individual contributions to the activity are recognized, so each student can be seen as a significant member of the class. Students feel at ease talking with each other one to one. They can be themselves. One to one, students are more likely to ask each other questions and are more likely to get answers they understand. The result is that they learn a great deal from their interactions with classmates. As with any other small-group or peer-teaching activity, the teacher has to remain vigilant so that the activity does not deteriorate into idle conversation.

EXAMPLE

It is the beginning of the school year, and the teacher of a high school speech class wants students to be introduced both to public speaking and to one another. Before dealing with the subject of public speaking, the teacher engages students in an activity that allows them to become acquainted.

Teacher: All right, now that we have formed a big circle around the classroom, I'd like for you students on this side of the circle (pointing to the window side of the room) to go over to a person you don't know on the other side of the circle. Get to know that person. Tell each other your name, what you like to do—that sort of thing.

Students on the window side of the circle move to the other side. Students talk in pairs for about three minutes.

Teacher: All right. Everybody take your original place in the circle. Now, students on the chalkboard side of the circle, you spot someone you don't know on the other side of the circle. Go over and get acquainted with that person.

This self-introduction procedure is repeated two more times.

Teacher: Now that the ice is broken, let's turn to another activity. It's an activity we begin in groups of four. So get yourselves together into groups of four students each.

The students form groups. The teacher expedites the group formation process by placing unattached students in groups. Four groups of four students each are formed.

Teacher: Take a good look at the students in your group. Know who they are. This is your home group. Each home group will be responsible for teaching part of today's lesson to everybody else.

Brad: How are we going to do that?

Teacher: Here's the way we'll proceed. First, I'll assign each group a different paragraph from our textbook chapter entitled "Basics of Public Speaking." Each group will study its own paragraph and make sure every group member knows its information well. Then the groups will break up and for a few minutes you'll get with someone from a different group. You'll teach each other your home group information. When I give the signal, you will find a person from another group and you two will teach each other your home group information. We'll proceed in this way until you've had a teaching-learning exchange with someone from every group.

Julia: How will we be able to pick out a person from a different group?

Teacher: By the color of the sheet of construction paper you'll carry. Each group will have its own color—red, green, blue, or white.

Maurice: So first we learn a paragraph of information in our home group and teach it to everybody else?

Teacher: That's right. In the last phase of the lesson, you will return to your home group and make sure every member knows the other home groups' information.

Rudy: We want to be the Red group.

Teacher: OK. You're the Red group (handing the group four sheets of red construction paper). And you are assigned the second paragraph, the one beginning with the words "Every successful public speaker knows. . . ."

The teacher assigns each of the other groups a color and a textbook paragraph to be responsible for teaching. All of the groups begin talking about how to proceed. The Red group decides immediately.

Rudy: I guess we've all read our paragraph now. Any ideas about how to deal with it?

Jeanne: I think we should make a list of the stuff it says.

Brad: It would help me if we numbered the things on the list and go over them again and again.

Vicky: We should quiz one another on the list.

Rudy: First in pairs, then round-robin.

The Red group produces and learns this list of information:

1. Every aspect of a speech should get a response. (Most important)
2. A speech is designed for a specific audience.
3. A speech makes a point.
4. The speaker uses simple, concrete examples.
5. A speech is intended to be heard, not read.

The other groups find similar ways to handle their own assignment. The teacher gives the signal for the groups to break up and students from different groups to teach each other their material. Two students who find each other are Rudy of the Red group and Verdin of the Green group.

Rudy: Our group's topic was about knowing the characteristics of a good speech.

Verdin: Ours was about making a speech have an interesting topic.

Rudy: We have a list of four characteristics of a good speech. Let me tell them to you and then we'll go over what your group has to teach about getting an interesting topic. OK?

Verdin: OK. Tell me the four characteristics.

Students talk in pairs for three minutes. The teacher gives the signal and students find a classmate who represents a different group.

Melanie: My Blue group is assigned the paragraph on organizing the main points of a speech.

Rudy: The Red group has a list of four characteristics of a good speech. Let me recite our list to you. Then you tell me what your group has to say about organizing the main points of a speech.

The paired teaching-learning phase of the activity continues until every student has met with a student from every other group. The teacher then directs students to reassemble in their home groups and make sure each member has learned the material taught by the other groups. The Red group carries out this part of the activity in about the same way the other groups do.

Rudy: I think we should take turns reciting what all the other groups had to say.

Jeanne: But I'm not sure what they all said.

Brad: Me neither. I could recite what the Blue group said. But I'm not sure about the Green group's material. And I'm totally unable to say what the White group said.

Vicky: I talked to a different person in the Green group and she made their stuff really clear.

Jeanne: And I can help you out with the White group's material, I'm sure. But I'm fuzzy about the Blue group's information.

Rudy: OK, let's take turns telling what we do know. Brad, first you go over the Blue group's material. Next, Vicky, you tell us about the Green group's stuff. And, Jeanne, you tell us about the White group's information.

The home groups sort out the information they heard during paired teaching-learning and drill their members so that everyone can recite the information of the entire lesson.

Basics of Public Speaking

Making a good speech is not easy. It takes a great deal of thinking and planning. But if you keep in mind a few basics of public speaking, you will find that you can prepare and deliver speeches quite effectively.

A successful public speaker knows the characteristics of an effective speech. These characteristics translate into essential rules of speech making. The most important rule is that every aspect of a speech is intended to evoke a response. It is this rule that all of the other rules serve. A speech is designed for a specific audience. It has a point to make. To make the point, the speaker uses simple, concrete examples. And the speaker keeps in mind that a speech is intended for the ear, not the eye.

To make a good speech, you must have an interesting topic. It is best if the topic is interesting to you. This means that your choice of topic should be something that you already know well and that you want others to know. You will probably have to limit the topic. Your major challenge is to make the topic interesting to your audience.

How you present your topic depends on your purpose. Once your purpose is clear, communicating with your listeners is a matter of organizing your main points. Your main points are the things you want to say. Make a list of these points. Then rewrite the list, arranging the points in the order in which they make sense and are most likely to affect listeners the way you want. With an ordered list of main points, write your speech.

It is important that you clarify the main points of your speech and support them adequately. To clarify your main points, define the key terms. You may find that an anecdote about a friend or teacher illustrates a point well. Visual aids are also helpful for illustrating a point. To support your points, offer details and statistics on important aspects of the topic. To give authority to your support, allude to sources of the information you cite.

Source

Dave Capuzzi. (1973). Information intermix. *Journal of Reading, 16,* 453–458.

24

Note Cue

Note Cue expands students' reading comprehension by stimulating discussion about the main ideas and important information of texts. It develops students' ability to formulate questions about assigned reading, to respond to questions asked by others, and to elaborate on issues presented in texts.

Note Cue provides examples of appropriate responses to a text. Students see written on note cards the kinds of questions the teacher would have them ask and the kinds of answers to give. Cues on the note cards serve as supports early in instruction, but are later withdrawn. Initially, students mimic the questions and answers on the note cards.

As they mimic these questions and answers, students become aware of what good questions and good answers are like. With Note Cue, students develop habits of active listening and participating. They become aware of what situationally appropriate responses are like. Eventually, the note card cues become unneeded. Note Cue is a text discussion activity for groups whose size is limited to a number that permits active participation by every student. It may be used with students in the middle grades and beyond. Note Cue is well suited for literature, social studies, and science classes.

Procedure

The teacher prepares for a Note cue activity by developing two sets of note cards, one for use before reading or with a first reading and one for use after reading or with a closer reading. Each set of note cards contains a number of cards with questions about the reading and an equal number of cards with corresponding answers. In preparing the cards, the teacher makes sure to phrase questions and answers so they can be easily matched. Also in each set of cards are cards that comment on the content of the text and cards that are left blank. Each card should be clearly labeled at the top as "Question," "Answer," or "Comment" card. The first set of cards may contain questions, answers, and comments about issues and events relevant to upcoming reading; or, if used following a first reading, the cards concern information that contributes to understanding the text. The second set of cards contains questions, answers, and comments about the main points and important issues raised in the reading. For each successive Note Cue activity, the number of blank cards is increased. Eventually blank cards should constitute as much as 80 percent of the cards.

The Note Cue activity itself is simple. Having introduced a reading assignment, the teacher asks students to skim or quickly read the text for gist. While students silently skim or read the text, the teacher places a note card on each student's desk. After skimming the text, students are asked to read silently the note card they have been given. Students with blank cards are asked to think of a question or comment that they might write on the card. The teacher then calls on students to read their cards aloud. If a question card is read, the teacher asks for the answer card to be read in response; if a statement or answer card is read, the teacher asks for the corresponding question card to be read. The teacher encourages students given blank cards to read what they have written on the cards, whether a question or statement. Card reading continues until the teacher deems that students are sufficiently prepared to read the text. It is not necessary that all the cards be read. The teacher then assigns students to read the selection silently.

While students are reading, the teacher places a second note card on each student's desk. After students have had time to read the text, the teacher asks for a student to read a question card aloud and then for the student with the answer to read that card aloud. After several question and answer cards are read, the teacher asks students to read comment cards. Students with blank cards are encouraged to offer spontaneous comments. Throughout the activity, the teacher encourages students to elaborate freely on the questions, answers, and comments that are read. Following the postreading discussion, the teacher may administer a written test. Questions for this test come directly from the postreading note cards.

Discussion

Note Cue provides a supporting structure of ready-made responses to assigned reading. It serves as an instructional scaffold for buttressing the confidence of reticent students and for building response behavior based on a footing of what is relevant and important in a text. Students may be disinclined to speak up in class due to shyness or due to a history of passively listening to lectures delivered by the teacher. Or students may be talkative, yet dwell on the trivial and peripheral aspects of the subject matter. Note Cue can be helpful in either circumstance. It gives students risk-free opportunities to respond overtly to assigned reading. Having text responses guided by note cues, students become more aware of the content in texts that merits attention. The teacher's goal should be one of replacing the scaffold of ready-made responses with responses structured by students themselves.

Reading questions, answers, and comments from note cards can become a dry exercise if the lesson is conducted mechanically. The teacher can enliven the activity by offering elaborative commentary and by encouraging students to add to the information they read and hear. The note cues are a device to stimulate discussion that is focused on the important aspects of assigned reading.

■ EXAMPLE

A high school English teacher attempts to show students how to respond to poems they are assigned to read. For each poem of the lesson, the teacher has prepared two sets of note cues, one to be used following the first reading of the poem, and the second to be used following a closer reading.

Teacher: So, enough of my talking about the background of this poem. More important is the poem itself. Let's do a first reading to understand the situation that the poet describes.

As students read, the teacher places a note card on every student's desk. Students who typically need no prompting get a blank card. When students finish reading, the teacher explains the purpose of the note cards.

Teacher: The note cards I've placed on your desk are to guide our response to the poem. They're like cue cards that television performers and public speakers use to help them know what to say. Some of the cards contain questions, some have answers, some present comments, and some are blank.

Sam: What do we do with these cards?

Teacher: As we go over our first reading of "Strange Fits of Passion Have I Known," be alert for an appropriate time to read your card. If you have an answer card, listen for the question it answers and read the answer. Also, think about what your card says and feel free to add your own remarks.

Annette: What do we do if we get a blank card? Is that just a foul-up or something?

Teacher: If you get a blank card, write a question or comment of your own.

Percy: On the card?

Teacher: Yes. Let's think about "Strange Fits of Passion Have I Known."

Alex: Weird title.

Teacher: It is intriguing. Anybody have a card that asks about the title?

Emily: I do. "What fit of passion is related in this poem?"

Teacher: Any other question cards that ask about the poet's fit of passion?

Ezra: This may be one. "What wayward thought slid into the poet's head?"

Teacher: I think that has to do with his fit of passion. Which of these questions should be answered first?

Arch: They're the same question, really. But the second one asks more about how the fit of passion takes place, by slipping into the poet's head as a dream. The first one should be answered first because that will tell what the poem is about.

Teacher: Who has the answer card?

Elizabeth: I think I do. "When dreaming about his lover, the poet is overcome with dread that she may die." That's about as much a fit as the poem tells about.

Teacher: It's a serious fit of passion for a romantic like Wordsworth. Who has the answer card for the other question?

Rupert: I do. It's pretty much the same answer. "The poet finds himself worrying that he may lose Lucy to death."

Christina: What about this one? It sets the stage for telling about his fits of passion. "What does the poet dare to tell in the lover's ear alone?"

Edna: I have the answer to that. "The poet dares to tell about strange fits of passion he has known." We've already said what fit of passion is told in this poem.

Teacher: Good. Are there any cards with questions about the action that takes place?

Gerard: My card asks, "Where did the poet go everyday beneath the evening moon?"

Marianne: And my card answers, "The poet says he went to his sweetheart's cottage everyday beneath an evening moon."

Oscar: I have a card with another question about what takes place in the poem. It reads, "On what were the poet's eyes fixed as he dreamt?"

Leonie: "In one of his sweet dreams, the poet kept his eyes on the descending moon." That's my card's answer.

Teacher: Edith, let's hear what your card says.

Edith: "Who is the poet's lover?"

Gene: My card has the answer to that. "The poet calls his lover Lucy."

Elinor: I have a comment card that probably should be read now. "This is one of Wordsworth's so-called Lucy poems, which are considered to rank among his finest lyrics. Who was Lucy? Nobody knows for sure. She may have been merely an imaginary character. Or she may have represented his sister, Dorothy, on whom he depended for emotional stability."

George: I got a blank card, but I have a question. Is this Wordsworth weird, or what?

Teacher: I suppose you mean weird with respect to his relationship with his sister.

George: That and writing poems about fits of passion.

Teacher: Wordsworth's time was the age of romanticism. And you have to keep in mind some facts about Wordsworth's life.

The teacher seizes the opportunity to tell about Wordsworth's being orphaned, his resisting ordination as a clergyman, his sympathy for the revolution in France and disillusionment with England's position toward France, his long separations from his wife, and so on. More cards are read that present questions, answers, and comments about the poem's rhyme and meter. The teacher than directs the class to read the poem again.

Teacher: Now let's examine the artistry evident in this poem. Annette, please read us your card.

Annette: "How do images of movement and stillness suggest death in this poem?"

Sam: I think I have the card with the answer. "Throughout the poem, motion is juxtaposed with stillness. The analogy of this juxtaposition is activity and life contrasted with inertness and death."

Teacher: To fill out this observation, other cards ask further questions about movement and stillness.

Percy: Here's one. "How are motion and stillness contrasted in the third quatrain?"

Emily: The answer is, "In the third quatrain, the poet's eye is fixed upon the moon, giving an impression of its stillness. In contrast with the still moon is the quickening pace of his horse."

Christina: I have another question like that. "What two sorts of motion are described in the fourth quatrain?"

Bill: Did you say fourth quatrain? Here's your answer. "In the fourth quatrain, the climbing horse is shown against the sinking moon."

Elizabeth: My comment card reads, "Something ominous is suggested by the sound and pace of the fourth quatrain."

George: My card asks another question about motion and stillness. "How are motion and stillness contrasted in the fifth quatrain?"

Edna: "In the fifth quatrain, the poet's conscious eye is on the sinking moon, while he is inwardly arrested by a dream."

Teacher: There's a question about the last two quatrains.

Alex: I have it. "What parallel movements are described in the last two quatrains?"

Elinor: "In the last two quatrains, the moon drops behind the cottage roof and thoughts of death slide into the poet's head."

Arch: These images do contrast motion and stillness, but it seems to me any motion occurs against a backdrop that has stillness in it.

Teacher: Your point is reasonable. You're not reading that from a card, are you?

Arch: No. I have a blank card. So for my blank card I ask this question: How can we be sure that the contrasts between motion and stillness were images deliberately crafted by the poet, and not mere observations interpreted by literary critics?

Teacher: That's an excellent question. And we don't have to rely on the text of the poem itself for the answer. There are other poems by Wordsworth that use exactly the same device, but we don't have to interpret those poems either to know that it was a deliberate device. In the Preface to his *Lyrical Ballads,* Wordsworth asserted that the reader derives pleasure from the perception of similitude in dissimilitude. The *analog universelle* is central to his theory of poetry. According to this theory, meaning arises from coupled images.

After discussing this poem, the class reads "A Slumber Did My Spirit Seal," another of Wordsworth's poems that suggest death by contrasting images of motion and stillness. For this poem, more of the note cards are blank.

> *Strange Fits of Passion Have I Known**
> *William Wordsworth*
> *(1770–1850)*

Strange fits of passion have I known:
And I will dare to tell,
But in the lover's ear alone,
What once to me befell.

When she I loved looked everyday
Fresh as a rose in June,
I to her cottage bent my way,
Beneath an evening moon.

Upon the moon I fixed my eye,
All over the wide lea;
With quickening pace my horse drew nigh
Those paths so dear to me.

And now we reached the orchard plot;
And, as we climbed the hill,
The sinking moon to Lucy's cot
Came near, and nearer still.

In one of those sweet dreams I slept,
Kind Nature's gentle boon!
And all the while my eyes I kept
On the descending moon.

My horse moved on; hoof after hoof
He raised, and never stopped:
When down behind the cottage roof,
At once, the bright moon dropped.

What fond and wayward thoughts will slide
Into a lover's head!
"O mercy!" to myself I cried,
"If Lucy should be dead!"

Source: Excerpt from *Adventures in English Literature,* Classic Edition by Paul McCormick et al., copyright © 1968 by Harcourt Brace Jovanovich, Inc., reprinted by permission of the publisher.

Source

Anthony V. Manzo and Ula Casale Manzo. (1990). Note Cue: A comprehension and participation training strategy. *Journal of Reading, 33,* 608–611.

Refining Concepts and Building Vocabulary

Teaching is an exercise in developing the concepts of a domain of knowledge. It is through efforts to develop concepts that the teacher gives shape to a subject and enables students to think usefully with its content. Essential to the endeavor is teaching the words that represent the concepts of a subject. These are the words that constitute a subject's vocabulary.

The vocabulary of a school subject can be quite extensive. Part of every subject's vocabulary are technical terms used only in connection with matters related to the subject. There are, however, many words that are in general use but represent special meanings in the context of an academic subject. Developing facility with words of both sorts is part of developing knowledge of a subject. As knowledge of words increases, thinking about the subject becomes more precise. Concepts become more highly differentiated, and features of concepts are brought into sharper relief. Having command of a subject's vocabulary is fundamental to communicating its ideas effectively.

Because students have to know the vocabulary of a subject in order to increase their knowledge, think with facility, and communicate about its ideas, the teacher is obliged to take deliberate steps to increase students' word power. Although it is possible for students to acquire new words through mere exposure to them, leaving vocabulary development to take place through incidental learning invites a host of problems. Most serious among them are that students' knowledge is likely to be left incomplete, misconceptions may be formed, and communication about content will remain inefficient and faulty. These are problems that can be averted with proper attention to teaching the concepts and vocabulary of the subject.

The teacher equips for such teaching by acquiring a repertoire of methods for accomplishing a variety of instructional tasks. In general, these are methods that provide for introducing new concepts and terms, giving practice in applying them, and refining understanding. More specifically, they are methods that have students:

- *Connect new concepts and terms to personal experience and previous learning*
- *Make use of context*
- *Categorize concepts and terms*
- *Discriminate shades of meaning*
- *Monitor their own understanding and learning*
- *Observe relatedness among newly introduced concepts and terms*
- *Analyze words*
- *Pronounce words*

- *Use the dictionary*
- *Review concepts and terms introduced in a lesson*

The methods presented in this section provide for accomplishing these purposes.

25

Concept of Definition

Concept of Definition (CD) helps students learn the vocabulary of a subject area. It is a vocabulary mapping strategy that helps students discover what they already know about a word and what they need to know in order to understand it and independently judge whether they have enough information for learning it.

The premise is that organizing information on a concept map increases the efficiency with which students gain new vocabulary. In CD, a concept map depicts three types of related information in answer to essential questions about a novel concept: category (what is it?), properties (what is it like?), and illustrations (what are some examples?). By internalizing this framework, students are able to engage in metacognitive reasoning. CD enables students to understand the nature of developing word knowledge.

Concept of Definition is well suited for vocabulary study across the content areas. It may be taught as early as fourth grade and extended to the college level. The activity may be used with any size group. The presentation to an entire class facilitates initial instruction in CD, but later the class may be divided into smaller groups or pairs for practicing with various aspects of the vocabulary mapping.

Procedure

The teacher provides students with strong initial support in studying the vocabulary of a subject. Gradually, management of word study is transferred to the students. The teacher begins by demonstrating how organization and structure can aid memory. Then, by having the class brainstorm about a familiar concept, the teacher shows students that they already have some of the information they need for CD mapping. The teacher lists students' ideas on the chalkboard, points out how much they know, and demonstrates that their ideas could be organized into three groups: the category to which it belongs, the properties that make it different from other members of the category, and illustrations of its use. Next, the teacher displays the basic CD map (see the figure in the Example). Discussing how it helps in learning the meaning of new concepts, the teacher maps one or two concepts used in a categorization task. Here, the teacher demonstrates how to arrive at a definition by combining information by moving clockwise around the map.

The remaining activities and discussions involve the use of complete and partial contexts to help students clarify the information needed on the CD map. When students become familiar with the structure, they begin using it as a guide to determine meanings of concepts presented in their textbooks. A discussion of the text leads to mapping and then to writing definitions. Passages giving partial context are used so that students may contribute any background knowledge they may have. Also, the teacher suggests where students might look to get more information.

Students then practice internalizing the structure. Students are given examples of partial context passages and related definitions, some of which are poorly written. Students evaluate the definitions. They look at the passage for more information, check their background knowledge, and consult other sources. They now write a more complete definition. After modeling this, the teacher has students work in pairs to complete other examples.

Discussion

CD instruction can be a useful approach to helping students evaluate their vocabulary knowledge. It helps direct their search for new information and aids their recall of other, related concepts. CD activities can have long-term value if students take responsibility for their learning and internalize the CD framework.

An advantage for the teacher is that CD offers an effective strategy for discussing new concepts with students. It allows engaging students in discussion of word meaning and having them search for components of definitions. Certainly it is a viable alternative to looking up vocabulary definitions when context clues seem not to help. Unless it becomes automatic, CD can become time consuming for students. Students do need long-term experiences and teacher modeling for CD to be effective. CD requires a good deal of teacher planning.

EXAMPLE

A fifth-grade social studies class is studying ancient Egypt. The teacher's aim is to acquaint students with the ancient Egyptian social structure and religion. When students read the word *pharaoh* there are several questions. The students want to know what a pharaoh is and how this word fits into Egyptian society. The teacher draws a Concept of Definition Map on the chalkboard and asks the students to supply information about category, description, and example.

Teacher: Looking at the text and thinking about what you already know about rulers, can you suggest a comparison for *pharaoh?*

Shane: A king.

Teacher: (writing *king* in the comparison circle on the CD map) Yes, exactly. A pharaoh is a type of king. All right. Can you name a category that a pharaoh could fit into?

Robert: A pharaoh was Ikhnaton.

Teacher: Ikhnaton was a pharaoh, but Ikhnaton would be an *example* of a pharaoh. What category could both pharaoh and king fit?

Jenny: Both lead the people. Maybe *leader* is the word?

Teacher: That's a great word, Jenny. (The teacher writes in the word *leader* in the top blank.) Now, how would you answer the question, "What is a pharaoh like?" What are some properties or descriptions of a pharaoh? Look for clues in the reading.

Keith: Well, sometimes they were very young.

Lynn: They were worshipped by the common people.

Amy: They had lots of gold and jewels. They were very rich.

Cory: They were buried in tombs with lots of their favorite jewels and pottery.

The teacher places more spaces on the properties side of the map. This shows the students that they can have as many spaces as they want. The teacher records all of the responses and encourages the students to keep their own list of properties. The teacher reminds them that there is no definite number of properties they should list.

Teacher: Those were all very good answers for describing a pharaoh. Our next task is to give examples. We already have one example, Ikhnaton, that Robert gave us. Who are some others?

Concept of Definition Map

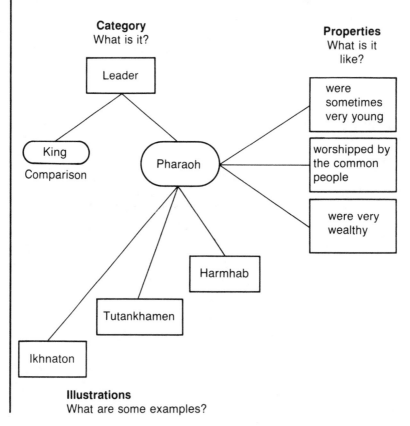

Category
What is it?

Properties
What is it
like?

Leader

King
Comparison

Pharaoh

were
sometimes
very young

worshipped by
the common
people

were very
wealthy

Harmhab

Tutankhamen

Ikhnaton

Illustrations
What are some examples?

Kelley: What about Tutankhamen?

Lori: And Harmhab!

Teacher: You're both correct. (The teacher writes these in the spaces for examples.) You could go to an encyclopedia if you needed others.

Completing the Concept of Definition Map, the teacher explains that this process can be used for all unfamiliar words. The teacher also tells students that as they practice this strategy, it will become so easy that they will not need paper and pencil. Then the teacher tells them that, after going through this process, they will be more likely to remember the unfamiliar word.

Ancient Egypt a Religious Society

In Ancient Egypt, the people worshipped nature and many gods who were believed to be the forces of nature. Religion was the greatest single influence on the culture. Art and literature were largely expressions of religious beliefs. Even the society was structured according to religious beliefs.

The most important religious leader was the *pharaoh,* who was the ruler of the society. Believed to have been given his authority by the gods, the pharaoh was worshipped by the common people. The pharaoh was all powerful and controlled most of the wealth. Among the most powerful of the pharaohs of ancient Egypt were Ikhnaton, Tutankhamen, and Harmhab.

The pharaoh ruled for life. When he died he was buried in a richly appointed tomb. The most powerful of the pharaohs were buried in the pyramids of Egypt. Buried with the pharaoh were the things that the people believed he would need in the afterlife. These things included jewels, pottery, pets, and sometimes servants.

Religious beliefs were explicit about the line of succession, and some Egyptians became the pharaoh at a very young age. The first line of pharaohs was established about 3200 B.C. The last line of pharaohs ended in about 500 B.C.

Sources

Robert M. Schwartz. (1988). Learning to learn vocabulary in content areas text books. *Journal of Reading, 32,* 108–118.

Robert M. Schwartz and Taffy E. Raphael. (1985). Concept of Definition: A key to improving students vocabulary. *The Reading Teacher, 39,* 198–205.

26

Contextual Redefinition

Contextual Redefinition is a method for teaching words that can be defined by the context in which they occur.

Often, textbooks and teachers describe for students certain kinds of context clues that aid understanding unfamiliar words. These clues include direct explanations, typographical aids, modifying phrases, synonyms, and restatements. Being able to name or identify context clues in sentences does not necessarily result in students being able to use these clues, however. Experiencing the importance of context in ascertaining word meaning is more effective than naming the type of context clue. Contextual Redefinition provides this experience. It is a method for teaching students to use context clues to define unfamiliar words. This in turn contributes to students' effectiveness as readers and learners.

This method is necessarily a group activity. It is effective with both large and small groups. Good students act as role models, and poorer students benefit from seeing the appropriate processes being used. The method can be used in any of the content areas. It would be particularly helpful with material that contains words that are unfamiliar yet necessary for communicating major concepts.

Procedure

Contextual Redefinition begins with the teacher identifying words likely to be unknown to students but necessary for understanding major ideas of the lesson. Using a transparency or the chalkboard, the teacher presents these words in isolation and has students guess the meaning. Students must defend their guesses and come to a consensus about the words' meanings. It does not matter how implausible the guesses are. For each of the words, the teacher writes a sentence with a clue to its meaning. If a clue is in the text to be used in the lesson, that clue is used. Otherwise, the teacher creates one. Students again are asked for the meaning of each word, and they must defend their guesses. Finally, students check the dictionary to verify the group's guesses.

Discussion

In Contextual Redefinition, students become actively involved with new words and take responsibility for learning them on their own. Students soon become aware that guessing in isolation is not effective. Their experience leads them to realize that the rest of the sentence or passage allows them to make more informed guesses. This is of particular importance to slow students who benefit from direct experiences.

Certainly it is more effective than passively memorizing vocabulary lists. Most students like group activities, and this adds to the method's attractiveness.

EXAMPLE

A high school general science class is involved in a unit on the senses. As part of a lesson on vision, the class is considering the nature of seeing when the eyes are closed. An important element of this lesson is teaching the words *phosphene, neural,* and *random.*

Teacher: When you think about a thing and try to picture it in your mind, you only *almost* see it. Now, there is a kind of seeing when our eyes are closed that is somewhat more like seeing with our eyes open. Before reading about this kind of seeing, let's try to guess the meanings of some words that are in the text. The first word is *phosphene.* I'll write it on the board. *Phosphene.* What's it mean?

Larry: It's seeing a meaning of something that happened a long time ago.

Julie: Yeah, but it's a hideously ugly memory that you can't help but see.

Vickie: I think it could mean seeing a sweet memory.

Teacher: A "sweet" memory?

Vickie: Like remembering the taste of something sweet and tingly to drink.

Teacher: Hmm. Here's another for you. *Random.* (The teacher repeats the word and writes it on the board.) *Random.* What does *random* mean?

Donnie: Maybe it means seeing things like they're all run together.

Jane: Or seeing things like little birds do. What do you call them, wrens? Like wrens see from high on a dome. It's like seeing from far away or high up.

Julie: It might mean mystical visions like mystics and religious people in the Middle East have.

Teacher: Hmm. OK. I have one more word for you. *Neural* (writing it on the chalkboard). Spelled like this. *Neural.*

Vickie: Oh that's like seeing something in your mind before you can actually see it.

Donnie: Like something new that you're waiting to see. It's like guessing what the new model of Chevies will look like before they let you actually see them on the showroom floor.

Jane: It could mean imaging things that are big and bulky and beastly. You know, like gnu. G-N-U.

Teacher: Well, these are certainly fun and crazy guesses. Let me give you more to go on.

The teacher writes on the chalkboard enough of the sentence in which each word appears in the text to allow inferring the meaning from context. For the word *phosphene,* the teacher writes: "Mysterious are those images known as phosphenes, the stars you see when you bump your head."

Donnie: Oh, wow! There's actually a scientific name for those things.

Julie: They're the dust-devils you see behind your eyelids sometimes.

Jane: And like the visions you see when you meditate with your eyes closed.

Larry: But *phosphenes?* Why are they called phosphenes?

Teacher: Let's check it out in the dictionary. The etymology should give us a good idea why they're called phosphenes.

The teacher thumbs through the dictionary. Finding the word, the teacher writes the etymology on the chalkboard:

<GK. *phos* light + *phainen* to show

Teacher: It says here "a luminous impression due to excitation of the retina."

Larry: I can understand that definition now that we already know phosphenes are the stars you see when you bump your head. But I don't think I'd get it if I didn't already know it.

Teacher: The dictionary is a tool that can give us the etymology and definition of a word. But it's a tool we use after we have something to go on, like how the word is being used. Often we use the dictionary just to verify a hunch about the meaning of a word.

As the lesson proceeds, the words *neural* and *random* are discussed in the same way. They are given in the context in which they appear in the text and they are looked up in the dictionary and discussed.

Phosphenes

Inner vision is a phenomenon not yet well understood. Particularly mysterious are those images known as phosphenes, the stars you see when you bump your head or squeeze your eyes shut tightly. Made up of the Greek words *phos* (light) and *phainen* (to show), phosphenes probably originate in the brain and retina and reflect the organization of the neural pathways of vision. A headache, certain drugs, or pressure on the eyeballs can ignite an array of phosphenes. These arrays are not random, but occur in patterns. Phosphene patterns may be classified as belonging to more than a dozen general categories.

Source

David W. Moore, John E. Readence, and Robert J. Rickelman. (1982). *Prereading activities for content area reading and learning* (pp. 38–40). Newark, DE: International Reading Association.

Related Reading

Sterl Artley. (1943). Teaching word meanings through context. *Elementary English, 23,* 68–74.

27

Analogical Reinforcement

Analogical Reinforcement is an effective approach to expanding students' knowledge of subject area vocabulary, especially its conceptual vocabulary. Through the development of analogical thinking, it encourages students to attach personal experience to novel terms, to discern shades of meaning, and to explain and resolve difficulties with words.

Teaching vocabulary analogically involves having students observe correspondences among words that might otherwise be regarded as dissimilar. By having students relate groups of words through comparison and contrast, teachers make clear which words can and cannot fit in an analogical pattern. Students are more likely to understand and remember word meanings after placing words in analogical relation to other words, because it is an exercise that demands attention not only to the meaning of individual words but to possibilities for connecting groups of words according to an underlying pattern of meaning.

Analogical Reinforcement is intended for teaching vocabulary at the middle grades and above. Although it has obvious applications in reading and language arts classes, it can be productively used in classes where many new terms are introduced daily, such as science, social studies, music, and foreign language. It can be effective in tutoring situations as well as in whole-class instruction.

Procedure

To begin the activity, the teacher makes clear that it is the context in which a word is used that often determines its meaning and pronunciation. The teacher writes on the chalkboard a word that may represent more than one meaning and that may be pronounced in more than one way depending on its context. Students are asked to pronounce the word, define it, and use it in a sentence or phrase that exemplifies its meaning. The teacher encourages sentences and phrases that represent different meanings of the word and call for its different pronunciations. The teacher emphasizes that there is no best meaning or pronunciation outside a specific context.

Next, the teacher orally introduces several very simple word analogies, such as *boy* is to *male* as *girl* is to *female, steam* is to *hot* as *ice* is to *cold,* and so on. The teacher follows this by having students supply the final term to further simple word analogies, such as *moon* is to *night* as *sun* is to *day, summer* is to *hot* as *winter* is to *cold,* and so on. The teacher than reverses the order of the stems of the same analogies, now having students probe their own reasoning processes and explain their answers.

Students' facility with analogies is increased by an exercise that moves concentration away from the last term and requires attention to each term of the analogy in relation to the others. This is done by presenting either on the chalkboard on a worksheet four-term analogies, each of which contains an incorrect term for students to identify. As each incorrect term is identified, discussion deals with the relatedness of terms and an explanation of the incorrect term's failure to fit. Here, the teacher may take up two or three basic kinds of relatedness, such as part-whole or member-class. The teacher solidifies students' conscious understanding of relatedness by having them explain how elements are related in "half-analogies" (i.e., pairs of elements that might appear in an analogy such as *goose–gosling, tire–wheel,* or *tree–oak*). If possible, the teacher uses terms from the material under study.

The discussion returns to whole analogies, with the teacher showing students how the punctuation is read in conventional analogy statements. Writing an analogy statement on the chalkboard, the teacher tells students that the colon *:* is read *is to* and the double colon *::* is read *as.* This is followed by presenting either on the chalkboard or on a worksheet a number of analogy statements to be completed by the students. The teacher explains how to complete the first two or three of these. Finally, students read about the topic under study and from what they read generate analogy statements on their own.

Discussion

Analogies are effective for teaching vocabulary because they provide a built-in context. And they afford students opportunities to think through words to be learned by several different angles. Students tend to be better served by game-like activities that call for thinking through terms to be learned within a self-contained context than by vocabulary exercises dealing with disparate bits of information.

▌EXAMPLE

An eighth-grade science class is being prepared for the concept of mechanical advantage. In this lesson, the teacher introduces simple machines. The immediate objective is to teach four terms, one for each of the simple machines: the lever, the inclined plane, the pulley, and the wheel and axle.

Teacher: Yes, it is easier to use machines to do these things for us. Did you ever think about how complex most of those machines are? They *are* complex for sure, but we can understand them if we keep in mind that they are a lot of simple machines that have been put together to work together. We're going to examine the mechanics of complex machines by observing the mechanics of the simple machines that they comprise. So let's start thinking mechanical. Let's think about these words that can be associated with machines and mechanical things.

The teacher writes on the chalkboard the words: *lead, incline, alternate, project,* and *reject.*

Teacher: You pronounce them and say what they mean. Use them in a sentence if you like.

Mack: The first word you pronounce /led/ like the heavy metal.

Bud: But you could also say it /leed/, as being out front or showing the way.

Sissy: /In-*cline*/. That's what you do when you lean back.

BillieSue: That's *ree*-cline, Einstein. In-*cline* means to lean *toward*, not lean back.

Leonard: Hey, you can't say in-*cline* and *in*-cline the same way you can re-*cline* and *ree*-cline. It really doesn't make any difference if you say re-*cline* or *ree*-cline. But with in-*cline* and *in*-cline, in-*cline* is something you do, but *in*-cline is something that *is*. And what an *in*-cline is is a slope.

Teacher: Leonard, you're quite alert. BillieSue's *in*-cline was her way of indicating that there was a discrepancy in that syllable. But if this word is just written on the board by itself, how can you tell how to pronounce it? How can you tell which meaning it has?

George: Well, really you can't. It takes other words with it to set up which—in-*cline* or *in*-cline—it will be.

Teacher: What about the other words?

Nancy: They're the same way. With these words you can't tell for sure how to say them by themselves.

Joe: You could say alter-*nate* or alter-*nut*.

Jill: Just like you could say *prah*-ject and pre-*ject*. The machine we used for the *prah*-ject helped us nail down the boards that had to pre-*ject* beyond the frame.

Teacher: Very imaginative. How about this one?

Terry: If you don't want something, you want to re-*ject* it, push the *ree*-ject button.

Teacher: So as Nancy said, when words stand all by themselves in print, you just can't tell sometimes how they are to be taken. They have to connect with other words. It's the other words that are there that help set the meaning. It's the other words there that let you know how all the words are to be connected.

BillieSue: You mean, it's like with one of these complicated machines? What any one part does depends on its role in working with the other parts. What they all do together has to do with what each one does by itself.

Teacher: Exactly. As one part—or smaller machine within the big machine—works, there is a corresponding action among the other parts—or smaller machines. Think of a machine that had a hammer for driving nails, but it worked along with the machine's screwdriver, stapler, and riveter. Each tool within the machine has a part to play, and what each tool does corresponds with what the other tools do.

Betty: So when the machine does its job it will have nailed, screwed, stapled, and riveted things to get a job done—like make a piece of furniture or something.

Teacher: Right. To express how the machine's individual parts and what they do correspond to one another, we might say something like: *Hammer* is to *nail* as *screwdriver* is to *screw*. *Stapler* is to *staples* as *riveter* is to *rivets*. We call these statements *analogies*. Analogies tell how things are related to each other in ways that correspond to the way other things are related to each other. To make an analogy, how would you complete this statement? *Drill* is to *bore* as *saw* is to . . . ?

Mack: Cut.

Teacher: Good, Try this one. *Scissors* is to *paper* as *can opener* is to . . . ?

BillieSue: Can.

Teacher: *Can* is to *can opener* as *paper* is to . . . ?

Mack: Scissors.

Teacher: *Dig* is to *shovel* as *cut* is to . . . ?

Joe: Knife.

Teacher: You see, it's the other words that let you know what word to fill in. But it's also the way those other words are ordered that clues you about how to complete the analogy.

At this point, the teacher writes on the chalkboard several analogies, each with an incorrect term:

> Screwdriver is to knife as saw is to cut.
>
> Wrench is to bolt as hammer is to pliers.
>
> Pull is to pliers as shovel is to axe.
>
> Drill is to hole as shovel is to spoon.
>
> Drill is to bit as knife is to spoon.

Teacher: What's wrong with these analogies? Let's take them one at a time.

BillieSue: In the first one, there are two tools, related, I guess, because they both have a blade, compared to a tool and what it does.

Teacher: What's wrong with that?

BillieSue: In an analogy, the things being compared have to correspond in like ways. In this analogy, you should either compare these tools according to their parts or according to their purpose.

Teacher: So what's the incorrect term?

Mark: According to what BillieSue said, either of two terms could be incorrect. It depends on what you're comparing. If you're comparing tools according to purpose, knife would be incorrect. But if you're comparing tools according to their parts, it is incorrect to say what they do—like to cut.

As the discussion proceeds, the teacher elicits explanations for the incorrectness of each analogy. Examining the flaws in the analogies, the teacher brings students to consider the nature of the correspondence in analogies (part-whole, member-class, instrument-function, agent-object, etc.). The class is now ready to generate analogies with information they encounter in reading about machines. Following the reading of the text, the class produces analogies that the teacher writes on the chalkboard. As these analogies are dictated, the teacher shows students how to punctuate (and to interpret the punctuation of) analogy statements. The class produces this set of analogies:

> pulley:rope::lever:fulcrum
>
> pedal:sprocket::crank handle:axle
>
> inclined plane:knife::lever:bottle opener

ramp:wedge::windlass:doorknob

oar:gunwale::lever:fulcrum

bottle opener:pliers::knife:chisel

lever:pulling a nail::pulley:hoisting an engine

wheel and axle:doorknob::inclined plane:porch ramp

Simple Machines

Machines have great practical value because they make work faster and easier. They reduce the effort required to do a job by changing the speed, direction, or amount of a force. Complex machines are but combinations of simple machines.

Simple machines are devices that reduce work with one movement. There are four very useful simple machines. These are the lever, the inclined plane, the pulley, and the wheel and axle.

A *lever* is a simple machine consisting of a bar that is free to move about on a point called a fulcrum. Examples of a lever include a bottle opener, claw hammer, and wrecking bar. The type and use of a lever vary according to the relative location of the effort force, resistance force, and fulcrum. With the most efficient lever, effort force is applied at one end of its bar to overcome resistance force at the other end. Two things affect the action of a lever—the amount of force at each end of the lever and the distance between the force and the fulcrum.

An *inclined plane* is a slanted surface used for raising objects to higher elevations or for cutting. Inclined planes that raise things include stairs, mountain roads, escalators, and ramps. Less effort force is needed to raise objects with inclined planes because the objects are moved along a slanted surface. When the same objects are lifted straight up, a larger effort force is applied through a short distance. Wedges, knives, lawn-mower blades, and can-opener blades are inclined planes. The longer and narrower these implements, the less effort force required to overcome resistance force.

A *pulley* is a simple machine that changes the amount, speed, and direction of a force. A kind of rotating lever, a pulley is a wheel that turns on an axle. A pulley can be either fixed or movable, and it can be used either by itself or in combination with other pulleys. A single pulley that is fixed in position changes the direction of resistance force but does not change effort force. The effort force still equals the resistance force. Movable pulleys offer mechanical advantage equal to the number of support ropes.

The *wheel and axle* is a simple machine that operates on the same principle as the lever and pulley. The direction of force is changed, and force is reduced by spreading it over a greater distance. The force applied to the wheel is applied to the axle, but the wheel turns through a larger distance than the axle. So the force on the wheel moves through a greater distance than the force on the axle. The difference gives the wheel and axle its mechanical advantage. A steering wheel, wrench, bicycle, and sprockets are examples of the wheel and axle.

Source

> Scott C. Greenwood. (1988). How to use analogy instruction to reinforce vocabulary. *Middle School Journal, 12,* 11–13.

28

Vocabulary Overview

Vocabulary Overview provides students with a structured approach to learning unknown words they encounter in reading. It shows students how to categorize new words, establish connections among these words, and relate them to personal experience. Emphasized is the importance of students' monitoring their own learning processes.

Vocabulary Overview incorporates strategies that have been shown to be effective for comprehending and learning subject matter. These are strategies that have students activate as much knowledge as they can about the topic, form associations between new material and personal experience, and monitor their own performance as they attempt to learn it. To make sure that all necessary steps are taken, a checklist is used. To help students organize new words and make connections to familiar experience, a chart is completed. The procedure can be adapted for most subject areas and for high school and college students of different abilities and backgrounds.

Procedure

The procedure to be followed by students is specified in a checklist called the "Vocabulary Overview Guide." The teacher hands out this checklist and leads students through its steps. For purposes of modeling the steps, the teacher uses an overhead projector to display the lesson's text and the chart for organizing new words.

Vocabulary Overview Guide*

Defining the vocabulary through use of context

1. Survey the material (title, headings) to see what it is about.

2. Skim the material to identify unknown vocabulary words and underline them.

3. Try to figure out the meaning of the word from the context of the sentences around it. Ask someone or use a dictionary to check the meaning.

4. Write the definition in the text (use pencil) or on paper so that it will be available when you read the text.

5. Read the passage with the defined vocabulary to ensure comprehension.

---

*Source: Eileen M. Carr (1985). The vocabulary overview guide: A metacognitive strategy to improve vocabulary comprehension and retention. *Journal of Reading, 28.* Reprinted with permission of the International Reading Association.

Completing the vocabulary overview guide

6. Fill in your vocabulary overview guide. Write:

   a. The title of the passage
   b. The category titles—decide on the categories you need by asking yourself the topics the vocabulary described or discussed
   c. The vocabulary word
   d. The definition underneath the vocabulary word (you can use synonyms here—make sure you leave room to add a few more synonyms as your vocabulary increases)
   e. A clue to help you connect the meaning to something you know or have experiences

Studying the vocabulary

7. Read the title and categories to activate background knowledge and recall words associated with each aspect of the story.

8. When you study the word in each category, cover the clue and word meaning—uncover the clue if necessary. If the clue doesn't jog your memory, then uncover the meaning.

9. Review your words frequently (each day) until you know them well. Review them once a week or periodically as you learn more words.

10. Add synonyms to old vocabulary words as you learn them. In this way, you will connect the old with the new words and that will help you remember them.

Discussion

Vocabulary Overview is a highly structured approach to teaching subject area vocabulary. It is an approach students are likely to find appealing because it has them develop personal clues to word meaning that they share with classmates. Teachers will find it attractive because, once modeled, the procedure will be carried out by students on their own.

Common sense should govern the use of Vocabulary Overview. Textbooks that present so much difficult vocabulary that students need to use the method on a regular basis may be inappropriate.

EXAMPLE

A high school class in U.S. history is discussing events of the 1960s. The topic of discussion is dissent and civil disobedience. Having observed several important terms in the textbook's treatment of the topic, the teacher has decided to give attention to these terms.

Teacher: The decade of the 60s was a time of intense dissatisfaction about a lot of things in American society. The ways people voiced their dissatisfaction were somewhat different from previous ways of expressing discontentment.

Mario: You mean by having sit-ins?

Joan: And burning draft cards?

Teacher: Sit-ins and draft-card burning were really a lot like protests that had previously taken place—against some specific government action or law or some particular circumstance. But protest in the 60s was different.

Bob: How do you mean?

Teacher: Let's turn to our text to find out. In the text there are numerous terms to which we should pay close attention. To guide your learning about these terms, I've prepared a checklist for you to follow and a chart for you to fill in.

The teacher distributes handouts of the vocabulary overview guide and the vocabulary overview chart.

Teacher: As the first three items of the checklist direct, you look over the material you're going to study and underline the words you don't know. For this section of the text, "Resistance to Authority," I've already identified the words you should learn. You'll notice that they're already listed on the chart you'll be completing.

Patsy: So if we were studying this on our own, we would look through the text for new words before we read it?

Teacher: Right. You scan the text for unfamiliar words and try to figure out what they mean by the surrounding words. Words whose surrounding context doesn't help you understand, you look up. Jot down their meanings. That way you'll have their definitions available when you read.

Mary Jane: Do we write the definitions on the chart somewhere?

Teacher: No. You write them on a separate sheet of paper. I'll show you how to fill in the chart after you've gotten the words' meanings and written them down on a separate sheet of paper.

Andy: Looking at the text, I see the first new word is *dissent*. It's with other new words, *civil disobedience*. The title makes me think they're both about resisting authority, probably the government.

Mario: I'd say civil disobedience means defying the government, maybe by disobeying its laws.

Joan: Dissent probably means something else. A writer wouldn't say the same thing twice with two different words side by side.

Patsy: It has something to do with resisting authority, but you can't tell exactly what just by the surrounding words.

Teacher: OK, then let's look it up in the dictionary.

Bob: Here, I have it: "to withhold assent," whatever *assent* means. It goes on to say, "to differ in opinion."

Mary Jane: So here it must mean disagreeing with the government.

Mario: Stands to reason. Disagreeing with the government is what causes people to defy it or disobey its laws.

Teacher: All right. Take out a sheet of paper and write down these words and their meanings.

As the discussion proceeds, the class determines the meaning of each of the unfamiliar words identified by the teacher either through context or with the dictionary. The teacher has students read the passage and then begins to lead them through filling out the vocabulary overview chart.

Teacher: Now we're ready to fill in the chart.

Andy: But we've already looked up the words and have understood them in the reading we just did.

Teacher: I know, but I believe that you may find that filling in the chart helps fasten the word meanings in your mind.

Several: So, OK. Show us how to fill in the chart.

Teacher: (turning on the overhead projector) On the screen I'm projecting the chart as you have it. Since this is the first you've worked with a vocabulary overview chart, I have already supplied information that ordinarily you would have to fill in — the title, the column headings, and the words from the text.

Mary Jane: I can see how you got the title. It was the section title of the chapter. But how did you get the column headings?

Patsy: I think I know.

Teacher: OK, Patsy, how?

Patsy: Each heading tells something that relates the words down the column to the title, to the overall topic.

Mary Jane: But they're all related to the overall topic.

Patsy: Yes, but each column of words is related to the topic in a certain way. The column head tells how.

Teacher: Right. And notice, too, that the column head serves to place the words themselves into a group and provide a label for that group.

Mario: OK. Well, what do we put in the box and lines attached to each word?

Teacher: On the lines you write either one- to three-word definitions or synonyms. In the boxes you write a one- or two-word personal association.

Joan: I'm not sure what you mean.

Teacher: We don't have to take the words in any special order. Let's fill in the lines and box for, say, *escalate*.

Andy: Earlier we wrote down that it means "to heighten" or "to increase."

Teacher: All right. We'll write "heighten" and "increase" on the lines beneath *escalate*.

Joan: You said we write a one- or two-word personal association in the box. What do you mean by "personal association"?

Teacher: What you think about when you hear or see the word. How it strikes you in some particular way.

Bob: It makes me think of Macy's department store. It has an *escalator,* which *escalates* me to the higher floors.

Teacher: OK. Bob, the word *Macy's* is a clue to help you connect the word to something you know. You would write "Macy's" in the box under *escalate.* For our example on the overhead, we can go with that, too.

Resistance to Authority

Forms	Action	Control
Dissent	Erupt	Martial Law
protest	volcano	National Guard
differ in opinion	break out	military rule
disagree		
Civil Disobedience	Precipitate	Curfew
Ghandi	weatherman	11 P.M.
defy government	to cause	time for clearing streets
resist authority		
Riots	Escalate	
prison	Macy's	
mob violence	heighten	
	increase	
Looting		
natural disaster		
stealing		
Jeering		
umpire		
heckling		
mocking		

As the lesson proceeds, the teacher continues to show students how to fill in the vocabulary overview chart, calling on students to share brief definitions and synonyms for the remaining words on the chart and to volunteer personal associations with those words. The teacher brings the lesson to a close by explaining to students how they can use the vocabulary overview chart as a study tool. In doing this, the teacher directs students' attention to items 7 through 10 on the checklist.

Resistance to Authority

Dissent and civil disobedience have long been part of the American scene, but in the 1960s the nature of dissent and civil disobedience changed. Riots and other forms of violence broke out in most of the large cities across the country. Hundreds of riots took place. These riots created a new problem for law enforcement, because they were unlike previous forms of civil disobedience.

The riots of the 1960s did not erupt in protest to any specific law or policy. Rather, they were expressions of frustration with poverty, unemployment, and hopelessness of inner-city citizens. They were initiated by young people who were largely idle. Their inability to find decent work created hostility, and this hostility was released in violent ways.

Typically the riots were precipitated by some incident involving the application of police authority. A crowd would gather as a police officer arrested someone in the street. The crowd would become angry and boisterous. Jeering led to starting fires and looting stores. They would then shoot at officials who came to put out the fires and stop the looting. The violence would escalate until eventually the state's governor dispatched the National Guard and ordered martial law. To restore order, a curfew was used to keep people off the street where they might gather and form mobs.

Source

Eileen M. Carr. (1985). The vocabulary overview guide: A metacognitive strategy to improve vocabulary comprehension and retention. *Journal of Reading, 28,* 684–689.

29

Possible Sentences

Possible Sentences is a technique for introducing new concepts and vocabulary. Through direct instruction, it helps students understand subject area terms and see how those terms are related to one another. It is also used for motivating students and setting purposes for reading.

Concentrating on words taken from material to be read, Possible Sentences emphasizes the vocabulary of particular topics. It has students rely heavily on the context of the material for providing clues to word meaning. Students observe the context in which words occur and then use the words in contexts that they themselves create in a reading-related writing activity. Because the technique involves prediction activity, it tends to motivate students and focus their attention.

The technique is appropriate for class-size groups (i.e., 30 or so students). Although the time required for the activity varies according to the number of words to be introduced, it should take no longer than a 50-minute class period. Possible Sentences may be used in any academic subject.

Procedure

A Possible Sentences lesson is carried out in four steps. In the first step, the teacher introduces terms to be learned by listing them on the chalkboard and pronouncing them several times. The teacher should make sure that the terms selected for teaching are essential for understanding the text and occur in a clearly defining context—that is, students are able to figure out the words' meanings by the way they are used.

In the second step, the teacher calls on a student to put any two words on the list into a single sentence. As the student dictates the sentence, the teacher writes it on the chalkboard (or overhead transparency) and underlines the two words from the list. The sentence is written exactly as dictated by the student, even if it contains inaccuracies. The teacher continues calling on students, each to dictate a sentence using any two words on the list. Students may use previously used words, but all words on the list should be used at least once. To the extent that time and group size permit, students may continue dictating sentences for the teacher to record.

In the third step, the teacher directs students to read the text and observe the way words listed on the chalkboard are used. The purpose given for reading is to check the accuracy of the sentences dictated to the teacher.

In the fourth step, the teacher leads a discussion in which students evaluate the sentences dictated prior to the reading: Which sentences used the listed words accurately? Which need modifying or elaborating? How does the text's use of the word tend to validate or fail to validate a sentence's use of target words? Students correct and modify the sentences, and then the teacher may ask students to produce additional possible sentences. As additional sentences are dictated, other students may challenge their accuracy or completeness in light of the text presentation.

Discussion

This method motivates students, sets a game-like purpose for reading, and provides a thorough consideration of terms to be learned. It concentrates on specific words and makes these terms vivid through meaningful associations developed by students themselves. In order for the method to work, students have to be able to determine the meanings of targeted words by the context of the material read. Context determines the meanings of words, but it does not always reveal their meanings. Thus, the teacher needs to select words that are *defined* by the context. Also, because words tend to be introduced in connection with subject matter at an abstract, symbolic level, the teacher needs to provide experiences that allow students to apply learned words at a personal and concrete level.

EXAMPLE

A middle-grade science class is beginning a unit on the seasons of the year. The teacher's objective is to acquaint students with concepts and terms used for understanding changes of the seasons. Before reading a textbook section called "The Tilting Spinning Planet Earth," the teacher introduces key terms.

Teacher: (holding a globe) So, to understand the change of seasons, we have to know some things about the Earth's movement and what happens when a place on Earth moves closer to or farther from the sun. These things are explained in our textbook. But before we read, let's get to know some words that we will see in our textbook. OK, the first word is *axis. Axis.* I'll write the word *axis* here on the board so you can see it. *Axis.* The next word is . . . .

The teacher introduces four more words, pronouncing each several times as they are written on the chalkboard. The words introduced are: *axis, rotates, pole, equator, hemisphere.*

Teacher: Let's have some fun with these words. Let's make up sentences that use them. But each sentence has to use not one, but *two*, of the words. OK, who'd like to be first?

Carla: The equator rotates around the earth.

Although the teacher recognizes the error of Carla's sentence, it is written on the chalkboard. As students continue to dictate sentences, the teacher writes them as stated on the chalkboard without regard for their correctness. The sentences recorded are:

> The *equator rotates* around the earth.
>
> At the top of the world is the North *Pole,* and the *equator* is in the middle.
>
> The *equator* divides the earth into two *hemispheres.*
>
> The South *Pole* is at the bottom of the world's *axis.*

Teacher: All right. We have on the board your sentences that have in them words you'll see in the text. Let's now read the text to see if the sentences on the board use the words correctly. Read the first two paragraphs of the section entitled "The Wobbling Spinning Earth."

Once students have apparently finished reading, the teacher asks them to comment on the dictated sentences.

Teacher: Let's look at the first sentence. Having seen the way the text uses the words *equator* and *rotates,* would you say this sentence is all right? Does the equator rotate around the earth?

Susan: Well, it does, sort of. I mean it's really the earth that rotates. But the equator, being part of the earth, rotates too.

Rick: But that's the problem with the sentence. If the equator is *part* of the earth, it rotates *with* it—not *around* it.

John: So it's not the equator that rotates around the earth. But isn't it the earth that rotates around the axis?

Teacher: What does the text say, exactly?

John: (reading from the text) "It rotates on its axis," *on* its axis.

Teacher: Let's write an improved version of the sentence here under a heading we'll call "modified sentences."

As the discussion continues, each dictated sentence is considered in light of the text's use of the target words. The discussion results in these modified sentences:

> The earth *rotates* on its *axis.*
>
> At either end of the earth's *axis* is a *pole,* the North Pole at one end and the South Pole at the other.
>
> The *equator* is an imaginary line that divides the earth into two *hemispheres,* the Northern Hemisphere and the Southern Hemisphere.
>
> The South *Pole* is as far south as one can go in the Southern *Hemisphere.*

In checking and modifying the sentences originally dictated, the students further consider the targeted words and are able to produce additional sentences:

> The *axis* and the *equator* are both imaginary lines.
>
> Every point along the *equator* is equally as distant from the North *Pole* as from the South *Pole.*

The Wobbling Spinning Earth

The Earth is the third planet from the sun. The Earth revolves around the sun, spinning slowly as it goes. It rotates on its axis, which is an imaginary line running in an up-and-down direction through the Earth's center. At each end of the axis is a point called a pole. At the top end of the axis is the North Pole. The North Pole is as far north as you can go on the Earth. At the bottom end of the axis is the South Pole. The South Pole is as far south as you can go.

Another imaginary line is the equator. It runs around the surface of the Earth at a distance exactly between the North Pole and the South Pole. The equator divides the Earth into halves, called hemispheres. The hemisphere above the equator is called the Northern Hemisphere. The hemisphere below the equator is called the Southern Hemisphere.

Source

David W. Moore and Sharon Arthur Moore. (1986). Possible sentences. In E. K. Dishner, T. W. Bean, J. E. Readence, and D. W. Moore (Eds.), *Reading in the content areas: Improving classroom instruction* (2nd ed.) (pp. 174–179). Dubuque, IA: Kendall/Hunt.

30

List-Group-Label

The purpose of List-Group-Label (L-G-L) is to help students develop skills for thinking about subject matter inductively. These skills are developed through the process of listing words related to a topic, grouping these words into different categories based on a shared relationship, and labeling each word group to indicate the characteristic that unites the words as a group.

L-G-L has students organize their existing knowledge into categories in order to see how different words within a topic are related. L-G-L helps students relate previously learned information with new information through the placement of information into categories. Although L-G-L was developed as an approach to teaching vocabulary in elementary-level social studies and science classes, teachers have found that it can be adapted for any grade level or content area. L-G-L may be used either as a prereading activity to find out how much students already know about a topic, or it may be used as a postreading activity to evaluate what students have learned from reading. Thus, the activity serves as a motivation ploy before reading or as a reinforcement activity after reading. L-G-L may be used with large or small groups of students. Small groups are preferred, however, because they allow students to cooperate with one another in creating word categories.

Procedure

The teacher initiates L-G-L by writing at the top of the chalkboard a term that identifies the material being studied. If L-G-L is used as a prereading activity, the teacher has students generate words or ideas associated with this term by drawing from their experience or knowledge. If L-G-L is used as a follow-up to reading, the teacher has students produce these associations by pulling information from the text. The teacher writes all word/idea associations given by the students beneath the topic word. In order to keep the list manageable, the teacher should stop listing after 25 to 30 words have been recorded.

The teacher reads the list of words to students orally and then directs students to make smaller lists from the large list of words on the chalkboard. The smaller lists are to contain at least three words that have something in common. The teacher explains that words in the large list may be used in more than one small list as long as the grouping is different. In addition to grouping words, students are to give the word-groups a label to indicate what they have in common. At this point, the teacher gives students an example of a labeled group of words to get them started. The teacher emphasizes that all words in a category should share a common meaning rather than a surface characteristic (i.e., number of syllables, same suffix, same prefix). The teacher may wish to divide the class into teams to do this part of the activity. If so, a recorder should be selected by each team to write down and report the labeled groupings to the class.

The final phase of the procedure begins once students have completed grouping and labeling the words. The teacher asks students or team recorders to read their lists and provide labels that explain the reason for grouping the words together. The teacher writes these groups of words and labels on the chalkboard. The purpose of the strategy is fulfilled once all categories are recorded on the chalkboard.

Discussion

L-G-L is an effective teaching activity for several reasons. It is flexible enough to be used with large or small groups of students in any grade level or content area. It can be used as a motivation technique for prereading or adapted as a reinforcing postreading technique. It helps the teacher find out how much students know about a specific topic and what additional instruction or clarification may be required. Most important, the strategy allows students to share and discuss worthy ideas concerning a topic and relate them to one another according to a common characteristic.

Although L-G-L has many obvious strengths, the strategy may prove ineffective for some students. The teacher may have to provide additional material for practice in categorizing for students who are younger or slower. Before the actual lesson occurs, the teacher should explain the process of categorizing as being based on a shared relationship; afterwards, the teacher gives students a list of words to group and label for practice. Another limitation of the strategy is that some words may not fit in any grouping. To deal with these words, the teacher may suggest creating a "misfit" list.

EXAMPLE

A high school geography class is beginning a unit on Japan. In the lesson, the teacher uses L-G-L as a way to initiate thinking about Japan and as an activity to follow reading an introductory section of the textbook's chapter on Japan. As a prereading activity, L-G-L indicates to the teacher how much students already know about Japan and has students organize that knowledge. As a follow-up to reading, L-G-L has students recall and organize information they encounter in the text. The teacher writes the word *Japan* at the top of the chalkboard.

Teacher: What words come to mind when you think of Japan?

John: I think of World War II because my grandfather fought in that war against Japan.

Holly: How about the movie *Shogun?* It took place in Japan.

Jason: I've seen pictures of the A-Bomb explosion over Hiroshima during World War II.

Teacher: Yes, all of these things are associated with Japan. Can you think of others?

Amy: My parents visited Tokyo and brought me back a geisha and a samurai doll.

Matt: Many things are imported from Japan to the U.S., like cars, stereos, televisions, and VCRs.

Julie: I enjoy Japanese food like sukiyaki, sushi, and saki.

Nancy: Japan used to have an emperor.

The teacher writes on the chalkboard all associations made by the students. The teacher ends the listing once all students have had a chance to respond. The teacher reads the list of words orally to the students:

Japan

World War II	Hiroshima	samurai
Shogun	Tokyo	cars
A-Bomb	geisha	stereos
sushi	saki	emperor
televisions	VCRs	sukiyaki

Teacher: I want you to use this large list of words to construct smaller lists containing at least three words that have something in common. I will give you an example to get you started.

On the chalkboard the teacher writes a list of words and labels it:

People Associated with Japan

geisha

samurai

emperor

Teacher: Notice that after grouping these words, I gave the group of words a label that indicates what they have in common. Now you try it. Write down the words in groups of at least three words each and then label each group. I will give you as much time as you need to group and label your words.

When students have finished grouping and labeling words, the teacher calls on students to share their lists and to provide a label that explains why the words have been grouped in the particular way stated.

John: World War II, Hiroshima, and the A-Bomb are aspects of Japan's history. That's my label, "Aspects of Japan's History."

Amy: Televisions, VCRs, stereos, and cars. I've labeled these "Things Imported by the U.S. from Japan."

Matt: My group of words includes sushi, saki, and sukiyaki. My label is "Japanese Foods."

The teacher records all groups and labels on the chalkboard.

Aspects of Japan's History	Japanese Foods
World War II	sushi
Hiroshima	saki
A-Bomb	sukiyaki

Things Imported by the U.S. from Japan	Misfit List
televisions	*Shogun*
VCRs	Tokyo
stereos	
cars	

Teacher: Obviously, you already know some things about Japan. Our textbook has a lot more information for us. Let's read the introduction to the chapter on Japan and go over its information the way we've just gone over what we already know about Japan.

John: By listing and grouping stuff?

Teacher: And by giving each group a label. First, let's read the chapter introduction.

Students silently read the introduction of the textbook chapter, "The Island Nation of Japan." When it appears that students have finished reading, the teacher asks them to identify the important information presented in the text.

Teacher: Here at the top of the chalkboard, I've written "The Island Nation of Japan," the title of this chapter in our textbook. Beneath, I'll jot down information about Japan you've learned from reading the chapter introduction.

Holly: Should we give the information in the order the text states it?

Teacher: At this point, our purpose is just to list the information—in no particular order.

Jason: Islands.

Amy: Cars.

Matt: Tokyo.

Julie: Electronic products.

As students continue giving information presented in the text, the teacher produces this list at the chalkboard:

The Island Nation of Japan

islands	Kyushu	Hokkaido
cars	iron	Ainus
Tokyo	steal	Sapporo
electronic products	hot springs	coal
rice	winter sports	Yokohama

Honshu	timber	tobacco
fishing	vegetables	copper
mountainous	Shikoku	camphor
volcanic	fruit	subtropical climate
Hiroshima	tea	earthquake prone

The teacher reads the list aloud so that every student recognizes all of the words on the chalkboard.

Teacher: Now let's arrange this information into smaller groups of information and give each group a label that tells what the group's words have in common.

Nancy: Should each one of us write this down?

Teacher: For this, I have something else in mind. I want you to do the grouping and labeling in teams. Students on the window-side of the room form one team, and students on the door-side of the room form the other.

Holly: So we decide as a team how we would like to group the information on the board?

Teacher: That's right. For your team, choose a recorder. The recorder's job is to write down the groups and labels that the team produces. It will also be the recorder's job to report and explain your team's word groups and labels to the class. Remember, each group should have at least three words.

The class divides into teams, and the activity proceeds. When the teams complete the assigned task, the recorders report the results. The following groups are explained by the recorder of the window-side team.

Main Islands	*Agriculture*	*Northern Japan*
Honshu	rice	winter sports
Kyushu	fruit	Hokkaido
Shikoku	tea	Ainus
Hokkaido	tobacco	
	vegetables	*Misfit List*
Cities	camphor	hot springs
Tokyo	timber	subtropical climate
Yokohama	fishing	cars
Hiroshima		electronic products
Sapporo	*Physical Features*	
	islands	
Minerals	mountainous	
iron	volcanic	
coal	earthquake prone	
copper		
steel		

The Island Nation of Japan

Introduction

Japan is an island nation that lies off the mainland of Asia between the Sea of Japan and the Pacific Ocean. It is a mountainous and volcanic country prone to earthquakes. Being a country of many islands, it has a long and indented shoreline. The four main islands of Japan are Honshu, Kyushu, Shikoku, and Hokkaido.

Honshu is the largest island. It is large enough that its climate ranges from subtropical in the south to cool temperatures in the north. Historically, Honshu has been the cultural and economic center of Japan. Most of Japan's important cities are in Honshu. Tokyo is the capital and largest city of Japan, with over 100 universities and a large industrial district. Honshu's important seaports include Yokohama, Nagoya, Osaka, and Hiroshima. Modern industries produce iron and steel, automobiles, chemicals, textiles, and electronic products. In the agricultural sector, Honshu grows rice, fruit, cotton, and tea.

Kyushu is the southernmost of Japan's four main islands. It is known for its subtropical climate and hot springs. The most important cities are Kitakyushu, Fukuoka, and Nagasaki, all industrial-seaport cities. In the northwest is a large rice-growing area. Kyushu also grows timber, fruit, and vegetables. Fishing is an important part of Kyushu's economy.

Shikoku is the smallest of Japan's four main islands. Surrounded by the Inland Sea, it lies between Honshu and Kyushu. The interior is forested, and most of its people live on the coastal plains. The major cities are Matsuyama on the western coast and Takamatsu on the northern coast. Copper is mined in the north. Shikoku's economy also depends on fishing and growing rice, tobacco, mulberry, and camphor.

Hokkaido is northernmost of the main islands. It is forested and its climate is cool. Winter sports are popular. The northern part of the island is sparsely populated. Hokkaido is home of the sizable population of Ainus, an aboriginal caucasoid people. The chief city is Sapporo. The economy is based on coal mining, farming, and fishing.

Sources

John E. Readence and Lyndon W. Searfoss. (1980). Teaching strategies for vocabulary development, *English Journal, 69,* 43–46.

Hilda Taba. (1967). *Teacher's handbook for elementary social studies.* Reading, MA: Addison-Wesley.

31

Capsule Vocabulary

Capsule Vocabulary develops students' word power by providing relevant contexts in which to use newly introduced words. It increases students' comfort and confidence in using unfamiliar words, and it enhances their ability to read and communicate about a topic by widening their range of words.

Most students are eager to improve their skill with words, when they find it possible. Many students have to search hard for words to express their thinking about a subject, and some students have to search for words even to express their most basic feelings. Capsule Vocabulary works well with students because it introduces words in a way that encourages their immediate use in discussing subject matter. It can be effective for building students' general word power by introducing words that can be used in everyday contexts. The method does not use lists of popular vocabulary words or vocabulary builders. Instead, the emphasis is placed on the utility of words. As students' facility with words increases, their enthusiasm for vocabulary building grows.

Capsule Vocabulary may be used effectively with students at intermediate grade levels and above. Language arts teachers find it an attractive method for teaching vocabulary and communication skills, yet it also lends itself well for instruction in all academic subjects. It may be used in whole-class teaching or in small-group exercises.

Procedure

Each Capsule Vocabulary lesson focuses on a specific topic. In a content area class, the unfolding subject matter largely determines the topic. The teacher may also choose the topic on the basis of previous discussion or, perhaps, on the basis of interviews aimed at finding out about students' personal interests related to the subject matter. With the topic of interest in mind, the teacher generates a list of a dozen or so words that students are likely to need for communicating effectively about the topic. The list should include any words that students are likely to have heard or read but have been reluctant to use. This list is the vocabulary capsule.

To begin a Capsule Vocabulary lesson, the teacher engages students in a discussion about the topic. During the discussion, the teacher uses the words from the vocabulary capsule as naturally as possible. As each word is introduced into the discussion, it is written on the chalkboard, and students are directed to record it in their notebooks. The discussion takes as long as is needed to introduce and repeat the listed words. This may take up to half an hour or so.

The teacher divides the class into pairs and assigns students to talk to each other, one-on-one, about the topic. A brief reading assignment can provide substance for these exchanges. Students are to try to use each word from the list as much as possible. The idea is to give students an opportunity both to speak and to hear the words in a comfortable situation.

The one-on-one talk is followed by a writing activity. The teacher assigns students to write a short composition on the topic under discussion. Students are directed to try to use all of the words from the topic word list. At the next meeting the teacher selects some of the compositions for reading aloud, and in the discussion surrounding these compositions the teacher uses the words from the vocabulary capsule. The teacher looks for opportunities to reinforce learning the words by using them and by eliciting their use by students.

Discussion

The basis for the vocabulary capsule is the topic selected by the teacher. If the teacher exercises care in selecting the topic, students will become truly interested and the Capsule Vocabulary activities will prove effective for building students' word power.

As with any activity that assigns students to pairs and small groups, there is the potential that idle conversation will take over. Also, once class is over and students are on their own, they may be without others with whom to practice their new words in conversation. The method is intended as a starting point for removing inhibitions about using new words. There is no guarantee that students will continue to use the words introduced in the lesson.

EXAMPLE

A seventh-grade science class is involved in a unit on water resources. In preparation for a lesson on surface and underground water flow, the teacher has identified some 13 words to be introduced into the discussion:

Vocabulary Capsule

Rivers and Groundwater

artesian flow	groundwater
aquifer	impenetrable
brackish	impermeable
delta	meander
encapsulate	porous
gradient	potable
rill	

The teacher begins the discussion by gulping down a glass of water.

Teacher: Ah, water. Cool, clear, potable water. It really slakes my thirst. (The teacher writes the word *potable* on the chalkboard.) Of course, I'd only drink it if it's potable.

Jeff: Right. You wouldn't want to drink water you can't carry around.

Mary: That's *portable*. The word is *potable*.

Teacher: You're right, Mary. *Potable*. No brackish, bitter, undrinkable water for me. (The teacher writes *brackish* on the chalkboard.) It's got to be potable.

Gina: Well, by potable you mean out of the faucet, right?

Teacher: Well, I certainly hope faucet water is potable. We assume that water from the faucet is fit to drink. But, did you ever wonder how water gets to our faucet? I mean, after it falls from the clouds, how it comes to us?

Mary: Don't we just pump it from the river?

Jeff: Yuk. I hope not. The river water is definitely not *potable*. We pour the city sewage into it. And Chem-Co pours its poisons in there, too.

Teacher: There was a time, long ago, when we took water from the river that meanders through our fair valley. (The teacher writes *meander* on the chalkboard.) But you're right, Jeff. It's too polluted for us to rely on it for drinking water.

Mary: But in Pine Summit, where we lived before we moved here, I know we got our water from Clear River. We swam in it, fished it, even panned for gold in it.

Teacher: But Pine Summit is in the mountains, where the river begins with melted snow running fresh from rills and streams, where the gradient is steep and the water flows rapidly. Here in the delta, at the mouth of the river, Clear River isn't so clear. The river brings to us the things people have dumped in it upriver. (The teacher writes *rills, gradient,* and *delta* on the chalkboard.)

Jeff: The words you're writing on the board. They're about this stuff about water?

Teacher: Right. I'm jotting them down as I say them so you can see how they're spelled. You should write them down in your own notebook so you can think about them later. I want you to see these words as we talk about water.

The teacher waits for the students to record the words already listed.

Mary: Well if we don't get our water from the river, where do we get it?

Teacher: From underground. There's plenty of groundwater here. And, thank goodness, it's still potable.

Gina: How did it get there? Where does groundwater come from?

Teacher: Good question. It's water that instead of flowing on the surface, sinks into the ground. Some of it becomes encapsulated in underground pockets. And some of it flows through aquifers. Aquifers are underground streams that run through porous rocks.

Jeff: It sounds as if we take two different kinds of groundwater. There's water encapsulated in pockets and water that runs through aquifers.

Teacher: We do take groundwater found in both ways. We take encapsulated water from *bored* wells. Bored wells are fairly shallow—about 50 feet. We tap into aquifers with deeper, so-called *drilled* wells. They're called drilled wells because to get to an aquifer you have to drill through underground rock. But there are other forms of groundwater.

Mary: Oh sure. A spring is groundwater.

Teacher: Yes it is. And so is an artesian flow.

Gina: What's that?

Teacher: It's water that flows forcefully out of the ground. Water flowing through an aquifer picks up velocity as the volume increases. If the water comes to an impenetrable barrier of underground rock and there are cracks in the rock above the aquifer, the water shoots up through those cracks.

The discussion continues until the topic has been introduced and each capsule word has been used and noted. The teacher then directs the class to divide into pairs and discuss the textbook section entitled "Water on the Surface and Underground." For homework, the teacher assigns students to write an account either of the formation and action of rivers or the accumulation and flow of groundwater. The next day, the teacher reads aloud selected students' compositions on each topic to stimulate further discussion, in which the capsule words are again used.

Water on the Surface and Underground

When rain or snow falls to the ground, different things can happen to the moisture, depending on the slope of the surface. If the gradient is steep, the water may flow on the surface and into a run-off. If the gradient is gentle, or if the surface is level, the water may sink into the ground and become groundwater.

Streams and Rivers

Streams and rivers form when surface run-off moves in the same channels. First, small rills form and flow together to make networks of creeks and brooks. These, in turn, flow together to form streams. When streams form networks and run together, the surface is eroded into wider and wider channels until, eventually, a river forms. As the number of streams flowing into the river increases, the river's volume becomes larger.

Water always flows toward lower elevations. When water flows downward into large depressions in the surface, lakes are formed. When the lakes fill, the water overflows and continues to move toward lower elevations. As the water moves, it cuts a deeper and deeper channel. When the slope becomes gradual, the water cuts sideward and widens its bed. Taking the course of least resistance, the river flows around obstacles and curves from side to side to form an s-shaped channel. As it meanders, the river cuts into the outside of each curve and deposits sediment at the curve's inside.

Sometimes water overflows its bed and floods the land next to the channel. When this happens, alluvial plains develop. Alluvial plains are usually swampy and layered with fertile deposits of sediments. The Mississippi Valley is an alluvial plain whose soil has been enriched by annual flooding from the river.

Once the river reaches its mouth, its rate of flow diminishes suddenly. Where the river meets standing water at the river's mouth, sediments are deposited and a delta forms.

Groundwater

Water that sinks into the ground moves downward through underground spaces. The water seeps through grains of soil and crevices in rocks until it reaches a layer of rock that is impenetrable. Reaching impermeable rock, the water accumulates underground. It may become encapsulated in pockets of underground rock, or it may accumulate to the extent that underground streams and rivers are formed.

The level to which groundwater rises is the water table, which is nearly always parallel to the ground. The water table is, however, somewhat deeper from the tops of hills, and is somewhat shallower from valley floors. Although the water table usually remains below the surface, it reaches the surface in swamps, springs, and rivers.

Like surface water, groundwater moves toward lower elevations, and it takes the course of least resistance. It moves through underground networks of porous rocks, sand, and gravel. Freely flowing underground water is called an aquifer. Holes from the surface are drilled into an aquifer in order to provide a well with a reliable source of water.

Groundwater continues to move downward until it meets resistance by impermeable rock. When this happens and there is pressure created by the water's flow, water is forced upward through cracks in the ground. A spring develops when the upward flow of groundwater reaches the surface and gurgles out. An artesian flow develops if the water spews out of the ground under pressure.

Source

Barbara I. Crist. (1975). One capsule a week—A painless remedy for vocabulary ills. *Journal of Reading, 19,* 147–149.

32

Feature Analysis

Feature Analysis employs a grid chart called a "Feature Matrix" to help students make fine discriminations among concepts or terms within a category. It helps students to see how ideas, objects, words, and so on within a category are alike and different. With this method, the teacher encourages students to examine features or properties of subject matter and to categorize the subject matter according to distinctive features or properties.

Feature analysis is based on the notion that information is processed by establishing mental categories and rules for operating within those categories. Importantly, the rules include comparing and contrasting distinctive aspects of category information. Feature analysis offers a concrete way to simulate the process. It has students fit information within categories, note shared attributes of the information and highlight unique attributes. Through active reflection on these attributes, concepts and the terms associated with them are learned with completeness and precision.

Feature Analysis is an effective method for any academic subject. It is especially useful in science and social studies. Appropriate times to introduce Feature Analysis are during vocabulary building or during review. As a vocabulary builder, it clearly shows the uniqueness of individual terms within a category. As a review device, it allows thorough exploration of a topic's major concepts. Once students are acquainted with Feature Analysis, it may be used effectively to spark interest in a topic or to emphasize distinctive features of subject matter as it develops during instruction.

Procedure

The teacher leads students to compare the terms (ideas, objects, words, etc.) of a topic. Comparisons are made with the use of a Feature Matrix, a grid in whose cells students indicate feature possession of a term. On the matrix, the terms to be compared are listed in a column down the left side. The features on which these terms are compared are listed across the top. Where the lines extending from terms and features intersect, feature possession is indicated.

To begin a lesson using Feature Analysis, the teacher writes on the chalkboard the topic to be examined. Below this, the teacher develops the Feature Matrix. As each term of the topic is presented in the lecture or discussion of the text, the teacher lists it down the left side. At the top, the teacher lists its descriptors. With the addition of each term, the teacher has students indicate whether it possesses features previously listed. Also, students indicate whether previously listed terms possess the features added. Thus, significant features are repeatedly considered, and terms are compared again and again.

To use the Feature Matrix as a review device, the teacher presents it with terms and features already present. The teacher leads students either to consider each term for its feature possession or, alternatively, to consider features one at a time, indicating whether each feature applies to the terms listed.

Feature possession may be indicated in three basic ways. The simplest way is merely to note whether features apply or do not apply. This is shown with marks such as +, −, 0, and so on. Another way to indicate feature possession is to show the extent to which features apply. This is accomplished with a rating scale by which gradations of feature possession are shown with numbers 0 through 4, 0 indicating no feature possession and 4 indicating maximum feature possession. A third way of indicating feature possession is to write within the term's feature cells brief notes explaining the conditions under which features may apply to terms. This approach is similar to the use of data charts (see pages 218–226).

Discussion

Feature Analysis offers a structured, systematic approach to the examination of subject matter. It departs from traditional methods in that its framework allows students to bear the major burden of the analysis and discussion. It is an activity that students themselves value as an enjoyable and productive way of learning. It facilitates their participation by the predictable direction of discussions, term by term and feature by feature. And it highlights significant information students need for making fine discriminations in the material they are studying. For the teacher, Feature Analysis offers a way to teach not only conceptual content but vocabulary and a highly useful study skill as well. The activity requires relatively little preparation.

As all approaches that examine subject matter thoroughly, feature analysis takes time. It can be time well invested, however, if the material calls for making differentiations and those differentiations are made appropriately. Students have to be able to understand the descriptors in order to make meaningful distinctions. Also, meaningful distinctions can only be made with indicators that can reflect feature possession correctly (i.e., as absolute presence vs. absolute absence or as present in degrees or as present under certain conditions).

EXAMPLE

A middle-school science class is learning about dinosaurs. The teacher's objective is to enable students to identify the distinctive features of different dinosaur species. Students have read the textbook's introductory paragraph on "Dinosaurs."

Teacher: During the 100 million years they were on the earth, dinosaurs evolved into a variety of species. (The teacher writes the word *Dinosaurs* on the chalkboard toward the top and middle.) What were some of the differences among dinosaurs that were mentioned in the first paragraph?

Fred: Some dinosaurs walked on two feet, but others walked on all fours.

Betty: Some ate meat.

Katie: Some ate plants.

Mark: Some lived in the water, and some lived on land.

Beginning a feature matrix, the teacher writes these differences just beneath the heading *Dinosaurs* horizontally across the chalkboard.

Dinosaurs

Walked on 2 Feet	Walked on 4 Feet	Ate Meat	Ate Plants	Water	Land

Teacher: Now let's find out about some specific dinosaurs whose fossils have been found. Let's silently read the next paragraph in our text.

Students read the paragraph.

Teacher: OK, Katie, tell us what this paragraph adds to our knowledge about dinosaurs.

Katie: It named the largest dinosaur. It's called Bronto, er, something.

Teacher: (pronouncing the word) That's Brontosaurus.

Katie: Oh, Brontosaurus. It was large and made a lot of noise. That's why they call it Brontosaurus. The name means "thunder lizard" to scientists.

At the left of the emerging feature matrix, the teacher writes the subheading *Species* and beneath the subheading lists Brontosaurus.

Teacher: Good. Beside the name and in parentheses I'll note "thunder lizard." How about these features that distinguished the different dinosaur species? Which apply to Brontosaurus?

Mark: The text said it was a water dinosaur.

Katie: But it didn't say Brontosaurus never went on dry land. It did have feet. And there's dry land in and around swamps.

Fred: Yeah. But mostly it was a water dinosaur.

Teacher: The text does say Brontosaurus lived in lakes and swamps. But Katie has a point. Having feet, not fins, it probably did walk on land sometimes.

Mark: It used the water to support its weight.

Katie: But not necessarily all of the time.

Teacher: This is not an either-or matter. Let's use a rating scale to show how much each describing feature applies. Let's let 0 mean the feature never applies, 1 mean rarely, 2 mean sometimes, 3 mean often, and 4 mean always.

Fred: Then let's give Brontosaurus a 3 for water.

Katie: But at least a 1 for land.

Teacher: Does anybody see a problem with giving Brontosaurus a 1 for land and a 3 for water? (Pause) Seems reasonable to me, too. (Writes 1 and 3 under land and water, respectively.) How about those other features?

Katie: It ate plants, not other animals.

Betty: It probably didn't eat meat at all, so give a 4 to "ate plants" and a 0 to "ate meat."

Several: Right. Yes.

The teacher enters these ratings.

Fred: It walked on four feet, not two.

Mark: So mark "walked on two feet" 0 and "walked on four feet" with 4.

Several: Right.

Teacher: Did Brontosaurus have features not listed on the board?

Fred: It was large, the largest dinosaur. So we should add the word *large* and give Brontosaurus a 4 for being large.

Katie: But it was gentle. I think we should write down *gentle,* too.

Teacher: How should we rate it on gentleness?

Betty: Well, it was a plant eater and lived in the water. It would have to be rated as gentle as a whale or gentler. I'd say give it a 4.

Teacher: Good. Let's read the next paragraph to find out about another dinosaur.

Students read the paragraph on Tyrannosaurs Rex. In the discussion that follows the teacher and students rate this dinosaur on the descriptors listed on the Feature Matrix and then add further descriptors. The added features are considered for their fit with the dinosaur previously discussed, Brontosaurus.

As the activity continues, the class discusses each dinosaur described in the text and builds the feature matrix. The feature matrix they finally produce looks like the one shown on the facing page.

Feature Matrix

Species	Walked on 2 Feet	Walked on 4 Feet	Ate Meat	Ate Plants	Water	Land	Large	Gentle	Ferocious	Fighter	Horns	Protective Collar	Crested Skull
Brontosaurus (Thunder Lizard)	0	4	0	4	3	1	4	4	0	0	0	0	0
Tyrannosaurus Rex (King of the Tyrants)	4	0	4	0	0	4	3	0	4	4	0	0	0
Triceratops (3 horns about eyes)	0	4	0	4	?	?	3	3	2	4	4	4	0
Lambeosaurus (Λ-shaped skull)	3	2	0	4	?	?	3	4	0	0	0	0	4

The text leaves open the possibility that two of the dinosaurs (Triceratops and Lambeosaurus) could have been either land or water creatures, but does not give enough information to permit an inference. The teacher assigns students outside reading to find the answer.

Dinosaurs

Dinosaurs roamed the earth for more than 100 million years. During that time a great variety of dinosaurs evolved. Some walked on two feet, some on four; some ate meat, others only plants; some lived in water, others on dry land. Although dinosaurs were extinct long before written history, their petrified remains tell us about many different kinds of dinosaurs.

The largest dinosaur was Brontosaurus, whose name means "thunder lizard." Weighing four tons and extending 70 feet in length, this dinosaur must have made quite a noise when it moved and ate. Brontosaurus had a small head and brain and stood on four feet. A plant eater, it was a gentle dinosaur. It lived in lakes and swamps where the water served both to provide food and to support the weight of its bulky body.

The most ferocious dinosaur was Tyrannosaurus Rex, "king of the tyrants." This dinosaur stood upright 20 feet tall and walked on its hind legs. Head to tail, Tyrannosaurus Rex was about 50 feet long. It ripped into its prey with tearing claws and rows of razor-sharp teeth. It fed mainly on animals that were plant eaters, including herbivorous dinosaurs.

Triceratops was an armored dinosaur well equipped for fighting. It looked somewhat like a rhinoceros, but with two horns extending from the head and one from the nose. *Triceratops* means "three horns about the eyes." It also had a neck collar to shield it from attack by meat-eating dinosaurs. Although it was an excellent fighter, it was a plant eater. Triceratops weighed over 10 tons and measured 30 feet in length.

Lambeosaurus was a duck-billed herbivore. Its crested skull resembled the shape of the Greek letter lambda, Λ. The hollow nasal passages of its duck-billed crest gave it a good sense of smell. It had rows of molars for grinding food, and cheek pouches for storing it. Lambeosaurus stood about 15 feet tall and was about 30 feet head to tail. It had strong back legs and small front limbs, and it often walked on all fours.

Source

Dale D. Johnson and P. David Pearson. (1978). *Teaching reading and reading vocabulary.* New York: Holt, Rinehart and Winston.

Related Reading

Patricia L. Anders and Candace S. Bos. (1986). Semantic feature analysis: An interactive strategy for vocabulary development and text comprehension. *Journal of Reading, 29,* 610–615.

R. Scott Baldwin, Jeff C. Ford, and John E. Readence. (1981). Teaching word connotations: An alternative strategy. *Reading World, 21,* 103–108.

Shelley Mattson Gahn. (1989). A practical guide for writing in the content areas. *Journal of Reading, 32,* 525–531.

John E. Readence and Lyndon W. Searfoss. (1980). Teaching strategies for vocabulary
    development. *The English Journal, 69,* 43–46.
Frank Smith. (1971). *Understanding reading.* New York: Holt, Rinehart and Winston.
Ezra L. Stieglitz and Varda S. Stieglitz. (1981). SAVOR the word to reinforce vocabulary
    in the content areas. *Journal of Reading, 25,* 46–48.

33

Mathematics Review Lesson

The Mathematics Review Lesson helps students gain a clear understanding of concepts and terms presented in mathematics instruction. The activity provides an intensive review of material that the teacher has previously presented and reveals problem areas so that the teacher may give proper attention to them.

Mathematics instruction poses special difficulties for students. By its nature, the subject matter is abstract, and the presentation of that subject matter is usually terse and highly compressed. Too often mathematics textbooks are too difficult for the grade levels at which they are used. The Mathematics Review Lesson helps students deal with these difficulties by encouraging them to analyze mathematical problems to generate examples and counterexamples of concepts and to use the language of mathematics. Since mathematics subject matter is usually presented sequentially and hierarchically, students who miss a class session are likely to have gaps in their knowledge. The mathematics review lesson can close these gaps. It restates and emphasizes major points covered during instruction, clarifies reasoning and corrects misconceptions, and provides repetition students need in order to gain mastery of the material under study.

The activity is appropriate for a wide range of situations in mathematics instruction. It is particularly indicated for teaching material that will be needed for subsequent learning. This might include, for example, mathematics facts, mathematics language, computation, factoring, and solving equations. The activity may be used successfully with entire classes as well as with small groups.

Procedure

The teacher begins the lesson by discussing with students the concepts and terms listed either on a prepared study sheet or on the chalkboard. During the discussion, the teacher clarifies major concepts developed during instruction and encourages students to ask questions about any they do not understand well. Two purposes are served by the discussion of concepts and terms. It indicates the areas in which students need to concentrate their study efforts, and it provides opportunities for correcting misconceptions. In the discussion, the teacher elicits explanations and examples and counterexamples. Once discussion of the listed concepts and terms has taken place, the teacher may lead a review of the text's presentation of the material. In this review, the teacher may either skim the text, highlighting pertinent information, or elaborate on information given in the text's summary section, if there is one. Finally, the teacher engages students in a follow-up activity that has them practice applying the material reviewed.

Discussion

The Mathematics Review Lesson gives an overview of a unit of instruction and at the same time focuses on students' needs in learning its content. Having been exposed to the content during initial instruction, students possess experience for applying it. As they do, they may solidify their understandings, yet may be confronted with their misunderstandings. For the activity, the teacher may evaluate students' progress and adjust future instruction accordingly.

The success of this method depends largely on the teacher's ability to clarify material that remains unclear to students. Students should be encouraged to make concerted efforts to contribute to the review so that they do not become passive and overly dependent on the teacher.

EXAMPLE

An eighth-grade mathematics class is reviewing an introductory unit in geometry. The teacher's objectives are to have students learn basic concepts and terms used in geometry and to be able to classify and label geometric figures. The teacher begins the review lesson by presenting a study sheet that contains a list of terms that are briefly defined.

Study Terms for Chapter on Introduction to Geometry

1. Point—an exact location.
2. Ray—a never-ending straight path in one direction.
3. Angle—two rays with a common endpoint.
4. Right Angle—an angle that measures 90 degrees.
5. Acute Angle—an angle that measures between 0 degrees and 90 degrees.
6. Obtuse angle—an angle that measures more than 90 degrees but less than 180 degrees.
7. Line—a never-ending path that extends in both directions.
8. Line Segment—formed by two points and the straight path between them.
9. Perpendicular Lines—two lines that intersect or cross to form right angles.
10. Parallel Lines—lines in a plane that never cross.
11. Polygon—a closed figure.
12. Scalene Triangle—a triangle with no equal sides.
13. Isosceles Triangle—a triangle with at least two equal sides.
14. Equilateral Triangle—a triangle with three equal sides.
15. Trapezoid—a quadrilateral with only one pair of parallel sides.

16. Parallelogram–a quadrilateral with two pairs of parallel sides.

17. Rectangle–a parallelogram with all angles equal.

18. Rhombus–a parallelogram with all sides equal.

19. Square–a parallelogram with all sides and all angles equal.

Teacher: Let's take a look at this study sheet I've made up for you. On it are listed the terms we've encountered in our introduction to geometry. The first item is the *point*. Geometric description begins with the point. It is a precise, yet imaginary, location.

Larry: By *imaginary* you mean that it can be real but you still have to imagine it? Or mark it with a dot where it would be if it was a physical thing?

Teacher: Right, Larry. When we draw things in geometry, the things we draw only represent the ideas of the things we can think about. They represent images. Now, if there's anything unclear to you, be sure to speak up.

The teacher proceeds through the list, encouraging students to comment on the items.

Teacher: So, Jan, what's the difference between a line and a ray?

Jan: Oh, a ray is a line. It's just one kind of line.

Teacher: What makes you think they're not different?

Jan: They're just not. Both are straight. They're both straight lines.

Teacher: What is a line, anyway, Jan?

Jan: Oh, you know. Like these lines on my notebook paper.

Teacher: Look at the study sheet, Jan. What does it say a line is?

Jan: (reading) "A never-ending path that extends in both directions." So?

Teacher: Now read what a ray is.

Jan: "A never-ending straight path in one direction."

Teacher: And the difference, Jan?

Jan: The words are different, but they're still the same thing to me.

Bill: No, Jan. A ray only goes in one direction.

Jan: That depends on how you look at it. If you're somewhere along the ray, you can look down it both ways.

Bill: True. But if you look hard enough, in one direction it ends. At a point. In the other direction it goes forever.

Jan: Oh, OK. I get it. Lines go on forever in *either* direction, but rays have an endpoint.

As the discussion continues, misconceptions about other terms are revealed and cleared up. When all the terms on the study sheet have been discussed, the teacher turns to the textbook chapter the class has been studying.

Teacher: Now let's look at the summary of the chapter on this stuff. Karen, the first paragraph tells us why we need to know the terms we've been talking about–

uh, the ones on the study sheet. In your own words, Karen, why do we need to know these terms?

Karen: They're like basic. You have to begin with the basics, and these *are* the basics you begin with.

Bob: It's like everything else seems to be in math. Things build on things. These are the bottom things in geometry.

George: And the "bottomest" is the old point. Without them you can't talk about angles and polygons.

Tony: And you can't talk about different kinds of triangles and quadrilaterals if you don't know angles from polygons.

When the discussion of the textbook chapter concludes, the teacher has the students complete a worksheet exercise that requires application of the terms discussed in the lesson.

Summing Up Introduction to Geometry

This chapter introduced concepts and terms that are basic to the study of geometry. Most basic of these are the *point, the ray,* and the *line.* These concepts and terms were used to describe *angles* and *polygons.*

Geometric description begins with the point. A *point* is an exact location. It is represented with a dot and named with one of the letters of the alphabet.

A straight path extending from a single point is called a *ray.* A ray extends from a point in only one direction, and its path is infinite.

Two rays that extend from a single point form an *angle.* An *acute* angle is one that measures between 0 degrees and 90 degrees. A *right* angle is one that measures exactly 90 degrees. An *obtuse* angle measures between 90 degrees and 180 degrees.

A *line* is the path of a moving point. Its length is never-ending in both directions. A line may be perfectly straight, or it may be curved. Lines that never cross are called *parallel* lines. Two lines that intersect to form right angles are called *perpendicular* lines.

A *line segment* is the straight path between two points. A line segment is finite; that is, it has a starting point and an ending point.

A *polygon* is a closed figure bounded by straight lines. The chapter introduced two kinds of polygons—the *triangle* and the *quadrilateral.*

A *triangle* is a polygon with three sides and, thus, three interior angles. A triangle with all three sides equal in length is called an *equilateral* triangle. A triangle with two sides of equal length is called an *isosceles* triangle. A triangle whose sides are not of equal length is called a *scalene* triangle.

A *quadrilateral* is a polygon with four sides. A quadrilateral with two pairs of parallel lines is called a *parallelogram.* There are three kinds of parallelograms: the *rectangle,* the *rhombus,* and the *square.* In a rectangle all four angles are equal (right angles). In a rhombus all sides are of equal length. In a square all four angles are equal *and* all sides are of equal length. A quadrilateral with only one pair of parallel sides is called a *trapezoid.*

Worksheet Exercise: Introduction to Geometry

Use symbols to name the following.

1. line XY

2. M   N

3. ray BC

4. T   U

5.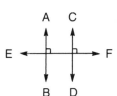

6. angle ABC

Measure each angle. Then classify each angle. Write ACUTE, RIGHT, or OBTUSE.

7.

8.

9.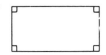

Use symbols to name the following. Use the figure at the right.

10. Perpendicular lines

11. Parallel lines

Classify each triangle and quadrilateral.

12.

13.

14.

15.

16.

17.

18.

19.

20.

Source

Margaret Godfrey. (1979). How to develop the mathematics review lesson. *Reading Improvement, 16,* 219–221.

34

Sound-Structure-Context-Dictionary

Sound-Structure-Context-Dictionary (SSCD) is an approach to understanding unfamiliar words that students encounter in reading. By this approach, word meaning may be determined in four possible ways: pronouncing the word, examining its parts, observing its context, and looking it up in the dictionary. Used on a regular basis, it increases students' sensitivity to words and fosters independence in word learning.

Vocabulary is developed as new words are encountered in meaningful contexts. In the ordinary course of living, people acquire words and shape their meanings through meeting and using words in a variety of situations. In school, the contextual aspects of word learning can be simulated only to a limited degree. Given the relatively meager contexts and infrequent use of words taught in school, especially technical terms, formal approaches to vocabulary building are necessary. Students can learn the words of a subject more efficiently under the guidance of an informed teacher than they can on their own. SSCD combines the contextual aspects of ordinary vocabulary acquisition with the advantages of a formal approach to word learning. As students attack new words with SSCD, they make use of four basic ways of determining word meaning. In the process, they acquire a formal strategy for dealing with new words independently. SSCD is appropriate for students in the upper-middle grades and beyond. It can be built into instruction across the academic subjects.

Procedure

SSCD is not a free-standing lesson framework. Rather, it is a word attack routine to be applied within lessons. It is incorporated into the ongoing instruction. As an unfamiliar word is encountered by students, the teacher reminds them of four ways to get to the meaning. The first way is to sound out the word. It may be a word in the students' speaking-listening vocabulary but that they have not previously seen in print. The second way to get to a word's meaning is through its structure. Its prefix, root, or suffix may reveal its meaning. The third way to word meaning is through context. Students may be able to determine a word's meaning by checking the words and sentences surrounding it. Finally, if students remain unsure about a word's pronunciation or meaning, they can look it up in the dictionary. The teacher reminds students that the dictionary is best used for verifying hunches about a word's pronunciation and meaning. Also, since there may be more than one pronunciation or definition given, the teacher has students see which of the ones given seem most likely for the word's context.

Discussion

SSCD is an eminently practical approach to dealing with new words. It is easy for the teacher and students to employ. There is nothing extra for the teacher to prepare, and there is nothing conceptually difficult or complex for students to grasp. The teacher needs to remain conscious about applying the approach in instruction at every opportunity. If students are to adopt the approach for themselves, they need to see it applied by the teacher on a regular basis. The teacher can facilitate the structural analysis aspect of the approach by providing students with a list of frequently occurring affixes and roots with their meanings. Whenever the dictionary is consulted, students should check the correctness of their structural analysis of the word by noting its etymology.

EXAMPLE

An eighth-grade science class has just finished reading a textbook segment on estimating travel time in outer space. The textbook segment contains the term *telemetry*.

Teacher: Our text says figuring out how long it takes to get to the next galaxy is no problem for space scientists. Why are they so confident that they can do it, Werner?

Werner: Uh, it says something about top rocket speed possible and using tel . . . . uh, I don't know how you say that word.

Several: How can we know what the text means if we can't even say that word?

Teacher: First, let's pronounce it. It's a word you may have heard before–te-LEM-e-tree, te-LEM-e-tree. Now *you* say it. All together, te-LEM-e-tree.

Class: Te-LEM-e-tree.

Christa: I've heard the word *telepathy* before.

Chuck: And *symmetry*.

Judy: But not *telemetry*.

Teacher: It's not a word you hear or read everyday. But you do encounter this word's parts quite often. You find them in words more common that *telepathy* and *symmetry*.

Bob: You mean like *tele* in *telephone?*

Werner: Or *television* or *telescope?*

Teacher: Right. What do all these words have in common?

Judy: They all begin with *tele*.

Teacher: OK, but what else do they have in common–that *tele* indicates?

Bob: They're things that involve long distances. Like television involves sending out a picture that can be seen far away.

Sally: By telephone, people who are far apart can talk to each other.

Teacher: OK, what about the last part of this word *telemetry?*

Christa: You see it in words like *geometry* and *trigonometry*.

Werner: And *optometry*.

Teacher: What common meaning does this word part have across these words?

Christa: Geometry and trigonometry are math classes.

Teacher: And what are math classes about?

Bob: Numbers, quantity.

Werner: How much, how many, how often.

Teacher: Right. An important aspect of mathematics has to do with measuring things—how much, how many, how often. Optometry is one of the health professions. It deals chiefly with measuring things that have to do with our eyes.

Sally: So the last part of the word *telemetry* is probably about measuring.

Christa: Oh, I think I know what it means. The text is about computing the time to get to the nearest galaxy. To do that, you need to measure the distance between here and there. So telemetry probably means distance measuring.

Chuck: Or measuring that you do from a distance away.

Teacher: OK. Let's be sure. Let's check our hunches about its pronunciation and meaning in the dictionary. Everybody, take out your dictionary and look up this word.

Judy: I've got it. It *is* pronounced te-LEM-e-tree.

Bob: And we were right about its meaning. It says: "Measuring at a distance; the measurement of faraway objects; the science of measuring the distance of an object from the point of the observer."

Teacher: Check the etymology. It's in the brackets following the pronunciation and preceding the definition.

Christa: It's from the Greek words *tele,* meaning far off, and *metron,* meaning measure.

Teacher: Now, Werner, what approach do space scientists take to estimate the time it will take to travel to the nearest galaxy?

Estimating Travel Time in Space

Calculating the time required to travel to the nearest galaxy is no great problem for space scientists. They know the limits of rocket technology and the speeds that rockets cannot possibly exceed. Coupling their knowledge of rocket technology with their techniques of telemetry, they can closely estimate the shortest time possible for a rocket to reach the nearest galaxy.

Source

Thomas G. Devine. (1981). *Teaching study skills: A guide for teachers.* Boston: Allyn and Bacon.

SECTION FOUR

Detecting Structure in Reading, Applying Structure in Writing

In instruction, the communication of subject matter is organized and orderly. Quite literally, it is formal. It has form and is intended, by its form, to add to and give form to knowledge. (The word instruction shares the same Latin root with the word structure, structus, meaning placed together in orderly arrangements). The materials and procedures of instruction are arranged so as to achieve a coherent, sensible presentation of subject matter. In short, they have structure.

Students who are aware of this structure can position themselves to understand and learn the subject matter they are presented more efficiently than students who are not. Awareness of structure allows students to establish a conceptual framework within which to fit the subject matter. Within such a framework, they can sort and place key ideas and supporting information, which in turn facilitates their making appropriate connections both within the material and to what they already know. With an organized grasp of subject matter, students can apply it with greater versatility. Without awareness of structure, they tend to regard all information as equal in weight and can make few connections. As a consequence, they can be easily overwhelmed by the volume and complexity of the information they are expected to take in. Clearly, discerning the structure of information is basic to students' formulating their own structures for understanding and using it.

Students can usually discern structure and importance in oral exchanges without having to pay conscious attention to talk's structural features. This is not the case with written presentations, however. Determining the importance of information presented in written form depends on giving attention to structural features of the text. It depends on knowing the conventions by which written presentations are constructed. Most students have to be taught these conventions.

Teaching students about the structure of written discourse takes two basic approaches, each of which complements the other. One of these approaches is to bring to students' attention the matter of organization in writing and have them make use of organizational features in studying texts. The other approach is to have students make significant use of organizational schemes in writing activities. Methods that take these two approaches have students:

- *Recognize the key features of conventional prose formats*
- *Recognize the characteristic elements of traditional rhetorical structures*
- *Recognize typical organizational schemes for communicating content within the literature of a discipline*
- *Recast the presentation of information according to one's own organizational plan*

- *Categorize questions to be answered in study*
- *Bring separate ideas together in a meaningful pattern*
- *Gather abstract information from different sources and cast it in one's own structure for presentation*

The methods presented on this section are useful for improving students' reading and writing skills. The methods highlight the role of structure in creating and interpreting written language.

35

Connection Questions

The purpose of Connection Questions is to help students focus on a text's distinctive organizational pattern in order to enhance comprehension of its content. Connection Questions are of two basic types. *Internal* questions help students see how ideas are connected within a text. *External* questions help students connect ideas in the text with their own experience.

Questions that encourage building connections among the ideas in a text and between those ideas and students' personal experiences lead students to think deeply about what they read. Internal questions encourage students to come to terms with the way ideas are related so that understanding can occur. If students can connect this understanding with their own experience, an even deeper understanding can occur. When a deeper understanding is achieved, students are better able to grasp the material they are to learn.

Connection Questions can be used in virtually every subject that uses expository texts (i.e., texts structured to present and explain subject matter). The method also has limited applicability with narrative material. It is best to use relatively simple materials initially and gradually move to more complex materials. The material may be used either with individual students or with groups. If it is used with groups, the size of the group should be limited to a number that permits significant participation by all students.

Procedure

Connection Questions follows the general algorithm for teaching suggested by the heuristic methods in this book. Students are prepared for the substance of a lesson, they are engaged with the material, and they are given opportunities to discuss and to participate in enrichment activities. The distinguishing feature of Connection Questions is its questioning students so as to have them interrelate the ideas represented in a text and connect those ideas with their own knowledge and experience. The questioning pivots from the text structure, or distinctive pattern of organization. Commonly used patterns include analysis, cause-effect, chronology, compare-contrast, definition, enumeration, illustration, and problem solving.

Having determined the text pattern in advance, the teacher poses to students questions about the material presented in the text. The questioning takes place before, during, and after students read the text. The teacher does not simply ask students to identify the pattern structure of the text. Rather, the teacher's questioning takes advantage of the text structure for asking questions that prompt students to see how ideas of the lesson are connected, both within the text to be read and to themselves. Throughout the lesson, the teacher interjects questions that lead students to build both *internal* connections among the content's constituent ideas and *external* connections between the content and their personal experiences and knowledge. In asking these questions, the teacher follows these guidelines: (1) try to build both *internal* and *external* connections, (2) treat each presentation of content individually in accordance with its context, and (3) model for students the types of questions they should think about and ask themselves when they study alone.

Discussion

Connection Questions help students build internal and external connections with the information they read. Because these questions are practical and foster effective reading, students are likely to create connection questions on their own when they read alone. Students may gain confidence in their ability to formulate effective self-questions when the teacher encourages and supports the formulation of such questions. To use Connection Questions in teaching requires little preparation time, and no instructional time is needed for teaching students about connection questions. However, time may need to be devoted to teaching students about commonly occurring text structures.

EXAMPLE

A middle-school language arts class is studying ways of testing the validity of beliefs that people hold. The class has just finished reading an article on two prehistoric monsters that many people believe exist. In order to prepare students for discussing beliefs that are held about the two monsters, the teacher first helps students grasp the content of the article. The teacher has students consider the article's information by asking connection questions which, following the article's compare-contrast pattern, have students observe information about likenesses and differences between the two monsters. Internal and external questions are indicated in parenthesis.

Teacher: The article describes two creatures, possibly prehistoric, that people believe are real. What are these creatures? (internal question)

Peter: The Loch Ness Monster and Bigfoot.

Teacher: Do you know anyone who believes either of these monsters exists? (external question)

Wayne: My aunt, she believes in them. She says, "Why not?" There's a heck of a lot of stuff we don't know for sure, but just because we don't know stuff doesn't mean stuff's not real.

Barbara: That's so, but we can't say something's for sure for real without good justification.

Sidney: Hey, but there *is* justification for these two creatures.

Teacher: How are the justifications presented in the article alike for both the Loch Ness monster and Bigfoot? (internal question)

Sidney: Both have been seen a whole bunch of times.

Barbara: People *say* they've seen them.

Wayne: There's pictures been taken of both.

Peter: But the sightings and the pictures have been taken from far away for both.

Teacher: We'll discuss the validity of the evidence in a moment. Are there differences in the evidence gathered on these creatures? (internal question)

Barbara: Sightings of Bigfoot have been reported in this century, but for the Loch Ness monster there have been sightings reported for hundreds of years.

Wayne: Since the sixth century.

Teacher: What about differences in the kind of evidence gathered? (internal question)

Peter: For Bigfoot, footprints have been obtained but the article didn't mention any tracks or other physical traces left by the Loch Ness monster.

Teacher: Now let's consider the evidence mentioned in the article. Do you know how a photographic image might be erroneously interpreted? (external question)

As the lesson continues, the teacher leads a discussion on weighing the kinds of evidence mentioned in the article.

Prehistoric Monsters

Are there in existence monsters that have survived since prehistoric times? Over the years numerous sightings of such beings have been reported. Two creatures most frequently claimed to have been observed are the Loch Ness monster and Bigfoot.

The Loch Ness monster is thought to be a plesiosaur or some descendant of the dinosaur family. It is described as being very ugly, blackish-green in color, and very long with humps in its back. It lives in the Loch Ness Lake in Scotland, and since the sixth century over 3,000 sightings of the monster have been made. In 1960, a young man, Tim Dinsdale, was able to record footage of what was supposed to be "Nessie." After the film was processed, an investigation bureau for the search of Nessie was formed.

Bigfoot is described as a humanlike creature. People who claim to have seen the creature say he is big, hairy, and muscular like an oversized gorilla. Reports concerning sightings of Bigfoot have been on file since 1924. In the early 1970s, many photographs were taken of the so-called Sasquatch. Footprints thought to belong to Bigfoot have been cast in plaster and have measured over 38 centimeters long. Roger Patterson conducted an investigation in the wilderness of northern California where he was able to film what he thought was Bigfoot, but no one can exactly say what was on the frame.

Although there have been photographs taken and many sightings reported, we still cannot know for sure whether these creatures exist, much less whether they are prehistoric monsters. Until scientists obtain sufficient evidence to identify them, the existence of prehistoric monsters will remain a mystery.

Source

K. Denise Muth. (1987). Teachers' connection questions: Prompting students to organize text ideas. *Journal of Reading, 31,* 254–259.

36

Structured Notetaking

Structured Notetaking is a technique by which the teacher uses a graphic organizer to help students recognize a text's structure and make use of that structure for taking notes from their reading.

Students who take notes on a text think more intensely about its content. They attend more actively to the message in order to select important information to retain in their notes. Students who use the text's pattern of organization to structure their notes tend to write notes that are even more helpful. Determining the text's pattern brings students' attention to the main ideas and their supporting details. Writing notes that are organized according to the text's organization enables students to retrieve information more easily and to remember the material for a longer period of time.

Structured Notetaking may be used in any academic subject area. It is particularly suitable for students of low ability who have difficulty comprehending and remembering expository material, though average and above-average students may benefit from the strategy as well. Notetaking skills become more important as students move through the grades, becoming especially important to students in the secondary grades. This technique may be used with any size group. It takes a good deal of time to teach and should be practiced over a long period of time.

Procedure

Teaching students how to take structured notes begins with the teacher discussing the purpose of notetaking and the difference between the structure of a presentation and the content of its message. With a passage selected in advance, the teacher points out words and phrases that signal the passage's particular type of text structure. The teacher then presents a graphic organizer for representing the text's structure. A graphic organizer is a visual aid for displaying the abstract organizational features of a text.

Together, the teacher and students enter the main idea and details on the graphic organizer. The teacher may repeat this process with a passage that exemplifies another text structure, encouraging students to point out clues to the text structure. The teacher introduces other text structures and graphic organizers for representing those structures. Students are told that the structure in texts is often unsignalled with explicit clues.

The teacher models the notetaking procedure using a read-think-aloud procedure with a passage 5 to 10 paragraphs in length. The teacher states the purpose for reading

Graphic Organizers for Common Text Structures

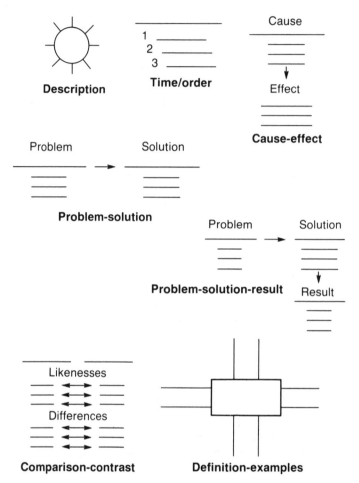

Source: Patricia L. Smith & Gail E. Tompkins (1988). Structured notetaking: A new strategy for content area readers. *Journal of Reading, 32,* p. 49. Reprinted with the permission of Patricia L. Smith and the International Reading Association.

and skims the material to identify the major structure. The teacher calls attention to information that supports the identified structure. The teacher then creates a graphic organizer and fills it in with the main idea and supporting details.

Students are given an opportunity to practice identifying text structure and taking notes. The teacher provides students one explicitly structured passage and one implicitly structured passage. Students work in pairs. One student reads the explicitly cued text and thinks aloud while taking notes. The other student gives feedback and encouragement. Then they reverse roles, and the other student thinks aloud and writes notes from the implicitly cued passage.

The teacher models a chapter-length passage using the read-think-aloud technique, drawing a graphic organizer that encompasses all the structures in the chapter. There is no single correct form, but the organizer should reflect the top-level structure as well as other structures in the passage.

Working in pairs, students read and make their own structured notes on a lengthy passage that has explicit clues. The teacher chooses the notes of two or three pairs of students to discuss and evaluate with the class. Then each student makes a set of structured notes independently.

The teacher again models the notetaking procedure. This time the teacher uses poorly organized material with implicitly cued structures. Students practice the procedure.

Discussion

An explicitly presented technique can be helpful to students who have difficulty taking notes. This technique gives students a beginning point, a purpose for reading and writing, and a structured form to guide them. Students who take notes on their reading necessarily spend more time thinking about what they read. Bringing to notetaking a visual dimension that captures the organization of process should lead to better comprehension and retention of the material they study. They may be able to transfer Structured Notetaking to other notetaking situations. They can use the text structures to organize their own personal writing. Ultimately, students who have mastered this technique should be able to invent new patterns that reflect the content they read.

The disadvantages of Structured Notetaking are that it takes considerable expertise on the part of the teacher and that a great deal of time is needed to collect appropriate materials and to teach the procedure. Below-average students may become discouraged with texts whose patterns are not cued explicitly. Poor notetakers are often poor readers, and the teacher may spend excessive time helping students identify the structure rather than aiding them in notetaking. Also, the teacher may not have enough time to complete all of the steps with poor readers.

EXAMPLE

A high school science teacher takes an opportunity to teach students how to take structured notes as they study a unit on bees. The teacher has already discussed with students the purpose and importance of taking notes. Now begins the task of leading students through the notetaking process step by step.

Teacher: Let me emphasize again the difference between the content and the structure of a text. The *content* consists of the facts and ideas it presents. The *structure* is the scheme by which that content is organized. In other words, content is the meat of a selection and structure is its skeleton. Let's look at a passage from our textbook and see if we can find its skeleton.

The teacher puts a passage on the overhead:

Honeybees Are Useful

Honeybees are among the most useful of the insects. They are useful both in nature and to people. They are useful in nature because they help pollinate flowers. As honeybees flit from flower to flower gathering nectar, they spread pollen. As a result of their pollen-spreading behavior, honeybees have not only played an important role in the reproduction of flowers but have helped create the wide variety of flowers we have in our world today. Honeybees are useful to people because they produce honey and beeswax. They make honey from nectar and fruit juices, which contain fructose, a natural sugar. Honey is a healthy sweetener since it contains fructose. Honeybees make wax by shedding oily flakes. Because beeswax is tallowy in its consistency, it is useful for making adhesives, candles, cosmetics, and polishes.

Teacher: Read the passage and ask yourself the question: What is the author trying to say about honeybees?

Mary: Honeybees are useful insects.

Teacher: That's right. The author then says why honeybees are useful. Saying why honeybees are useful is the purpose served by the passage structure. Notice that in this passage certain words tell us that the author is trying to support the statement that honeybees are useful. These words are clues to the passage structure.

Joe: You mean like the word *because?*

Teacher: Good. Do you see other words or phrases that are clues to the structure?

Sue: *As a result of.*

Gordon: *Since.*

Teacher: Excellent. These are words that tell the purpose. They are words that offer us clues for determining the structure of a text. Words like *because, as a result of,* and *since* are words that signal causes and effects. A cause-effect structure in a text can be represented visually, as shown on this overhead.

The teacher uses the overhead projector to display a schematic representation of the cause-effect relations in the passage.

Teacher: In this graphic, the direction of causation is represented by the downward pointing arrows. Causes have effects that are themselves causes. All the information leads to the main idea, which is to be written on the bottom line.

Rosalind: So on the bottom line you write the main idea of the passage, "Honeybees are useful."

Teacher: Exactly.

Don: On the next lines up, you could write on one line that they're useful in nature and on the other line that they're useful to people.

Teacher: OK. I'll enter that information on those two lines.

Joe: If you get to the basic reason that bees are useful in nature, you say that honeybees flit from flower to flower.

Teacher: Where should we write that?

Don: On the top line, up from where you've written "useful in nature."

Sue: It's the basic reason because that's how they spread pollen.

Mary: And that's what causes flowers to reproduce.

Don: And has created the wide variety of flowers.

Joe: Write those causes and effects on the lines according to the cause-effect directions shown by the arrows.

Teacher: All right.

Rosalind: If we write on the other top lines what honeybees do that's behind their being useful to people, we can follow the cause-effect direction for each and fill in the other lines with the important information from the passage.

The teacher notes passage information on the graphic organizer as students suggest, and the following example of structured notes is developed:

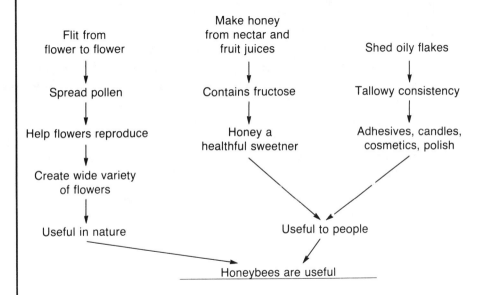

Teacher: All right. We've extracted the content of this passage and displayed it on a frame that represents the passage's cause-effect structure. We've arranged our notes on the content in a form suggested by the text structure.

Gordon: Do notes from all cause-effect passages fit on a form like this one?

Teacher: Good question. You don't have to use a form exactly like this one. You can use any configuration of lines, arrows, boxes, and the like that plausibly depicts a text's structure. The form we used here is a variation of one that has been suggested for depicting cause-effect information. Ways of depicting other common text structures are shown on a handout I have for you. We can use the handout to practice structuring our notes on other passages.

The teacher distributes a handout that shows graphic organizers for common text structures. With it, the teacher distributes another passage from the textbook.

Teacher: Here's another passage on bees. See if you can discern the text structure of this passage:

Bees

Bees are hairy, broad-bodied insects with sucking mouth parts and four wings. They are of the order *hymenoptera*. Of thousands of kinds of bees, several are well known. Honeybees provide us with honey and beeswax. Stingless bees have small stingers but do not use them as weapons. Bumblebees are black with orange or yellow bands. Carpenter bees build their nests from twigs and wood chips. Leafcutting bees pack pieces of leaves into small nests. Mining bees make nests of tunnels they dig in the ground. Mason bees fashion their nests out of bits of clay and stone. Cuckoo bees lay their eggs in the nests of other kinds of bees.

Sue: I don't see any clue words like in the other passage we just did.

Teacher: To detect the structure of many texts you have to read between the lines. Most texts, in fact, don't use clue words that explicitly reveal the structure.

Don: This must be one of those texts.

Teacher: It is. With a text like this, you have to determine what the purpose is and then see if you can match a structure with that purpose.

Mary: Seems to me the purpose of this text is to tell what bees are.

Joe: It tells what bees are generally like and places them in the *hymenoptera* order of insects.

Gordon: And it gives examples of different kinds of bees.

Rosalind: So it's probably a "definition-example" structure.

Teacher: Let's see if notes we take on this passage fit the definition-examples pattern.

The teacher puts on the overhead an organizer for the definition-examples text structure. Information from the passage is placed on the organizer to produce structured notes for the definition-examples structure:

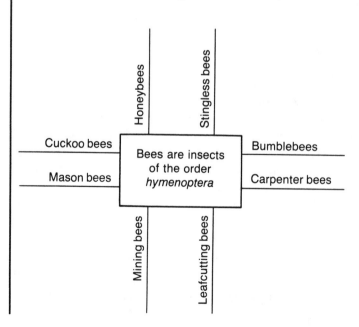

Having introduced structured notetaking with brief passages, the teacher now demonstrates how to take structured notes on a passage composed of several paragraphs.

Teacher: OK, I think you're getting the idea of organizing your reading notes according to the structure of the text. Now let's open our textbook to the section entitled "Do Bees Communicate?"

Do Bees Communicate?

It can be observed that if one bee discovers a feeding place, many other bees will appear at that place within a short period of time. The question this observation raises is whether bees can communicate. Does a foraging bee actually report her find to other bees? Or do other bees find the same nectar source by happenstance? If a foraging bee does communicate the location of a nectar source to other bees, how does that communication take place? What kinds of information are communicated? These are questions that naturalist Karl von Frisch has answered.

Von Frisch dealt with the basic question of whether bees communicate by finding out whether a foraging bee returns to the hive before other bees fly to the nectar. By daubing a foraging bee with a spot of paint and observing her movements, von Frisch found that this was indeed the case, that apparently bees do scout the location of a nectar source and communicate with other bees before they go there. But how does a scout bee do this?

Von Frisch dealt with questions of how and what bees communicate by observing scout bees and their interactions with other bees. He noticed that bees in the hive cluster closely around a returning scout bee, which moves about in a pattern like a dance. Could it be that bees take information from the scout by touching her and that the scout bee communicates through the dance pattern? Setting dishes of differently scented sugar water around a bee hive, von Frisch found that the dish that a scout bee visits is visited in significantly greater numbers by other bees in the hive. Von Frisch concluded that one way the scout bee communicates is by carrying the odor of the nectar. The bees that cluster around her taste the nectar and smell it with their antennae. Placing dishes of sugar water at different directions and distances from the hive and controlling the ones visited by scout bees, von Frisch found that scout bees vary their dance according to the direction and distance of the nectar source. The direction of the nectar source is indicated by a figure-eight dance in which the axis of the figure eight is pointed up the vertical axis of the comb at the same angle the other bees must fly in relation to the sun. The distance of the nectar source is signaled by the speed of the dance. The closer the nectar, the faster the dance.

Teacher: As I glance over this passage, I see that it asks whether bees communicate and, if they do, how do they do it. The passage seems to be about dealing with these questions, so it is likely to be one of two types of structures. It could be a problem-solution passage that develops these questions and answers to them. Or it could be a time-order passage that tells how the questions were addressed by recounting a sequence of events.

The teacher reads the first paragraph aloud and then pauses to think aloud.

Teacher: Yes, this is about the question of communication among bees. Is there such a thing, and if there is, what's it like? Still, I can't tell yet whether the passage will discuss an answer or will recount events leading to an answer.

The teacher resumes the oral reading, and at the end of the second paragraph, pauses again to think aloud.

Teacher: OK, the passage seems to be shaping up as a problem-solution text. It alludes to what vonFrisch did, but not in time-order fashion. It gives an answer to the basic question, saying generally how it was obtained. Then it takes the question to another level. How does a scout bee communicate the location of a nectar source?

The teacher continues to read and think aloud about the structure of the passage. Reasoning that the passage has a problem-solution pattern, the teacher structures notes on the passage accordingly:

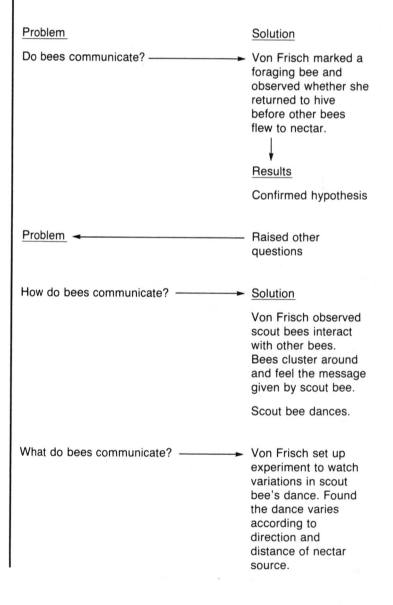

Problem

Do bees communicate? ──────────▶

Solution

Von Frisch marked a foraging bee and observed whether she returned to hive before other bees flew to nectar.

Results

Confirmed hypothesis

Problem ◀──────────── Raised other questions

How do bees communicate? ────────▶ Solution

Von Frisch observed scout bees interact with other bees. Bees cluster around and feel the message given by scout bee.

Scout bee dances.

What do bees communicate? ────────▶ Von Frisch set up experiment to watch variations in scout bee's dance. Found the dance varies according to direction and distance of nectar source.

Once the teacher has demonstrated structured notetaking through this read-think-aloud procedure, pairs of students practice the procedure with two shorter passages. First, one student in each pair reads and thinks aloud to the other student about the structure of one of the passages. Then, the second student reads and thinks aloud about the structure of the other passage. One of the passages contains words that are explicit clues to its structure. The other passage does not have such clues, so its structure has to be inferred.

Swarming

Bees swarm when they leave their hive to begin a new colony. The search for a new location begins with scout bees going out to find possible building sites for a hive. The scout bees inspect rotted stumps, hollows in trees, holes in the ground, and other such places. The scout bees return to the swarm and give information about the new locations to the other bees, who narrow the choice among locations to two or three sites. The scout bees then go out to these favorite sites to inspect them further. The scout bees make their report, and the swarming bees decide where to relocate. Finally, the swarm flies to the new building site.

Honeybees and Bumblebees

Honeybees and bumblebees are both of the order *hymenoptera*. Honeybees are of the genus *apis*, and bumblebees are of the genus *bombus*. Both are completely metamorphic and both are social bees. Colonies of honeybees typically number 50,000 in a hive. Colonies of bumblebees seldom have more than 400 bees. Among honeybees, both workers and queens survive the winter. Among bumblebees, only fertilized queens survive the winter. Honeybees range in color from black to shades of light brown. Bumblebees are black with orange or yellow bands.

Mary thinks aloud to Joe about "Swarming."

Mary: This is definitely a time-order passage. It tells how bees swarm by doing one thing after another. A search for a new hive *begins*; scout bees *then* go out; *finally* the swarm flies to the new place.

Joe: The passage does have words to tip us off that it has a time-order structure.

Mary: So let's structure our notes from this passage to show the time order of swarming.

Notes on Swarming

Leave the hive to begin a new colony is swarming
  1. Scout bees search for possible building sites.
    2. Scout bees inspect rotted stumps, hollows in trees, etc.
      3. The swarm narrows the choice.
        4. Scout bees make final choice.
          5. Swarm flies to new site.

Joe: The other passage doesn't have any certain words to clue us to its structure. But it looks to me like a comparison-contrast structure.

Mary: It sure does. All through the passage it tells about honeybees and bumblebees.

Joe: *As, like, whereas, on the other hand* are words that could be used here but aren't. They are sort of implied. The purpose of the passage is to compare and contrast bumblebees all right.

Mary: We can organize our notes on the passage in comparison-contrast form. We can list the ways honeybees and bumblebees are alike and different, point by point.

Notes on Honeybees and Bumblebees

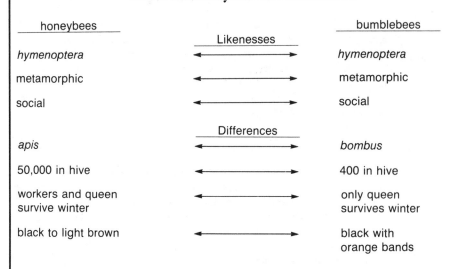

As the lesson continues, students are assigned to read a portion of the textbook chapter independently and take their own structured notes. Following this assignment, the teacher models structured notetaking with other passages.

Source

Patricia L. Smith and Gail E. Tompkins. (1988). Structured notetaking: A new strategy for content area readers. *Journal of Reading, 32,* 46–53.

Related Readings

Gordon Alley and Donald Deshler. (1979). *Teaching the learning disabled adolescent: Strategies and methods.* Denver, CO: Love Publishing Company.

Lori L. Conrad. (1989). Charting effect and cause in informational texts. *The Reading Teacher, 42,* 451–452.

Rosalind Horowitz. (1985). Text patterns: Parts 1 and 2. *Journal of Reading, 28,* 448–454, 534–542.

Lea M. McGee and Donald J. Richgels. (1988). Teaching expository text structure to elementary students. *The Reading Teacher, 38,* 739–747.

Robert A. Palmatier. (1973). A notetaking system for learning. *Journal of Reading, 17,* 36–39.

37

Expectation Outline

The Expectation Outline method heightens prereading anticipation and develops skills in formulating specific questions about material to be read. Students gain facility in categorizing questions and finding answers to them.

Expectation Outline encourages students to ask questions, to set their own purposes, and to find proof for their answers. Students may be encouraged to consult various sources of information. Critical and inferential reading skills may also develop as students offer different kinds of proof to answer their questions. Expectation Outline may be used as a class activity that involves the participation of all students present. It is especially useful with factual material, such as that found in science or social studies texts.

Procedure

First, students are to ask questions about what they expect to be answered from reading about a specific topic. As the students offer their questions, the teacher writes them on the chalkboard. The teacher groups related questions together without commenting on them.

Once the questions have been asked, the teacher directs students' attention to one group of questions at a time. Students are asked to make up a heading or title for each question. Next, the students read the text to find the answers to the questions. For each question/heading, students give an answer for which they find support in the text. The teacher asks students to read aloud portions of the text that prove the correctness of the answer. Questions not answered in the text are noted and displayed, perhaps on a bulletin board, to stimulate investigating other sources of information.

Discussion

The Expectation Outline is excellent for increasing students' interest in the material to be learned. In advance of reading, students ask questions concerning what they expect to learn. When they do read, they do so in order to answer their own questions. As questions are being written on the board, vocabulary words can be brought to students' attention. The teacher can discuss these terms while writing them down, thus making sure that the terms are understood as well as recognized in print. As the Expectation Outline is being developed, the teacher may assess students' readiness to deal with the lesson's concepts. If students appear lacking in necessary background, the teacher can provide it.

This method cannot be used in all situations. Its use is largely limited to dealing with factual information for which anticipatory questions can be generated. Also, students of below-average reading ability may experience difficulty in finding answers to questions. For these students, reading aloud the proof, or merely being called on to read aloud, could be embarrassing.

EXAMPLE

A middle-grade science class is studying space science. In this lesson, the teacher's aim is to introduce the topic of satellites. The teacher has identified a textbook section to help provide basic information about satellites. Before having students read the section, the teacher has students anticipate its content by asking questions.

Teacher: Before we read, let's ask outselves questions we expect to be answered by the text. What questions will probably be answered? Buck?

Buck: I think it'll say what satellites are. Books usually define stuff.

Teacher: Could you put that in the form of a question?

Buck: What is a satellite?

Teacher: Good. I'll write your question here on the board. Let's hear other questions that you expect the text will help you answer.

Werner: What do satellites look like?

Sue: What are they made of?

Bobbie: How do they get there?

Phillip: How do they stay there?

Lois: What keeps them from colliding?

The students continue offering questions that they expect the text to address. The teacher writes each question on the chalkboard, grouping questions that are related. Questions are grouped into categories of appearance/makeup, purposes, maintenance, and orbits. When it appears that students have no more questions to suggest, the teacher points out that the questions have been grouped and directs students' attention to one group of questions—on the orbital paths of satellites.

Teacher: You'll notice that I've written your questions in groups that have something in common. Let's look at this group of questions. What do these questions have in common?

Sue: They're about satellites.

Teacher: Yes. All of the questions on the board are about satellites. How is this group of questions distinguished from the others?

Werner: They have to do with the paths that satellites take.

Teacher: What are the paths of satellites called?

Phillip: They're called "satellite paths"–"SPs" for short.

Teacher: Good try.

Bobbie: I believe they're called "orbits."

Teacher: Orbits. That's right. Orbits. I'll write the word *orbit* as a heading above this group of questions.

Phillip: Why not just say "satellite paths"?

Teacher: Scientists do refer to them as satellite paths, I suppose. But the scientific term is *orbit*. Like a great many scientific terms, *orbit* comes from Latin. In Latin, *orbita* means track or rut. *Orbita* came from the word *orbis,* which means wheel. Let's now read for the purpose of getting answers to our questions having to do with the orbit of a satellite.

Students turn to the assigned section of the text, seeking answers to these questions under the heading *orbit:*

How are satellites put onto a path around the earth?

How do satellites keep to their path?

What happens if a satellite veers from its path?

What keeps satellites from colliding?

How can a satellite's path be altered?

Teacher: Now that we've read the text, we can answer some of our questions about the orbital path of a satellite. Let's take the first question.

Bobbie: Satellites are shot into orbit by rockets.

Teacher: Read aloud what the text says about how satellites are put into orbit.

Bobbie: (reading) For a rocket to enter orbit around the Earth, . . .

As the discussion proceeds, each question is considered. Not all of the questions can be answered by reading the text.

Teacher: That's another one of our questions that will require looking elsewhere for an answer. This text doesn't say. It's a good question, though. Let's post it with the other questions we'll try to answer by reading other texts. Now let's move on to our next group of questions. What would be an appropriate heading for these questions?

Werner: What do satellites do?

Teacher: Good. Could we reduce that to a heading of a single word.

Sue: Purposes

The lesson continues.

Earth's Satellites

A satellite is an object that revolves around a planet or other heavenly body. In recent years it has come to mean a rocket that has been shot into space and continuously circles the Earth.

For a rocket to enter orbit around the Earth, it must tilt sideways slightly, near the top of its path, and fire its engine. The return path of the rocket as it falls back to Earth will be curved. If it is aimed correctly, the curvature of the path will meet that of the Earth's, thus, it will never fall back to the Earth's surface. It will fall continuously in an orbit around the Earth, becoming a satellite of the Earth.

The orbit of a satellite is circular, unless the satellite meets with some sort of resistance that alters its speed. When this happens, the orbit becomes elliptical. An elliptical orbit causes the satellite to come closer to the Earth at certain times. At these points, the Earth's gravitational forces work on the satellite, pulling it closer each time it passes. Eventually, the satellite will enter the Earth's atmosphere, where it will burn upon entry.

Using electronic sensors, satellites can respond to wavelengths in the electromagnetic spectrum. Using these sensors, satellites have helped locate previously unknown oil and mineral deposits. Plants are detected easily with electronic sensors. In a matter of hours, a satellite can detect the type of crop in a large area of farmland. Also, weather forecasts are obtained daily with satellite images.

Source

Dixie Lee Spiegel. (1981). Six alternatives to the directed reading activity. *The Reading Teacher, 34,* 914–922.

38

Array Procedure

The Array Procedure helps students identify separate ideas of a topic and fit them together into a meaningful pattern. In the procedure, students process subject matter by constructing a free-form outline called an *array,* which shows how key words and phrases of a lesson are related. Constructing an array contributes to students' comprehension and memory of a topic's main ideas and their supporting information.

The premise of the Array Procedure is that relating ideas is the essence of understanding. In relating ideas, students observe how each separate idea contributes to an overall representation. Constructing an array is one way for students to identify and relate information and ideas. As students arrange information into an array, they learn how to recognize the relative importance of different pieces of information and to see how they are connected. In the process, their understanding is enhanced. The better the students understand something, the more likely they are to remember it. Since discussion usually turns on significant ideas and information, the procedure is best used with groups of students. The size of the group may be as large as will allow significant participation by each student. The procedure is best used with topics in science and social studies.

Procedure

The teacher selects 10 to 20 key words and/or phrases of a lesson and formulates questions that lead students to organize what they know in relation to the material. Some of the questions should be related to concrete conceptions or experience. The teacher presents the key words and phrases to the class, writing them on the chalkboard and directing students to copy these down on slips of paper. The teacher makes certain that students have some understanding of all the key words and phrases.

In response to the teacher's organizing questions, students hypothesize answers. Then students read on the topic and check their answers. Working in groups, students figure out how the key words and phrases fit together. Students lay out the slips of paper in an organized array, beginning with the slip of paper whose key word or phrase represents the most important idea. This slip is placed by itself in the center of the desk to stress its importance. The other slips are positioned around this slip so as to display relatedness to the most important key word or phrase and to other key words and phrases.

The teacher provides assistance during the procedure by answering students' questions and asking students to justify their arrays. When students appear satisfied with their arrays, the teacher asks students to copy their group's arrangement onto a larger piece of paper or the chalkboard. To show how key words and phrases are related, students add lines and arrows, showing the direction of relations. Finally, students are asked to share their arrays and to discuss reasons for placements and connections.

Discussion

The Array Procedure gives students experience in searching to round out details and to resolve inconsistencies in their understanding of a topic. The teacher leads students through the process step by step, answering questions, correcting misconceptions, and helping with the formulation of an outline that aids memory. Useful for teaching a wide range of content, the procedure fosters the development of effective organizational skills.

A possible difficulty in carrying out the procedure is getting students to discuss the material. Open communication in the classroom is desirable, but sometimes students find it hard to discuss things freely. Related to this difficulty is one of inhibition about trying out different possible arrangements of information. Both stem from an excessive concern about correctness. In order to encourage students to use an array as an approach to learning, notions about correctness of outline form should be diminished and occasions that call for outlining should be increased. The development of productive thinking requires conjecture that may very well prove incorrect. And certainly it is incorrect to believe that an outline used as a study tool must be "correct." The teacher needs to stress that usually there can be more than one correct way of thinking about a topic.

EXAMPLE

A middle-school class is studying birds. Using pictures taken from old magazines, the teacher has introduced a very unusual bird, the penguin.

Teacher: I have some words and phrases that have to do with penguins. As I say and write each on the board, you copy it on one of the slips of paper I have given you. The first word is *penguins. Penguins.*

The teacher writes this word on the board, and then presents the other words and phrases of the lesson to produce the following list:

penguins

Emperor

Adelies

reproduce in spring

reproduce in coldest part of winter

rookeries

nesting place

fish, squid, and shrimp

Antarctica

continent of snow and ice

surrounded by icy water

Teacher: Penguins certainly are strange-looking birds. Besides the way they look, in what ways do you think penguins are different from other birds?

Ronald: We copied from the board stuff about reproduction. So probably a difference is that other birds reproduce in the spring, but penguins reproduce in the coldest part of winter.

Debbie: They don't fly. They're like chickens. They're birds but they don't fly.

Gary: And their skin is like leather, slick and black.

David: No, they have feathers, like all birds. It is their feathers that look slick and black.

Todd: Their feathers are called rookeries.

Gary: Penguins are sacred to the Adelie people and are protected by order of their Emperor.

Tim: Penguins look like bowling pins.

Teacher: Besides the way they look, how are penguins different from other birds?

Tim: Well, if they don't fly, they don't live in the tree tops.

Bill: Very funny. Since they're birds, I'd say they live in nests, all right. But their nests are on the ground.

Mary: It could be that they don't have nests at all. Birds don't have to have a nest to be birds, do they? Since most birds do have nests, it would make penguins different if they don't.

Teacher: Where do penguins live?

Gary: Tim says they don't live in tree tops, and Mary says they don't live in nests. Maybe they live in birdhouses.

Paul: I know that some live at the zoo.

Teacher: I mean, in what part of the world do they live?

Bill: Where it's real cold and snowy.

Sadie: Like the North Pole.

Mary: That would mean they don't live in nests. There isn't anything there to make a nest out of.

Bill: Sure there is. Ice. Maybe they build nests of ice.

Gary: That would certainly be different from other birds.

Teacher: Penguins *are* birds of a different sort. Do you think there are different kinds of penguins?

Sadie: Penguins are penguins, as far as I know.

Tim: Mostly you just see pictures of penguins, and they all look alike.

The teacher has the students wondering about penguins, particularly about where and how they live and about whether there are different kinds of penguins.

Teacher: Now let's read to find out what our text has to say about penguins.

Ronald: What are we supposed to do with these slips of paper?

Teacher: When you've finished reading, you'll use them to go over what you've learned about penguins. Let's read now.

When it appears that students have finished reading, the teacher breaks the class into groups of four students each.

Teacher: Now we're going to use those slips of paper. You know now that the information on the slips of paper is information the text presented about penguins. Your group's task is to arrange the slips of paper on the top of a desk so that together they indicate what the text had to say about penguins. Use all of the slips of paper. How do you think we should begin?

Gary: Because this is all about penguins, we would lay down the slip of paper with the word penguins written on it.

Teacher: Right. Begin by establishing your topic—penguins—as the beginning point. Then, what would you do?

Mary: Lay down other slips of paper beside each other so that they make sense about penguins.

Teacher: Sounds as if you know what to do. The information can be grouped in lots of different ways. Let's see what the different groups come up with. Think about what the text said and talk over how you should place your slips of paper.

As students work in groups, the teacher circulates among them, clarifying the instructions and answering questions. The teacher notices one group that seems to be stuck.

Sadie: We're having a hard time here.

Mary: These words just won't fit together in sentences that make any sense at all.

Teacher: You probably *can't* get these words to fit into sentences. I should have given clearer directions. The idea is to show how the different pieces of information are related. For example, you might put underneath "penguins" the two kinds of penguins, "Emperors" and "Adelies," side by side. Under "Emperors" you could put that they "reproduce in the coldest part of winter." Under . . .

Sadie: (interrupting) Oh, I get it, I get it. You sort of put things next to each other that belong to each other.

The teacher continues to circulate among the groups, having students explain the placement of their slips of paper. Then the teacher has students show the array on a sheet of paper.

Teacher: If the groups are satisfied with the positioning of their slips of paper, we'll proceed. Now copy the arrangement onto a sheet of paper. Then draw lines to show how the information is connected.

Circulating among the students, the teacher notices that some students have drawn connecting lines that are winding and criss-crossed.

Teacher: Drawing those lines helps us to see how the information is interconnected. To get a clear picture, your lines should be straight and uncrossed. If your lines are winding or criss-crossed, you need to back up and rearrange your array.

With assistance from the teacher, problems with the arrays are cleared up. The teacher then has each group put its array on the chalkboard. Here is an example of one group's array for "Penguins."

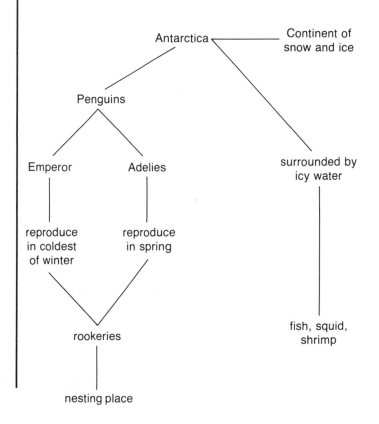

Penguins

Penguins are birds but they cannot fly. To get from place to place, they swim, they slide on their stomachs, or they take short steps the way a duck walks.

Emperor penguins and Adelie penguins live in the coldest, windiest place on earth—Antarctica, a continent of snow and ice surrounded by ice water. Few penguins are found in other places because they will not cross into the warm ocean water from the cold Antarctic currents. They spend much of their lives in the water, where they feed on shrimp, squid, and other fish. But every year, they come out of the water and go to their rookeries, or nesting places, to mate and have their young. A single rookery may contain as many as a million birds. Most penguins make their nest on the bare ground or in the grass. Sometimes, to reach a rookery, a penguin travels miles through water and over icy land.

Emperors have their young in the coldest part of winter, but Adelies wait until spring. Then they return to the icy water to feed until they go back again to their rookeries the next year.

Source

T. Stevenson Hansell. (1978). Stepping up to outlining. *Journal of Reading, 22,* 248–252.

39

Clustering

Clustering gives students a way to begin writing assignments. Through clustering, students turn random thoughts into patterns that can be written down and developed. Students become increasingly motivated to complete a writing task as their ideas emerge in organized form.

Many students find writing difficult, and they find getting started the most difficult part of writing. Clustering reduces this difficulty by giving students an organizing strategy to get them started. Ideas are freely associated and written out without pressure, thereby reducing tension and resistance often associated with writing. The product of this prewriting activity is an organized cluster of thoughts, which helps students stay on task when they write.

Clustering may be used effectively with students beyond the primary grades and in any class that requires writing. It is obviously most appropriate for English and language arts classes. It may be taught to large groups. Teaching students clustering takes about 10 minutes of demonstration time.

Procedure

The teacher begins by writing a nucleus word or phrase near the center of the chalkboard. To heighten students' concentration on the topic, the teacher circles this word or phrase. Students follow along at their seats by writing down the nucleus word or phrase and circling it. The teacher makes the point that other words and phrases are to be associated with the nucleus word/phrase, and with these words and phrases still other words and phrases are to be associated. The teacher demonstrates free association by saying aloud words and phrases that come to mind and jotting them down rapidly. These words and phrases are circled and connecting lines are drawn to show how they are associated.

The teacher invites students similarly to let their thoughts about the nucleus word or phrase flow freely and to offer them for addition to the cluster being constructed on the chalkboard. As more words and phrases are generated, they are added to the cluster. The teacher distributes a sheet that displays a cluster and shows a composition developed from it. Students are assigned to write a brief exposition, story, or poem with the cluster generated during the class demonstration.

Discussion

Clustering encourages students to write from their own experiences and associations, which encourages authenticity in the expression of their thoughts. Clustering is attractive to students because it is fun and because it allows them to be themselves as writers. Clustering is attractive to teachers because it improves the quality of students' writing. With the opportunity to associate freely about the topic prior to writing, students produce compositions that are more highly developed with relevant details. And by clustering associated information, they produce compositions that are better organized.

Because clustering is fun, a few students may not see its serious purpose. They may see it as simply a game. With encouragement, however, these students may begin to appreciate the advantages of free-associating and clustering ideas prior to writing. A few writing experiences that involve clustering may be needed before these students feel comfortable with it.

EXAMPLE

A high school English class is talking about their recent field trip to a local vineyard. The teacher's aim is to show students how they can organize their recollections of the trip in order to write a composition.

Teacher: It *was* a lot of fun to visit La Gallina Vineyard. And we learned a lot about an important part of the community's economy. For our next writing assignment, let's write about something we learned on the field trip.

Ernesto: It's one thing to talk about our field trip, but it's hard to write about it.

Julia: This assignment won't be hard as far as having things to write about. But putting all those things down on paper is the hard part.

Teacher: Getting started is usually the toughest part. One way to get started is to brainstorm the topic by free-associating about it.

Alma: What's free-associating?

Teacher: It's kind of like letting your thoughts flow freely, except you don't just let your thoughts flow entirely at random. It's letting thoughts trigger other thoughts on the topic. These thoughts trigger still other thoughts, and so on.

Aaron: How's that not just random brainstorming?

Teacher: Because each thought is associated with a previous thought and sticks to the subject.

Ernesto: Could you show us what you mean?

Teacher: Sure. Take La Gallina's basic product: grapes. When I think of grapes, I think immediately of edible fruit. The edible fruit is the berry. The berry grows in bunches. They may be red, purple, or green. They may be dried into raisins.

Julia: Oh, I get it. You don't wander off the subject like saying grapes, then purple, then bruise, then pain, then aspirin. But what if the first word, *grapes,* makes you think of other things?

Teacher: You go back and start another line of free associating.

Aaron: But how do we use all this free-associating to write about grapes?

Teacher: You keep it organized and then turn your organized thoughts into written form. To keep your thoughts organized, you have to jot them down. Let me show you what I mean. I write the word *grapes* in the center of the board, as you would in the center of your paper, and circle it. Beside the word *grapes,* I write down *edible fruit* and circle that and draw a line between the two circles. Then, next to *edible fruit,* I write the word *berry.*

Alma: Then you circle it and connect it with a line to *edible fruit.* And you go on circling the associated words and connecting your chain of associations.

Julia: When that chain runs out, you go back to the central word, *grapes,* and start a new chain.

Teacher: Right. And each word or phrase in a line of associations can itself be a term around which several associations can be clustered. Let's go back and start another line of associations from *grapes.*

Aaron: *Vitis vinafera.* The tour guide said that's the plant grapes grow from.

Teacher: Excellent. This is an associated technical term around which several describing words can cluster.

Ernesto: It's a twining plant.

Julia: That grows up to 90 feet long.

Alma: And has dense flowers.

Aaron: And lob-toothed leaves.

As the class continues free-associating about grapes, the teacher develops this cluster at the chalkboard:

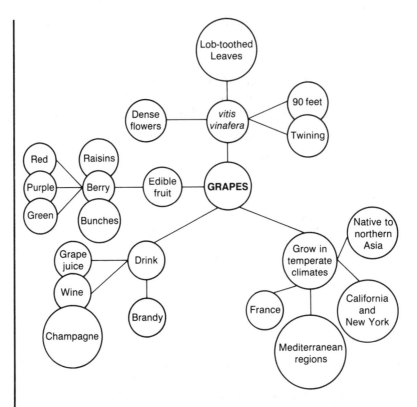

Ernesto: Couldn't this cluster about grapes be part of a large cluster?

Teacher: It sure could. If you were to write about local agriculture, grapes would be only one of several crops to include in your composition. For each crop you would develop a cluster.

Aaron: What do clusters have to do with writing?

Teacher: They help you keep your writing organized. They help you present intact information that belongs together. By keeping you from saying things willy-nilly, clusters help you from confusing and annoying your reader.

Alma: In other words, the cluster from which a composition is written is made up of other clusters. These clusters contain the information that get turned into paragraphs.

Teacher: Correct. It just so happens that I have an example of a paragraph that contains the information shown in one of the clusters making up the larger cluster on the board. It's a paragraph on grapes as an edible fruit.

The teacher distributes copies of this paragraph:

> Grapes are a delicious fruit. Their berries are red, purple, and green. They may be eaten fresh or dried. Fresh, they are usually consumed in bunches. In dried form, they are raisins.

Teacher: Now let's see if you can put clustering to work for you. Your assignment is to convert the cluster on the chalkboard into a composition on grapes.

Your composition will have four paragraphs. One of the paragraphs – the one on grapes as an edible fruit – is already written for you.

Source

G. L. Rico. (1983). *Writing the natural way: Using right-brain techniques to release your expressive powers*. Los Angeles: J. P. Tarcher.

40

Hierarchical Summary Procedure

The Hierarchical Summary Procedure builds skill in organizing the information of textual presentations. Students improve their ability to comprehend and remember the content of texts, and they develop skills essential for writing well-organized compositions.

The procedure stresses the organizational aspects of both reading and writing. Students are engaged in reading activity that gives emphasis to recognizing main ideas and their supporting details and examples. With information extracted from a text, students produce a summary. As they produce the summary, students develop ideas by organizing them into structures whose superordinate and subordinate elements are clearly shown. Taking notice of text organization in reading, students come to appreciate the importance of organization in their own writing. They come to realize that writing is more understandable to readers if it is organized.

The Hierarchical Summary Procedure is appropriate for students in the middle grades and beyond. It can be employed effectively in social studies, science, and English/language arts classes. Since the teacher's close guidance is essential throughout the procedure, small-group instruction will yield the best results. Used weekly, the procedure should produce discernible positive results for most students in about eight weeks.

Procedure

Using the class textbook, the teacher implements the lesson with a chapter whose sections and subsections are clearly marked with headings and subheadings. The lesson begins by having students peruse the headings and subheadings to speculate about the material – to say what the content will be and, perhaps, to comment on the bias or angle that will be taken. At this point, the teacher's purpose is to arouse interest in the topic and to have students begin to get the gist of the content.

The teacher then explains to students how to use the headings and subheadings to form an outline. The teacher can point out that textbooks present their content so that most important ideas are advanced first and then suported by tiers of facts and discussion. Since these tiers of facts and discussion are orderly, just writing down their headings and subheadings would usually result in a well formed outline.

However, since the idea of the exercise is to foster skill at summary writing, students are instructed not to copy these headings and subheadings. Instead, the teacher directs students to attempt a skeletal outline of the text by substituting Roman numerals and capital letters in the place of headings and subheadings. Specifically, the teacher directs students to write down, on the left margin of their paper, Roman numerals to represent headings; under each Roman numeral and to the right a half dozen letter spaces, students are to write down capital letters to represent subheadings. Spaces of a half dozen or so lines should be left between the capital letters.

While students attempt to make outlines at their seats, the teacher simultaneously constructs an outline at the chalkboard. With the first demonstration of this phase of the procedure, students may be unsure about the teacher's directions, so it is important that the teacher's outline provide a clear model of the explanation. To be clear about this phase of the procedure, the teacher may jot down beside a Roman numeral the heading given in the book, but once it is seen by students, erase it, saying that only the Roman numeral should be present.

Once a skeletal outline is formed, the chapter's material is considered section by section, subsection by subsection. For each subsection of the chapter, represented by a capital letter on the outline, the teacher guides students in writing a summary statement. The teacher assigns students to read a subsection silently and then to attempt a written summary of it in their own words. When it is apparent that students have finished writing, the teacher asks students to volunteer their summary statements. The merits of these statements are noted, and once discussed, the statements' best elements are incorporated into a subsection summary that the teacher writes on the chalkboard. Students are then directed to list and discuss details that support their summary statement. This procedure is repeated for each succeeding subsection—B, C, D, and so on.

Once students have written a summary statement for each subsection, an attempt is made to produce a synthesis statement of the entire section. The section summary distills the information of the subsection summaries. The result sought is a general statement that captures the essence of the subsection summaries. Students are then asked to group subsections that seem related. For each group of related subsections, students are to generate a descriptive phrase, which the teacher jots down in the left margin. It may help students to see how the subsections are related if the teacher draws connecting lines between each phrase and the subsection summaries it describes.

After reading and writing hierarchical summaries of the chapter, students review their summaries. They distinguish among topic sentences for sections, key phrases for connecting subsections, main idea statements of subsections, and supporting details. Finally, pairs of students tell each other everything they can remember about the chapter. While one of the pair recites, the other uses the summary for prompting unrecalled information.

Discussion

The Hierarchical Summary Procedure offers a straightforward approach to teaching the conventional organization of expository texts. Teaching about text organization is basic to teaching students how to study and write. Students who can recognize how textual information is organized can better understand and remember that information, because they can formulate an analogous mental scheme for doing so. They can write more comprehensibly because they can present their thoughts in patterns they see typically followed in the texts they read. Although the Hierarchical Summary Procedure is to be used initially with textbook chapters whose sections and subsections are clearly marked with headings and subheadings, the procedure can be modified over time to teach students how to discern the organization of texts without headings.

To observe gains on students' organizational skills takes only about three lessons using the Hierarchical Summary Procedure. To observe gains in content learning and writing proficiency may take as many as eight weekly lessons. Able students who already possess organizing skills and are aware of text patterns may find the routine use of the procedure wearisome. For these students, the teacher may need to provide alternative activities.

EXAMPLE

An eighth-grade social studies class is studying change in American society. As part of the lesson, the teacher aims to show students how to make use of the hierarchical arrangement of information in the textbook. The class is going over the chapter on the topic, section by section and, within each section, attending to the content subsection by subsection. The class has reached the end of discussion on the introduction to a chapter section entitled "Changes in Family Life."

Teacher: Our textbook says that the American family changes with changing economic forces. Looking ahead at the subheadings of this part of the chapter, how do you suppose the textbook will develop this idea?

Jay: The first heading is "Families of the Young Nation." There's a heading about modern families and the last one on this part of the chapter is about families in the future. So, I'd say it will tell the history of change.

Several: Yes, it will tell the history of American families.

Teacher: I think you may be right. You've already begun making an outline for the chapter by writing a Roman numeral for every section heading and a capital letter for every subsection. For this section on your outline, write, under the Roman numeral, a capital letter for every subheading.

Mike: There are four subheadings, so we should have four capital letters—A, B, C, and D, right?

Teacher: That's correct. As you can see on the board, I've outlined this section of the chapter to show that the subsections are parts of the section.

Lilly: You show that by indenting the capital letters under the Roman numeral.

Teacher: Right. So that you can see how the Roman numeral and capital letters correspond with the section heading and subheading, I'll copy the heading beside the Roman numeral and the subheadings beside the capital letters.

The teacher writes out the heading and subheadings beside the corresponding Roman numeral and capital letters.

Barbara: Do we copy the heading and subheadings on our outline too?

Teacher: No. I only wanted you to see what the Roman numeral and capital letters stand for, to see how we represent the subsections as parts of the section on the outline.

Barbara: I see. The whole section is shown by the Roman numeral. Each part of the section is shown by a capital letter.

Teacher: You have the idea. Now I can erase the heading and subheadings that I've written out and leave the Roman numeral and capital letters in place. One of our tasks in the lesson will be to write sentences in place of the subheadings as we read. Beside the Roman numeral we'll write a topic sentence for the entire section after we've covered it.

Sandra: It's like we're rewriting the textbook, only making it shorter.

Teacher: We are summarizing it in our own words. Let's read the first subsection, entitled "Farm Families of the Young Nation." When you have finished reading, turn your book face down and, beside capital letter *A*, write a sentence that summarizes what you have read.

The students read silently and then write their summary sentences.

Teacher: Lilly, please read your summary sentence to us.

Lilly: "Early American families worked together to produce the things they needed."

Teacher: Mike, what's your reaction to Lilly's summary sentence?

Mike: It's OK, but it doesn't say they were *farm* families. For my summary, I wrote, "In the early years of America, families lived on farms."

Lilly: But your sentence leaves out the most important point–that they worked together cooperatively. Besides, not *all* families lived on farms.

Barbara: I think both Mike's and Lilly's sentences tell the important information, but neither one by itself tells enough.

Teacher: So, are you suggesting that the summary sentence should include the information of both?

Barbara: Yes. The two sentences could be rewritten into one sentence that combines the information of both.

Bob: How about this sentence? "In the early years of America, most families lived on farms and worked together to produce the things they needed."

Barbara: Great! But I suggest making it clear that it was the family members who worked together, not families working together with other families.

Bob: I get your point. OK, how about this? ". . . lived on farms and depended on parents and children working together."

Teacher: (writing beside letter *A* on the chalkboard) Let's let this be our main idea statement for the subsection: "In the early years of America's history, most families lived on farms and depended on parents and children working together to produce the things they needed."

Sandra: Should we write that sentence on our paper beside letter *A*?

Teacher: Beside capital letter *A,* you should have a main idea statement like this one on the board. Now, in the space underneath the statement, let's jot down specific information that supports the statement.

Bob: In complete sentences?

Teacher: Words and phrases will do.

Jay: Boys worked with their father.

Lilly: They cultivated the soil.

Mike: And harvested the crop.

Bob: And worked on buildings and fences.

Sandra: The girls worked with their mother.

Lilly: They cooked and sewed.

Barbara: And made soap.

Jay: The kids didn't have much time for play.

Lilly: Or for going to school.

Teacher: Good. (writing on the chalkboard) These details do support our main idea statement for this subsection. Now let's move on to the next subsection, entitled "Families move to the Cities." Again we'll read silently, formulate a summary statement, and jot down details that support our summary statement.

The class repeats the procedure for the succeeding three subsections of the chapter section "Changes in Family Life."

Teacher: Having closely studied these four subsections, we should be ready to write a topic sentence for the entire section. Beside the Roman numeral at the top of your outline, write a sentence that tells what this section is about. Then we'll write on the outline on the board.

Katrena: I have one.

Teacher: All right. Let's hear it.

Katrena: "There are many reasons for the changing nature of the family."

Teacher: The section's introduction did say that, and it did mention some different reasons.

Barbara: But this part of the chapter was about one reason mainly – the economic reason.

Teacher: The final sentence in the section's introduction supports your comment, Barbara.

Barbara: My topic sentence is this: "Economic forces bring about changes in the family."

Bob: That's good, but the American family hasn't changed just because of economic reasons. Katrena is right to say there are many reasons.

Barbara: So my sentence should be revised to say "Economic forces *importantly* bring about changes in the family."

Mike: The subsections got into the changes of roles and relationships among family members.

Teacher: (writing at the chalkboard) OK, let's try this: "Economic forces importantly determine family roles and relationships."

Several: Good. That's it.

Teacher: Let's look at our outline. Which of the subsections seem to go together? I mean, how could we put these subsections into categories?

Mike: As Jay said earlier, the book develops its point about the economics of family life by telling about the history of family changes in America. Subsections *A* and *B* tell about changes that have happened in the past. *C* and *D* tell about changes that either are currently happening or are likely to take place in the future.

Several: That's right.

Teacher: OK. In the left margin beside *A* and *B*, let's write the key phrase "Changes of the past." Beside *C* and *D*, let's write the key phrase "Current trends." Now let's draw lines to connect *A* and *B* to their key phrase and to connect *C* and *D* to their key phrase.

At this point in the lesson, the class has completed an outline that summarizes one section of the chapter. The outline looks like this:

I. Economic forces importantly determine family roles and relationships.

Changes of the past

A. In the early years of America's history, most families lived on farms and depended on parents and children working together to produce the things they needed.

Boys worked with father, cultivated soil, harvest, tended livestock, buildings, fences; girls worked with mother, cooked, sewed, made soap; little time for education.

B. When families moved into cities to work in factories, they did not have a strong sense of family cooperation.

Current trends

C. Even though modern families are prosperous and comfortable, they have problems of separation and the generation gap.

D. Changes taking place in families today indicate that families will be very different in the future.

As the lesson continues, the class studies each succeeding chapter section in the same fashion. The class reviews the chapter by discussing the outline's topic sentences and key phrases. In the discussion, the teacher has students distinguish among topic sentences of chapter sections, subsection sentences, supporting details, and key phrases that connect subsections. Finally, the teacher breaks the class into pairs, who tell each other everything they can remember about the chapter. While one partner recites, the other refers to the outline to prompt recollection.

Changes In Family Life

One of the most significant changes in American society has been in the character of families. So great has this change been that the term *family values* can only be interpreted with reference to some particular time period in American history. Many reasons can be given to explain the changing nature of the family. Immigrants of different cultures have brought with them a variety of family traditions. Expanding educational opportunities have raised awareness of numerous possibilities for family life. Advances in technology allow different lifestyles. The list of reasons could go on and on. Basically, changes in the family are the result of changing economic demands.

Farm Families of the Young Nation

During the early years of the nation, most families lived on farms. On farms, families were able to produce for themselves most of what they needed in order to survive. But to do so, all members of the family had to pitch in and work together.

Because the relative prosperity of a farm depended on the size of the family, children were valued. The boys performed the heavy work necessary on a farm. With their father, they cultivated the soil, gathered the harvest, tended the livestock, and worked on the buildings and fences. The girls' work was also hard. With their mother, they cooked, sewed, made soap, and did heavy household chores. Life on the farm was hard, and children had little time for play or education.

Families Move to the Cities

As farm machinery developed and new factories were built, more and more families moved into cities. Families did not work as teams in the cities. Factory jobs separated family members during working hours. The mother stayed at home with the young children while the father and the older children worked in the factories.

From early in the morning until late at night, the father and the children toiled in factories. Working apart from other family members, children did not develop a strong sense of family cooperation. The spirit of togetherness diminished and family ties loosened in the cities.

Families In Modern America

In modern America, most families live either in cities or in suburbs. On average, they have fewer than two children. Because they often move great distances, grandparents seldom live with or near the family. Both the father and the mother typically commute long distances to work. Very young children are left in daycare centers. The older children do not have to contribute to the family income, so they spend much of their time in school.

Family life is easier and more comfortable than in the last century. Families are more prosperous. They live in better homes, eat better, and are healthier. They enjoy a great deal more leisure time.

The modern family is not without problems, however. Many of its problems stem from a difference between parents and children in the attitudes and values they hold. This difference is called the *generation gap*. Things change so rapidly that children grow up in a world different from the one their parents knew when they were growing up. The generation gap is widened as children communicate less intimately with their parents and are influenced mainly by peers and television.

Families of the Future

Whether the family will survive as a significant social unit remains to be seen. Until the present, economic forces have fostered the institution of the family and the establishment of traditions that family members are expected to keep. For generations, traditions were sustained in *extended families* in which grandparents and other relatives were always nearby. But as economic forces change, traditions disappear and new kinds of family roles and relationships emerge. Economic demands, not long-standing traditions, shape the affairs of today's *nuclear families,* which are composed of parents and children only.

Just as the extended family is an arrangement of the past, so also are features of the nuclear family fading into history. Religious faith is all but gone as an important factor in marriage. Race is becoming less important. Families are becoming less permanent. As people remarry several times, children are likely to gain membership in several step-families. And they are likely to be reared largely by childhood professionals in daycare centers and schools.

Source

Barbara M. Taylor. (1982). A summarizing strategy to improve middle grade students' reading and writing skills. *The Reading Teacher, 36,* 202–205.

41

Guided Writing Procedure

The Guided Writing Procedure (GWP) incorporates writing into instruction without changing the subject matter objectives or adding substantially to demands on time. The procedure satisfies several objectives: It tests students' existing knowledge related to material to be taught, it provides for evaluating samples of students' writing in the content area, and it improves students' writing. The procedure also facilitates students' understanding and remembering the subject matter. Because students discuss and write drafts about subject matter both before and after they read about it, they retain more of the information presented to them.

The Guided Writing Procedure is designed specifically for content areas in which instructional demands often crowd out instruction in writing. These are content areas other than language arts, such as those in the social studies and sciences. GWP can be adapted to any grade level, inasmuch as writing instruction may begin when reading instruction begins. The teacher can adapt the writing instruction to fit the needs of the classroom. For younger students, the teacher can help with organizing material to be written; older students can usually organize their own material. Although the writing is individualized, this procedure is practical with larger groups as long as all students are given a chance to participate in initial discussions in which the material to be written is generated.

Procedure

Just as writing takes time, so does teaching writing. The Guided Writing Procedure involves several steps, some of which take more time than others. The procedure described here spans several days. The teacher begins by having students brainstorm the upcoming topic. All of the students' ideas are written on the chalkboard. After all ideas are exhausted, students vote on the main ideas and details. Using the results, the teacher works with students to organize these ideas into an outline.

Next, the teacher instructs students to write two short paragraphs, using the outline as a guide. For younger students, paragraphs of three or four sentences will suffice. The teacher collects these paragraphs and analyzes each for content, style, and grammar. The teacher records evaluative information on a diagnostic checklist, leaving students' papers unedited. This checklist is the teacher's guide to charting students' improvements in writing and comprehension.

The teacher assigns reading on the topic that students have brainstormed and written paragraphs. After the students have completed this reading, the teacher returns the unedited first drafts. Using the checklist as a guide for the students, the teacher shows a student's draft on the overhead projector and asks students for suggestions for revising it. This serves as an example for students to revise their own drafts. Having read about the topic as well as having observed an example of the revision process, students' second draft should show some improvement in content, style, and grammar; however, the teacher may have to use the procedure for an extended period of time before seeing any appreciable change in the writing samples. The teacher sets up individual conferences for students whose writing does not improve over several lessons using the procedure.

Discussion

Regularly using the Guided Writing Procedure aids in students' writing development in the content area. If used in the early grades, students become accustomed to writing, and their writing skills may increase greatly. The major strength of GWP is in its holistic approach to instruction. By the time the teacher has worked through the procedure, students will have used all of the four communication arts: speaking, listening, writing, and reading. In addition, the method is flexible enough for the teacher to incorporate it into the classroom routine. The brainstorming exercise gives the teacher some idea of the students' existing knowledge of an upcoming topic so that instruction can be adjusted.

This brainstorming session can produce misinformation. If it does, the teacher is then faced with having to decide whether to correct it immediately, rely on the reading material to set things straight, or wait to correct the misinformation until after the reading. Because the procedure spans several days and involves homework, the teacher cannot closely monitor all of the students' efforts or offer constant, direct feedback.

As for the reading aspect of the procedure, the teacher has to rely on a follow-up quiz to determine whether students have read the material, and if they have, to check their comprehension. The postreading steps do give attention to the reading material, but the major emphasis of this method is on developing writing skills. Because the procedure is intensive, its use should be limited to no more than once every one or two weeks.

EXAMPLE

A seventh-grade history class is about to begin a unit on Franklin Roosevelt's leadership during the Great Depression and World War II. The teacher is unsure of students' knowledge about the era. They had little background knowledge about the last unit, the Roaring Twenties. The teacher writes "Franklin Delano Roosevelt" on the chalkboard.

Teacher: Class, I'd like you to tell me what you may already know about our upcoming topic. Speak clearly, but do not shout out your comments. I'll write each of them on the chalkboard.

Susie: FDR!

Teacher: Great, Susie. Next?

John: He was in a wheelchair.

Teacher: Okay, next?

Ben: He had polio.

Teacher: Thanks, Ben.

Mary: Well, he was President during World War II.

Jenny: He was also President during the Depression. My grandmother talks about that.

Mark: He died in Georgia, at Warm Springs. I went there with my parents.

Jason: We studied Theodore Roosevelt. They were related, weren't they?

Teacher: Yes. We're doing great. Let's get a few more ideas.

John: He had a plan called the New Deal.

Mary: His wife was named Eleanor.

Teacher: All right, I'll take one more idea. Anybody?

Leigh: We studied Prohibition in the Roaring Twenties. It ended during Franklin Roosevelt's presidency.

Teacher: Good, Leigh! Now, let's organize these ideas into an outline.

The teacher and students organize the list into the following groups:

President during Depression	"FDR"
New Deal	had polio
ending of Prohibition	was in wheelchair
President during WW II	related to Theodore
died in Warm Springs	married Eleanor

Teacher: Now I want each of you to write one or two short paragraphs using these ideas.

After the students have written their paragraphs, the teacher collects them and assigns students to read the textbook selection on Franklin Roosevelt. Before the class meets again, the teacher analyzes each student's paragraph. Rather than edit directly on students' papers, the teacher notes strengths and needs on a diagnostic checklist.

In the following draft, Mary has separated her ideas into two distinct paragraphs. Although the sentence structures are correct, the paragraph's punctuation is inadequate. Mary needs to work on her spelling.

Mary's Draft

Franklin Delano Roosevelt also called FDR was maryed to Elener he was in a weelchar he had polio.

He was presdent during the depression and WW II. He died in Warm Springs Georgia.

The next day, the teacher displays a representative draft on the overhead, along with the major areas included on the checklist:

Writing Checklist

Name	Sentence Structure	Paragraph Structure	Correct Spelling	Correct Punctuation
Mary	X	X		

The class helps the teacher edit the example using the checklist as a guide.

Teacher: Let's look at this paper. It's not bad for a first draft, but it does have some problems.

Mary: It looks OK to me.

Teacher: It does communicate information about FDR. The words are arranged in correct sentence structures and it presents its information in two paragraphs according to the way we grouped information on the board yesterday.

John: Yeah, but it's run together too much.

Leigh: I agree with John. The paragraphs would be clearer to me if some of the information were separated by commas or periods or something.

Jason: I don't think the writer really wants to say that Franklin Delano Roosevelt called someone named FDR after calling someone else. As a reader I could take it that way and get off track. I think the writer wants to say "Franklin Delano Roosevelt was called FDR for short. Franklin Delano Roosevelt and FDR are the same."

Mark: So "also called FDR" needs parentheses around it.

Leigh: Or just commas.

Teacher: Either would be correct, but punctuation *is* needed here. Probably commas would be less distracting to a reader.

On the overhead transparency, the teacher inserts commas to set off the appositive.

Susie: The first paragraph also needs a comma or something after Elener, which is misspelled.

Teacher: You're right on both observations. *Elener* is a misspelling. But for right now, let's stick to talking punctuation since we're already on that subject. Why is punctuation needed here?

Jason: Cause there's where a sentence ends and a new one begins. The word *he* begins a new sentence.

Teacher: OK. So, we'll put a period here. We use a period to separate sentences—really to *end* them—not a comma. The comma already has enough work to do separating other things without having to separate sentences, too.

Inserting a period, the teacher also capitalizes the first letter of the following word.

John: There's some problem after wheelchair. The sentence ends with "wheelchair" and a new one begins with "he."

Teacher: Good observation, John. We'll put a period in there, too.

The class continues discussing ways to fix problems with this draft and then examines another one together. Following this exercise, the teacher returns the first drafts to students and assigns them to revise this draft, keeping in mind the improvements made on the illustrative drafts. The teacher will refer to the initial checklist to determine whether improvements are made. For the second draft, the teacher will also note content. The students should incorporate new material into the revised draft.

Source

Christine C. Smith and Thomas W. Bean. (1980). The guided writing procedure: Integrating content reading and writing improvement. *Reading World, 19,* 290–294.

42

Data Charting

Data Charting is a highly structured technique for teaching students how to write topical reports. The technique involves teacher modeling and a worksheet designed as a tool for report writing. Students learn three primary skills: to abstract pertinent information from several sources, to organize the information for comparison, and to synthesize that information into a coherent summary.

With the aid of a worksheet called a "Data Chart," the teacher leads students through the basic steps of report writing. Specifically, the teacher shows students how to formulate questions, how to seek answers to those questions in an organized way, and how to compose the report from one's own notes. The worksheet makes clear the inadequacy of any single source of information and thus encourages students to consult multiple sources. Further, it helps students decide which information to exclude and which information to include in the report. Students can organize and compare information, evaluate the information, and write the report all from the worksheet.

Procedure

The teacher distributes copies of a blank worksheet divided into a calendar-like grid of 9 or 12 cells. To lead students through the steps of completing it, an overhead transparency of the worksheet has been prepared. Students are told that the worksheet serves as an aid to writing a report, and are directed to follow along with the worksheet at their seats.

First, the teacher shows students how to label the worksheet. This begins by writing the topic of the report at the top of the worksheet. Writing a report, the teacher explains, is essentially an exercise in answering questions that the report's readers will likely have. To be clear about these questions and to avoid digressing from them, students are led by the teacher to write them on the worksheet. For the topic given, the teacher suggests three or four questions that could be addressed and writes them across the worksheet transparency, one question at the top of each column. To get information for answering these questions, the teacher points out, several sources usually have to be consulted. In the demonstration, copies of three sources are provided. The bibliographic information on these sources is written on the far left side of the worksheet, one source for each row of cells.

The teacher demonstrates how information collected from one of the sources is entered in the worksheet. The class first reads this text for the purpose of getting information related to the first question. Eliciting this information from students, the teacher jots it down in abbreviated form in the worksheet's first cell. The class then reads the same text for the purpose of getting information on the second question, and again the teacher elicits the information from students and enters it in the worksheet in the appropriate cell. This is repeated for the remaining question or questions.

Having been shown how to take information from a text and place it on the worksheet, students are directed to gather information related to the questions from the other two sources and to enter it in the worksheet as demonstrated. The teacher stands by to assist individual students who may need help.

Once students have filled in the worksheet, the information from the original sources is abstracted and organized into a form that facilitates comparison. The teacher directs students to compare information down the first column for the purpose of identifying the main facts upon which all the sources agree. With these facts, the teacher writes a sentence that summarizes a common answer to the first question. This sentence serves as a topic sentence for a paragraph that deals with the first question. The other information in the cells of the first column includes facts, examples, and conflicting statements. The teacher uses this information to demonstrate writing sentences that expand or clarify or qualify the topic sentence. At this point, the teacher has, through demonstration, written the first paragraph of a three- or four-paragraph report.

For the information recorded in the remaining columns of the worksheet, the teacher asks students to repeat the procedure. Students compare the information, generate sentences that summarize an answer to questions at the column heads, and complete a paragraph for each.

As students become proficient in the basic procedure, the teacher can build report-writing skill by adding new demands to the task. Students can be assigned to propose their own questions. The sources can be longer and more numerous. Sources can be provided that contain substantial amounts of conflicting information. And students can be given sources with more irrelevant information to be screened out.

Discussion

Many students need to be shown how to write reports. Merely having students carry out assignments to write reports on given topics mistakenly assumes that all students can independently figure out the specific steps of report writing. Students who do figure out what to do by the sink-or-swim approach do so only inefficiently at best. Data Charting offers a reasonable approach to introducing the basic skills of report writing. It shows students the specific steps to take in a highly prompted activity that provides practice in taking those steps.

Not all teachers feel comfortable with Data Charting, however. Advocates of open-ended learning may see the highly structured activity and the use of a device to prompt thinking as unnecessary crutches that reduce creativity and inhibit the discovery of personal writing strategies. For these teachers, Data Charting provides at the very best an assignment format that facilitates grading. It also provides, perhaps, a remedial method for dealing with individual students who need extra clues in their search for writing strategies.

EXAMPLE

High school students in a U.S. history class are assigned to write a report on the invention of the cotton gin. The teacher demonstrates how to write the report using a data chart.

Teacher: We'll see that the cotton gin was a great boon to farming as well as to industry.

Jeb: You've already told us that. So why do we have to write a report on it?

Teacher: Writing a report on the cotton gin should fasten in your mind the important facts about this simple device and its effect on the course of history.

Beth: It's easier if you just tell us.

Lester: I don't know how to write a report.

Alex: I don't either, actually. I always just copy from an encyclopedia.

Several: Me, too.

Teacher: We'll do the assignment together. I'll write a report, too, and show you how to write yours.

Beth: That's better than leaving us to muddle through on our own.

Teacher: First, let's gather information. As we gather it, we keep it organized. To help us do that, we can use this worksheet. It's called a data chart.

The teacher distributes blank data charts to students.

Teacher: I'll work with my data chart here on the overhead projector. At the top of the chart I write the topic.

Bart: The topic on the top. On the top, the topic.

Jean: The cotton gin.

Teacher: Right. The cotton gin. Now doing a report is a matter of getting information that answers questions about a topic. Over here in the far left column of boxes, we write down where we get our information. We label the top of that column "Sources."

Fran: What are the questions?

Teacher: We have to formulate them, based on what we think the reader of the report needs to know. We write the questions at the top of the other columns on the data chart.

Fran: Oh, I get it. In the boxes below the questions, we answer the questions with information from the books named on the left.

Teacher: Right. It's there we note the information for answering them. As a history teacher, I believe the reader should know about the problem that the cotton gin solved. So, at the top of the first column for questions, I'll write, "What problem did the cotton gin solve?"

Bart: I'd like to know what the cotton gin did to solve the problem.

Teacher: Good question. I'll write it at the top of the next column.

Emory: You said that the cotton gin affected both industry and farming. What were those effects?

Teacher: Ah, Emory, you're thinking like a historian. Let's ask the question separately for industry and for farming. Answering these questions should round out our report.

The teacher adds these two questions to the data chart and then hands out copies of the first selection on the cotton gin, a segment taken from a U.S. history textbook.

Teacher: This is the first source we'll consult for our report.

Fran: We write the name of it in the first box under "Sources." Right?

Teacher: Yes, we do identify it in that box. We should note the author's name, the title, the page numbers, and the date of its publication.

Beth: Seems like an awful lot of stuff just to name your source.

Teacher: You'll need that information to put in a reference list at the back of your report. You include a reference list in case the reader wants to check your information. Now, let's read this passage to get information about the first question, "What problem did the cotton gin solve?"

Students silently read the first selection.

Teacher: What was the problem?

Alex: Cotton seeds had to be picked out of the cotton by hand.

Jean: That took a long time. In a whole day only about two pounds could be cleaned.

Teacher: All right. I'll jot down this information under the first question in the box for the first source. Now, let's read the passage again to get information about the second question, "How did the cotton gin solve the problem?"

Students again silently read the first selection.

Teacher: Well, what did the passage say about the second question?

Lester: It said that the cotton gin separated the fibers from the seeds.

Jean: And with it a worker could clean 50 pounds of cotton a day.

Fran: There's information about the other questions, but really not any more about the second question.

Bart: When I asked the question, I had a lot more in mind, like how did the cotton gin do what it did? The passage said that it separated cotton fibers from seeds, but not how it did it.

Teacher: That's exactly why we have to consult more than one source when we investigate a topic. Seldom does any single source provide adequate information on all of the questions we have. Sometimes they provide no information at all on a question.

In the cell for the second question, the teacher enters information students have taken from the first source. The teacher continues to demonstrate filling out the data chart as students read and tell information this source has for answering the remaining two questions. Then, the teacher distributes the second and third selections and directs students to use them to complete the data chart as has been demonstrated. With the overhead projector turned off, the teacher completes the data chart transparency and assists students who are having difficulty.

Teacher: Now, let's turn the information on your data chart into a report on the invention of the cotton gin. The report will have as many paragraphs as there are questions on the data chart.

Emory: So, we'll have four paragraphs, one for each question. To write each paragraph, we use the information in the column of boxes under a question. Right?

Teacher: Right. For each paragraph, we have to come up with a topic sentence. That's a sentence that generally sums up all of the information to be included in the paragraph. To get a topic sentence, we have to look closely at the information in the question's column of boxes and see what's common among them. In the column for the first question, Lester, what seems to be common?

Lester: Before the cotton gin was invented, before 1793, getting the seeds out of cotton was hard and slow.

Jeb: And that caused other problems.

Beth: Different problems are mentioned by different sources.

The Cotton Gin

Sources	What Problem Did the Cotton Gin Solve?	How Did the Cotton Gin Solve the Problem?	How Did the Invention of the Cotton Gin Affect Industry?	How Did the Invention of the Cotton Gin Affect Farming?
Johnson, Clarence. "Cotton in the North and South." *The History of Our Country.* 1989, p. 182.	Cotton seeds picked out by hand. Slow work, 2 lbs. cotton a day. This before 1793.	Pulled fibers from seeds. 50 lbs. cotton a day.	Allowed textile factories to use more cotton.	Made cotton farming very profitable in South. Growers started new plantations, moved westward—Atlantic Coast to Texas.
Whiskers, Charles. "Cotton Becomes the Dominant Cash Crop." *The Economic History of America.* 1965, p. 218.	Cotton products too expensive. Cotton seeds removed by hand. Little cotton fabric produced.	Eli Whitney invented gin to separate cotton fiber/seeds efficiently 1793. Cotton became cheap.	Could get cotton cheap—turned out more and cheaper cloth.	Cotton became most profitable cash crop (over rice & tobacco) Encouraged slavery. Slavery increased, moved west.
Edison, Timothy. "The Cotton Gin." *Great Inventions.* 1973, p. 128.	Separating cotton from seeds slow, tedious work—1 lb. cotton a day.	1793 Eli Whitney invented gin. Gin has 3 working parts: cylinder with hooks, metal plate with slots, brush. When cylinder turns, hooks snag & pull cotton through slots of metal plate, but not seeds. Seeds break off. Brush sweeps off fiber. Gin could clean 50 lbs. cotton a day.	American cotton industry became largest in world.	
Topic Sentence	Before 1793, separating the seeds from cotton fibers was hard and slow work.	In 1793, Eli Whitney invented the cotton gin, which could efficiently separate cotton fiber from the seeds.	The invention of the cotton gin made the American cotton industry the largest in the world.	Cotton farming became very profitable in the South.

223

Teacher: But the basic problem, the one mentioned by all of the sources, was getting the seeds out of the cotton. So, let's write that in a sentence and let that sentence be the topic sentence of the first paragraph.

Beneath the column of boxes for the first question, the teacher writes the first paragraph's topic sentence: "Before 1793, separating the seeds from cotton fibers was hard and slow work."

Teacher: We'll use the other information in the column under the first question to develop the paragraph. Before we do that, however, let's write a topic sentence for the information on each of the other questions.

Together, the class writes topic sentences for the remaining questions' columns of information.

Teacher: Now, we have four topic sentences, one for each paragraph that we'll include in our report. Returning to the first topic sentence, we'll write a paragraph with the information in the column under the first question.

Lester: We should put in it the facts about the problems with cotton.

Alex: The fact that cotton seeds had to be taken out by hand.

Jean: That only one or two pounds of cotton could be cleaned in a day.

Emory: And that these facts caused another fact: Cotton products were too expensive.

Teacher: Yes. We should include these three important facts about the cotton problems. I suggest writing a sentence for each fact.

Bart: Then, with the topic sentence, our first paragraph will have four sentences.

Beth: Hey, things are falling into place.

The teacher copies the first topic sentence from the overhead projector onto the chalkboard. There, the teacher composes three additional sentences, one for each important fact related to the cotton problem. Having demonstrated the development of the first paragraph, the teacher assigns students to complete the remaining three paragraphs by the same procedure.

Sources Used in Data Chart

Cotton in the North and South

In New England, textile mills required large quantities of raw cotton. The problem was, however, cotton's seeds were buried deep in the fibers and had to be picked out by hand. A worker could clean only about two pounds of cotton per day. In 1793, the invention of a new machine solved the problem. It was the cotton gin. Eli Whitney created a machine that could pull the cotton fibers away from the seeds. Using the cotton gin, a person could clean nearly 50 pounds per day. The invention of the cotton gin allowed textile factories in New England to use more and more cotton, and it made growing cotton very profitable in the South.

Large plantations in the South produced most of the cotton. With the invention of the cotton gin, cotton became king in the South. Cotton growers moved farther west to start up new plantations. In little time, cotton plantations stretched from the southern Atlantic coast to Texas. (page 182)

Cotton Becomes the Dominant Cash Crop

The cash crops of the South's plantations were cotton, rice, and tobacco. With the invention of the cotton gin, cotton became much more profitable than rice and tobacco. Cotton became the most important cash crop.

Until the end of the eighteenth century cotton products were too expensive for most people. Removing the seeds from raw cotton had to be done by hand. Because the process took a long time, little cotton fabric could be produced. In 1793, New Englander Eli Whitney invented a machine that could separate seeds from raw cotton efficiently. It was the cotton gin. Cotton soon became cheap, and textile mills of New England turned out more and cheaper cotton cloth.

The cotton gin made cotton a very profitable crop. It also encouraged slavery. Before the invention of the cotton gin, many people expected slavery to end soon. But as Southern planters began to reap huge profits, slavery increased. And as growers moved west to get more land to grow cotton, slavery moved west too. (page 218)

The Cotton Gin

For many years one problem held back the American cotton industry. It was the problem of separating the fibers of cotton from the seeds. Workers had to pick the seeds out of the fibers by hand. This was slow, tedious work. A worker could clean only about a pound of cotton in a day.

In 1793, Eli Whitney solved the problem with his invention of the cotton gin. The cotton gin was a machine with three working parts: a revolving cylinder with rows of stiff wire hooks, a metal plate with slots, and a brush. Its operation was so simple and efficient that the basic idea is still used today. When the cylinder turns, its rows of wire hooks pass through the slots of the metal plate and snag the cotton fiber. The wire teeth pull the fiber through the slots, which are too small for the seeds to pass through. The metal plate stops the seeds and they snap off. The brush sweeps the fiber from the cylinder and the cleaned cotton falls into a large pile.

With Whitney's invention, as much as 50 pounds of cotton could be ginned in a day. It was an invention that started the American cotton industry on its way to becoming the largest in the world. (page 128)

Teacher's Example of Completed Report

The Cotton Gin

Before 1793, separating the seeds from cotton fibers was hard and slow work. Cotton seeds had to be removed by hand. Only about one or two pounds of cotton could be cleaned in a day. This made cotton products too expensive.

In 1793, Eli Whitney invented the cotton gin, which could efficiently separate cotton fiber from the seeds. The machine did this by pulling cotton through slots small enough to block cotton seeds. The cotton gin could clean as much as 50 pounds of cotton in a day. Cotton became cheap.

The invention of the cotton gin made the American cotton industry the largest in the world. Factories could get cotton cheap, so they used more cotton. They produced cheaper cloth and more of it.

Cotton farming became very profitable in the South. There, it was king. Growers moved westward and started new plantations. Slavery increased and extended westward with the new plantations.

Source

    Gary R. McKenzie. (1979). Data charts: A crutch for helping pupils organize reports. *Langauge Arts, 56,* 784–788.

43

Guided Reading and Summarizing Procedure

The principal use of the Guided Reading and Summarizing Procedure (GRASP) is to model the process of composing original summaries of reading. In the process, students extract information from a text, organize that information, and summarize it in their own words. Students improve skills of monitoring their comprehension, organizing information, and writing reports.

Writing reports about subject matter focuses students' attention on significant information and forces them to reflect on that information. Unless the teacher shows students how to carry out writing assignments, however, students may resort to mindless copying. Through GRASP, the teacher can give students a few simple guidelines and demonstrate the use of those guidelines in a step-by-step procedure. Students come to understand the process of summary writing and become equipped with a skill they can apply in independent study situations.

Although GRASP is intended for large- and small-group instruction, it may also be used effectively with individuals. It may be used in any academic subject at the intermediate grade level and above. The length of the text to be summarized varies according to students' maturity and reading ability, from about 500 words for intermediate-grade students to about 1,500 words for upper-grade students.

Procedure

The teacher distributes copies of a text like the ones students consult for making reports. An encyclopedia article on a topic of interest to students is ideal. The length of the text ranges from 500 words for middle-grade students to 1,500 words for older high school and college students. The teacher explains that the text will be used for demonstrating the steps students might take in carrying out an assignment that calls for summarizing the information of such a text. The teacher emphasizes that the steps taken in the exercise closely resemble the steps that students are to take when they write text summaries on their own. The steps the teacher then demonstrates are to read for information, to organize that information, and to convert organized information into a presentation in their own words.

Reading for information begins with the teacher directing students to read the text for the purpose of remembering as much of its content as they can. When they are finished reading, they are to look up and turn the text face down. Once students have finished reading, the teacher asks them to tell everything they can remember, no matter how trivial or incomplete they may think it may be. The teacher lists the re-called information on the chalkboard. When students' recollection of the text is exhausted, the teacher has them reread the text in order to catch important information they may have left out and to correct mistakes in the initial recall.

The next step is to organize the material taken from the text. The teacher shows students how to group the information that belongs together and then how to organize the information within groups. The teacher leads a discussion aimed at identifying and labeling the text's major topics. These topics serve as categories within which to group the information listed on the chalkboard. The class considers each piece of information and decides the category to assign it. The teacher has students further organize information within each category by having them figure out which pieces of information are components or conditions of other pieces of information. As these decisions are made, the information is fashioned into an outline.

Converting the outline to a prose summary begins with the teacher informing students of three ways to handle the material. One is to include in the summary only the important information, leaving out details that are not necessary for summing up the reading. The second is to compress the information by combining it. And the third is to add information necessary for achieving coherence. The teacher then works with students to turn each group of information on the outline into a single sentence. Some groups of information may require two sentences. The teacher models the procedure by writing on the chalkboard a sentence for the first group of information. The teacher explains why some information is omitted, how information is combined, and why certain language may be added.

For the next group of information, the teacher tells students to write their own sentence. While they write, the teacher simultaneously writes a sentence that summarizes the same information at the chalkboard. The teacher then asks for volunteers to share their sentences with the class. The teacher points out strengths in the students' sentences and asks them to say why they made the composition decisions they did. If a student has a better sentence or sentence part, the teacher uses it to replace or revise the sentence on the chalkboard. Nothing is erased. The teacher marks through writing on the chalkboard and inserts revisions above. This leaves a visible record of the revision process. Together, the teacher and students convert succeeding groups of information into sentences, examining and revising each. This procedure results in a paragraph that summarizes the reading in about as many sentences as there are groups of information in the outline.

Discussion

Through GRASP, students acquire a step-by-step procedure for extracting information from a written source and summarizing it in their own words. Knowing *how* to summarize the information of a source, students have no need to copy it verbatim. As students discuss the processes of organization and composition, they learn that effective writing reflects a community's consensus about what constitutes effective communication.

GRASP is intended to simulate the process of extracting and summarizing the important information of a text. The lesson's procedure does differ, however, from what one does when actually summarizing a text. In order to force students away from writing down information taken directly from the text and possibly indulging the old habit of copying it, the procedure involves a memory task for extracting the text's information. In an actual summarizing task, one ordinarily takes notes directly from the text. And for the purpose of class demonstration, the text's length is limited to 500 to 1,500 words.

Most texts that students need to summarize are much longer. Another limitation worth noting is that GRASP keeps the teacher busy at the chalkboard. As in any activity that involves a great deal of work at the chalkboard, the teacher has to balance attention between the chalkboard and the students.

EXAMPLE

A high school anthropology class is considering human characteristics that have proved advantageous for the development of civilization. This lesson focuses on the human hand. To highlight the versatile structure of the hand, the teacher has decided to have students write a summary of an encyclopedia article on the hand. Having observed excessive copying in a previous writing assignment, the teacher takes an opportunity with this lesson to demonstrate the steps of writing a summary of one's reading.

Ralph: I guess I'd never thought about the part our hands have played in humans becoming what we are. I had always thought before that humans are just smarter than other animals.

Virginia: Me, too. I always thought that it was our brain that let us control the environment.

Ruth: And our ability to talk.

Teacher: Certainly our ability to think and reason and communicate should not be understated. But then neither should our physical characteristics. As we've pointed out in today's lesson, among our physical characteristics, our hand has contributed significantly to the development of civilization.

Franz: But what is it about the hand that lets us do so many things with it?

Teacher: The human hand is structured in a very special way. I have copies of an encyclopedia article that tells about the structure of the human hand.

The teacher hands out copies of the encyclopedia article.

Ralph: So you want us to read this for our homework assignment?

Teacher: I'd like for you to know enough about the human hand that you can write a description of its structure. Your assignment is to take information from the encyclopedia article and write a description of the human hand.

Franz: That's easy.

Teacher: I want you to *summarize* the encyclopedia article, not copy it. You are to write your summary in your own words.

Franz: That's not easy.

Teacher: No, it's not easy. But you can do it if you know how.

Franz: But I really don't know how.

Several: Me neither.

Teacher: Well, then, let's summarize this encyclopedia article together. Let's do a class activity with the article that takes you through the steps of writing a text summary. That way, you can learn about the human hand and at the same time find out how to write a text summary.

Virginia: What *are* the steps you take when you summarize a text?

Teacher: Basically there are three steps. The first step is to pull bits of information out of the text you're summarizing. The second step is to organize this information into an outline. And the third step is to turn the outline into your own written summary.

Ralph: Pulling out bits of information and making an outline seem like a lot of unnecessary bother to me.

Teacher: This is not the only way to write a text summary. The reason for including these steps in the activity here is to show you how to write a summary with the information you glean from the text, not with information you see in the text itself.

Ruth: That makes sense. When I see how something is written in a text, I know I couldn't write it any better. So I just go with the way it's already written.

Teacher: Let's begin to break you of that bad habit. Let's begin our activity. Read the article and try to remember as much of it as you can. When you've finished, turn the article face down and look up.

Students silently read the article on the hand.

Teacher: Without looking at the article, tell me everything you can remember about what it says about the hand. Tell me everything you can remember, even if you think it's unimportant or not quite correct. I'll jot down the information you give me here on the chalkboard.

Ralph: The hand is at the end of the arm.

Ruth: It grasps objects.

Franz: Bone, muscle, and skin have special features.

Harry: Four types of nerve endings.

Virginia: The wrist is a huge joint.

The teacher lists recollections on the chalkboard until students can recall no more of the article. In a column beside the first recollections listed on the chalkboard, the teacher will note additions and corrections until students have no more to offer.

Teacher: Good. You've remembered quite a bit of information from the article. Now read it again quickly to see if you've left out anything important or if you need to correct any of the information listed on the board.

Again, students silently read the encyclopedia article.

Teacher: Are there any additions or corrections we should make?

Virginia: The fingers roll under.

Harry: And stick out straight.

Franz: Bone, muscle, and skin are structured in a special way.

Ruth: They work together.

Ralph: It is the skin of the fingers and thumb that has the four types of nerve endings.

Teacher: Now let's begin to organize this information by sorting it into categories.

Ruth: The stuff on the board is about how the hand is a special structure of bone, muscle, and skin. There's a lot of detail about these three basic parts of the structure, so I think we should have a category for each—bone, muscle, and skin.

Remembered Information

First Recollections	Additions/Corrections
end of arm	fingers roll under
grasps objects	fingers stick out straight
bone, muscle, skin have special features	special structure
	work together
4 types nerve endings	skin of fingers & thumbs
wrist is hinge joint	feel slight differences in surfaces
wrist connects forearm w/ hand	wrist is upper part of hand
digit bones called phalanges	hand mobile & sensitive
5 carpal bones on palm	meta
tendons contract, hand closes	along palm
tendons—slender cords of muscle	connect at joints of phalanges
thumb rotates	hand opens when back of hand tendons contract
thumb opposes fingers	each
19 bones below wrist	manual skills possible
	carpal bones separate, movable
fingers have 3 phalanges	carpal bones in two rows
thumb has 2 phalanges	carpal bones allow rotation
35 muscles move hand	carpal bones allow side to side movement
20 muscles in hand itself	carpal bones allow back & forth movement
thumb's distant phalange bends back	distal
tendons extend from wrist	
thumb nearest digit to wrist	

Several: Me, too.

Franz: But there's other information, too. There's information about the function of hand and the things it does with all three of those parts working together.

Teacher: You're right. We do need a category for that information. Shall we call it "Functions of the Hand"?

Franz: We could, but the functions of the hand are possible because of its structure. The article is about the structure of the hand. Let's just list functions and other details in a category called "Structure of the Hand."

Harry: OK, but the main idea of the article is that the structure of the hand is special.

Teacher: Good point. Let's have as our first category one that includes general information related to the special structure of the hand.

Franz: We should put in it that the bones, muscle, and skin work together.

Virginia: That it can grasp objects.

Harry: And that it can feel surfaces.

Ruth: If it's a general information category, we'd better put in it that the hand is at the end of the arm. That sort of works there, but it won't fit in the categories about bone, muscle, and skin.

Several: Right.

Teacher: Now, what about the bones category? Which of our information fits under "Bones"?

The class continues to sort the information remembered from the article. Once all the information is sorted, it is further organized within each category. The result is this outline:

Structure of hand special
    Bone, muscle, skin work together
    Grab objects
    Feel surfaces
    End of the arm
Bones
    Wrist is hinge joint
        Connects forearm with hand
        8 separate, movable carpal bones
           Carpal bones positioned in 2 rows
        Rotate, back-and-forth and side-to-side movement
    19 bones below wrist
        Palm has 5 metacarpal bones
        Finger digits have 3 phalanges each
        Thumb digit has 2 phalanges
        Thumb is digit nearest wrist
Muscles
    35 muscles move the hand
        20 muscles in hand itself
        Below-wrist muscles called tendons

Slender
Connect with joints of phalanges
    Contraction of palm tendons closes hand
    Contraction of tendons of back of hand opens hand
    Fingers and thumb roll under
    Fingers and thumb stick out straight
    Thumb's distal phalanges bend back
    Thumb rotates
    Thumb opposes each finger
        Makes manual skills possible
Skin
    Fingers and thumb have 4 types nerve endings
    Extremely sensitive
      Can feel slight differences in surfaces

Franz: We have an outline of all the information we remembered from the article, but is all this necessary just to write a summary?

Teacher: It's really up to each writer how to organize the information to be summarized. But it does need to be organized. Organizing information is an essential aspect of composing a summary. The word *composing* comes from Latin and means "putting with" or "putting together."

Virginia: Like we just got through putting information together with other information in categories.

Teacher: And within each category, we put closely related information together. With related information put together in categories, we can write the summary by turning each category into a sentence or two.

Ralph: You make it sound so easy.

Teacher: With practice, it does become less hard to do. As you write, you have to keep in mind three rules of summarizing: (1) include only the information important for your purpose, (2) combine information where possible, and (3) add information or language to help complete and smooth out the summary.

Franz: Those three rules are fine for guiding your writing, but they don't change the outlined information into sentences.

Teacher: No, they don't. You still have to write the summary. By the approach we're taking here, you apply these three rules as you put each group of information into writing. You proceed through the outline one group of information at a time, writing a sentence or two for each group. To get us started with the actual writing, I'll turn the first group of information into sentence form.

The teacher pauses to take stock of the outline's first group of information and then writes this sentence on the chalkboard:

Bone, muscle, and skin of the hand are structured so that it can grasp objects and feel surfaces.

Teacher: Notice that I did not include all of the information. What's important is that the hand's structure makes its functions possible. So I left out the obvious fact that the hand is at the end of the arm. The rest of the information is combined.

Franz: You also left out that bone, muscle, and skin work together.

Teacher: Yes, I did. Another writer might include that. But I decided to let that information be implied.

Virginia: But how do we know what to leave out, what things can be implied?

Teacher: It takes practice to get the hang of it. The next group of information we've already organized into two subgroups. Let's take the first subgroup and turn it into a sentence or two. You write at your desks while I write at the board.

Simultaneously, the teacher and students write out the information of the outline's second group. On the chalkboard the teacher writes this sentence:

> Connecting the hand to the forearm is the wrist, which is a hinge joint with eight uniquely shaped bones positioned separately into two rows so as to allow the hand to rotate and to move from side to side and back and forth.

Before directing attention to this sentence, the teacher has students share the sentences they have written. In the discussion, the teacher observes strengths of each sentence.

Teacher: Your sentences are effective and, importantly, they are your own. You've used the rules for summarizing better than I have. My sentence seems too long and cluttered.

Harry: You could leave out information about the wrist connecting the hand and forearm. The wrist is not just a connector. It is the upper part of the hand.

Teacher: You're right. It is.

Virginia: Besides, this group of information is about bones. So the sentence should be about bones.

Teacher: You're right. It should. I can revise my sentence by deleting information about the wrist as a connector and hinge joint.

Ruth: It still seems hard to read: ". . . eight uniquely shaped carpal bones positioned separately into two rows. . . ."

Teacher: Maybe I can improve it by moving some words around and leaving some out.

Ralph: You could try this: "Eight separate carpal bones are shaped and positioned so as to allow. . . ."

Franz: Great. But you still need to put in that the carpal bones are in the wrist.

Teacher: (making the suggested revisions at the chalkboard) Excellent improvements. But the end of my sentence still seems awkward. It's got too much information packed into it.

Ruth: Maybe you could fix it by taking out "from side to side and back and forth" and substituting the words "in different directions."

Teacher: That's better, yes. Now let's write a sentence or two for the second subgroup of information on Bones. Again, you write at your desks while I write at the chalkboard.

As the lesson continues, the outline is converted to prose, part by part. The teacher makes no erasures as the summary on the chalkboard is discussed and revised. At the end of the lesson, students have before them an original summary with a visible record of the revisions made as it was written.

Summary Showing Revision Process

Bone, muscle, and skin of the hand are structured so that it

can grasp objects and feel surfaces. ~~Connecting the hand to~~

~~the forearm is the wrist, which is a hinge joint with~~ Eight
Separate carpal bones of the wrist are

~~uniquely~~ *and* shaped ~~bones~~ positioned ~~separately into two rows~~ so

as to allow the hand to rotate and ~~to~~ move ~~from side to side~~ *in different directions.*

~~and back and forth.~~ *Extending from* ~~Below~~ the wrist are ~~10 bones including~~ *five sets of bone segments that form the*

palm and the digits. ~~five metacarpal~~ Bones of the palm *are called metacarpals, and bones* ~~three phalanges of each~~

of the ~~finger~~ digits *are called* ~~and two~~ phalanges *The hand is moved by* ~~of the thumb. Thirty-five~~

~~muscles move the hand, 20 in the hand itself. These are~~

slender muscle cords, called tendons, that *extend from the wrist and* connect *at* the joints

of the phalanges. Contract*ing the* ~~of the palm~~ tendons closes the

hand, and contracting the tendons of the back of the hand

opens the hand. *Both* The thumb and the fingers can roll under *as well as* ~~and can~~

stick out straight, but the *end of the* thumb~~'s distal phalanges~~ *can also* bend

backwards. *Because* The thumb *can* rotates and opposes each finger ~~and~~

~~makes~~ *are* manual skills possible. ~~In the skin of the fingers and~~

~~thumb there are~~ four types of nerves *in the fingers* ~~that are extremely~~

~~sensitive and~~ *and thumb* heighten the sense of touch so that ~~you can~~

~~feel~~ slight differences in *a* surfaces *can be felt.*

Finished Summary

Bone, muscle, and skin of the hand are structured so that it can grasp objects and feel surfaces. Eight separate carpal bones of the wrist are shaped and positioned so as to allow the hand to rotate and move in different directions. Extending from the wrist are five sets of bone segments that form the palm and the digits. Bones of the palm are called metacarpals, and bones of the digits are called phalanges. The hand is moved by slender muscle cords, called tendons, that extend from the wrist and connect at the joints of the phalanges. Contracting the tendons of the palm closes the hand, and contracting the tendons of the back of the hand opens the hand. Both the thumb and the fingers can roll under as well as stick out straight, but the end of the thumb can also bend backwards. Because the thumb can rotate and oppose each finger, manual skills are possible. Four types of nerves in the fingers and thumb heighten the sense of touch so that slight differences in a surface can be felt.

The Hand

The hand forms the terminal end of the arm. Because of the hand's special structure, it can be used for grasping and exploring whatever may be within its reach. This structure comprises bone, muscle, and skin, each with unique features and combined so as to permit functioning in concert with one another.

The wrist forms the upper part of the hand. In the wrist are eight movable bones. These are the carpal bones. The shapes of the carpal bones and the way they articulate with the forearm form a hinge joint that gives mobility to the hand below the wrist. The carpal bones allow the hand to rotate and to move both back and forth and side to side.

Below the wrist, the hand consists of nineteen bones. Five of these bones are in the palm of the hand. The bones of the palm are the metacarpal bones. Extending from the palm are five digits, one digit extending from each metacarpal. The bones of the digits are called phalanges. Four of the digits have three phalanges each, and one digit has two phalanges. The digits with three phalanges are the fingers. The digit with two phalanges is the thumb.

The hand is moved by 35 powerful muscles in the forearm and hand; 20 of the muscles are in the hand itself. These muscles are structured so that many different movements can be made with precision. From the wrist, muscles become slender cords called tendons. Tendons extend along the palm and back of the hand and connect at the joints of the phalanges. When the tendons along the palm are contracted, the hand closes. When the tendons along the back of the hand are contracted, it opens.

The thumb is the digit nearest the wrist. It is shorter and thicker than the other digits, and it is more flexible. Whereas the fingers can roll under and return to an extended position, the thumb's distal phalange can bend backward as well as forward. The thumb can also be rotated to touch and oppose each of the fingers. Basically, it is this opposable feature of the thumb that makes manual skills and the use of tools possible. Adding to the hand's versatile mobility is its remarkable sense of touch. Skin with four different types of nerve endings allow the fingers and thumb to discern minute differences in the texture of a surface. So sensitive is the skin of the fingers and thumb that it is possible to read by feeling the shapes of slightly raised letters of Braille texts.

Source

David A. Hayes. (1989). Helping students GRASP the knack of writing summaries. *Journal of Reading, 33,* 96–101.

44

React-Then-Analyze

React-Then-Analyze encourages students to express and support their opinions both orally and in writing. As students interact in this procedure, they clarify and express their reactions to subject matter. Because the procedure involves writing, it contributes to the improvement of writing skill.

Although students seldom lack opinions, logic, or insight in reacting to subject matter, they tend to be unsure of their own ideas. And they tend not to value their written opinions because they are vulnerable to criticisms of spelling, grammar, and neatness. React-Then-Analyze provides students with a safe atmosphere in which to explore their ideas and to practice framing them in writing.

React-Then-Analyze may be used appropriately in a variety of situations at the upper-elementary grades and beyond. It may be used in reading classes to improve comprehension and sharpen critical reading skill. It may be used to heighten understanding and sensitivity to social and moral implications of topics in science. The method is especially effective in language arts and social studies classes where controversial topics are addressed.

Procedure

React-Then-Analyze has four phases. In phase 1, the teacher and students work together as a class so that the overall procedure can be demonstrated efficiently and so that students can begin to gain confidence with it. In phase 2, students work first in groups and then individually with teacher guidance. In phase 3, students progress from depending on a group to formulating and supporting their own positions. In phase 4, students use charts as aids to writing critical analyses of subject matter issues.

Phase 1 – Teaching. The teacher presents a controversial topic from a textbook, newspaper, or magazine and asks students to express their opinions about the issue. The teacher lists all student responses on the chalkboard or overhead transparency without placing value on the quality of the responses. All are listed as if they have equal value. Together, the teacher and students group the responses within five categories: experiences, pro, con, attitudes, and importance. The teacher then has students skim the textual material once for its general ideas and follow up with a more careful reading to discover the main viewpoint.

Following the reading, the class discusses ideas in the text that support the main concept and come to a single statement that summarizes the material. The teacher broadens the discussion, encouraging students to take divergent positions on the issue. Here, the teacher asks leading questions: Do you agree with the author? How does your view correspond with that of the author? The teacher lists reactions on the chalkboard or overhead transparency and assists students in developing them into basic viewpoints, pro and con, with reasons supporting the opinions. From these viewpoints, the teacher leads students to create a composite reaction that begins with a position statement. The position statement is written down, along with a list of reasons to support the position. From this, an essay is developed.

Phase 1 is the most time-consuming part of the method. Once students are taken through this phase, however, they can move through the other three phases with relative ease.

Phase 2–Guided Practice. For this phase, students build on what they have learned in phase 1. Students are offered a choice of textual materials (newspaper or magazine editorials, textbook commentaries, etc.). Topics may range from lightweight matters to serious issues. Students skim the material they select and, in preparation for writing, categorize their reactions to it in terms of experience, pro, con, attitude, and importance. Students then read and reread for the major theme and produce a summary statement. Following this, the teacher divides students into topic groups in which they discuss their opinions and reactions to the topic. After participating in group discussion, students individually write an essay from position statements and supporting reasons.

Phase 3–Independent Practice. In this phase, students advance from working in groups to completing the process alone. Students complete the following Personal Reaction Chart to prepare for writing a supported reaction.

Personal Reaction Chart

Author and Title _____

Issue/Topic _____

Before Reading

In the following categories, note your feelings about the issue/topic

Experiences _____

Pro _____

Con _____

Attitudes _____

Importance _____

_____

After Reading

In a single sentence, write the main point of the selection.

_____

After thinking about and/or discussing the selection, develop your personal reaction to it in writing. First, state your overall reaction. Then defend your position.

After writing their individual reactions, students discuss opposing points of view in topic groups. Students then add two pararaphs to their individual written reactions. One of these paragraphs presents an alternate point of view and its supporting arguments. The other paragraph presents the student's response to the alternate point of view.

Phase 4—Analyzing Selections.   Given sufficient practice in writing reactions under the foregoing conditions, students should be able to analyze a selection independently for an author's point of view and for the rationale used to support the author's position. To develop skill in identifying elements of persuasion, students' own reactions can be used to examine the process of determining an author's intent. The charts shown below help students formulate paragraphs that discuss almost any selection and its author.

Author Intent Chart

Who is the Author?

Name _____

Reputation _____

_____

Qualifications to comment on the issue _____

_____

Writes for readers who _____

_____

Other _____

_____

Author's Perspective

Pro side _____

Con side _____

Author's side _____

Author's Purpose

To inform the reader that _____

_____

To convince the reader to _____

_____

To persuade the reader to _____

_____

Critical Analysis Guide

List the facts given in the selection:

List the opinions stated in the selection:

The selection seems:

_____ serious	_____ humorous	_____ ironic
_____ formal	_____ happy	_____ tongue-in-cheek
_____ sad	_____ cordial	_____ sarcastic
_____ motivational	other _____	

List loaded words, euphemisms, slogans:

The selection attempts to persuade through:

_____ logic:	_____ name-calling/ridicule:
_____ facts/evidence:	_____ plain folks/common sense:
_____ appeal to authority:	_____ bandwagon:
_____ testimonial:	

Discussion

React-Then-Analyze has several strengths. Students enjoy discussing differing points of view. They become confident with taking risks, with being the only person in a group with a particular point of view. With successive writing experiences, students become more sensitive to the issues related to a topic and deepen their level of response to these issues. Reacting to issues through a routine process helps students become better organized and more skillful in writing. Writing is treated as part of the learning process, not as an end product.

The major limitation of the method is the amount of time it takes initially. Once students learn the process, however, they can move through it rapidly.

EXAMPLE

An eighth-grade health class is beginning a unit on teen pregnancy. Having introduced the topic, the teacher asks students what they think about teen pregnancy.

Teacher: We certainly hear a lot about teen pregnancy these days. How do you feel about it? Sandra?

Sandra: Well, pregnant is something I don't intend to be while I'm a teenager.

Donna: Me neither.

Billy: But it could happen.

Sandra: Not to me.

Andy: It seems that, from a physical standpoint anyways, the teenage years are the best time to have a baby. That's when a girl has her youth and strength and everything like that going for her.

Donna: Going against her really.

Teacher: What do you mean, Donna?

Donna: I don't think teenage girls are physically stronger than women in their twenties. And because they *are* teenagers, they don't have a husband to help take care of the baby when it comes.

The teacher is writing students' comments on the chalkboard.

Teacher: These are points worth noting. Let's hear some more of what you think.

Janie: A teenage pregnancy could wreck your whole life. It could mess up things with your parents. You'd have a hard time going to school.

Sandra: And that means your job possibilities aren't going to be there later on.

Johnny: It don't always mess you up. Look at Sharon. She's pregnant and still in school. And her parents didn't throw her out.

Donna: But everybody thinks she's a trollop.

As students continue giving their reactions to the matter of teen pregnancy, the teacher continues writing them down on the chalkboard.

Teacher: Now that we have a long list of your feelings about teen pregnancy, let's sort out the things you've said. Over here on the side of the board, let's make five columns and head them like this: Experiences, Pro, Con, Attitudes, and Importance. Let's transfer the items in the list to the column where it best fits.

Andy: What I said about teenage girls being physically fit for having babies–that's a *pro*.

Donna: And what I said about having no husband is a *con*.

Janie: I said pregnancy messes up a teenager's education and stuff–that goes under *con*.

Teacher: What about Sandra's comment that she doesn't intend to become pregnant as a teenager?

Billy: Attitude. That's definitely an attitude.

Teacher: And your pointing out that there is a teenager you know who is pregnant–that goes here under *Experiences*.

Once the class has categorized the list of comments about teen pregnancy, the teacher presents students with copies of an editorial from the school newspaper about teen pregnancy.

Teacher: You may remember this editorial that appeared in your student newspaper last fall. Very quickly skim the editorial to get its gist and then read it carefully to get the main point.

The students skim and then carefully read the editorial as directed. When it appears that students have finished reading, the teacher engages students in a discussion that leads them to write a statement that summarizes the editorial.

Teacher: How closely do your feelings about teen pregnancy, the ones we listed and categorized on the board, agree with this editorial?

Sandra: The writer and I are of the same mind.

Donna: That goes for me, too.

Teacher: Tell us, Donna, what *is* the point, or the main point, of this editorial?

Donna: That teen pregnancy is a problem.

Teacher: And what do *you* think? Do you agree that teen pregnancy is really a problem?

Donna: You know I do. I already said having a baby when you're a teenager messes up your life.

Johnny: Didn't mess up Sharon's.

Donna: Did, too.

Sandra: I agree with Donna. It's definitely a problem.

Janie: Me, too.

Several: It's a problem.

Teacher: Apparently most of you agree teen pregnancy is a problem. All right. Let's write that here on the chalkboard.

The teacher writes: I AGREE THAT TEEN PREGNANCY IS A PROBLEM.

Teacher: You have already given your own reasons why you think teen pregnancy is a problem—and some of you why you think it's not. The editorial argues that it is. Can you cite some of the points the editorial gave to make that argument?

Janie: In the United States, the birth rate is declining in every group except teenagers.

Andy: Four out of ten girls who turn fourteen this year will have a teen pregnancy.

Johnny: Television, rock music, and peer groups have been shown to influence sexual promiscuity.

Teacher: (listing these points of information at the chalkboard) All right. Is there anything said in the editorial to suggest that teen pregnancy is *not* a significant problem?

Johnny: It mentions the AIDS scare. That's the real problem—AIDS.

Billy: Yeah, AIDS makes it risky to have sex nowadays. People have always had sex and got married as teenagers, which I guess has been a problem. But AIDS is a new thing, and it makes us more aware of sex and teenagers having sex.

Teacher: All right. Underneath the list of points supporting the editorial's main argument, let's write down this *alternate point of view.*

The teacher writes: TEEN PREGNANCY ALWAYS A PROBLEM. AIDS DRAWS OUR ATTENTION TO IT.

Teacher: Now let's turn our position statement and supporting points into a short essay. Let's include in the essay a paragraph on the alternate point of view having to do with AIDS. Following this paragraph, though, add a paragraph that answers the alternate point of view.

From the students' essays, an example is selected to share with the class. Subsequent activities resemble this teacher-guided, whole-class exercise. Students progress to working in discussion groups and finally to working independently.

Teen Pregnancy a Problem
by Laurel Boykin

On Thursday, September 29, I attended a talk on teen sexuality at Charter Winds. My mother, along with some of my friends and their moms, also went to the meeting. I felt that the statistics were very surprising and thought I should report them. I realize that this is a very sensitive topic, but I think you can handle it.

Teen pregnancy is obviously a problem in Oconee County, just as it is everywhere, whether we want to admit it or not. Four out of 10 girls who turn fourteen this year in the U.S. will likely have a child while they are still in their teenage years. Do you realize that this includes the eighth-grade girls at our school now? Who knows what the statistics will be for future fourteen-year-olds? I don't know about you, but I find this absolutely appalling!

Another fact is that the birth rate is going down in every age group except teenagers.

Recently, Emory University and Grady Hospital did some surveys involving teenagers and sex. By asking the teenagers, they found that the three major influences for sexual behavior among teens were, in order: (1) TV—from soap operas, nightly shows, and MTV; (2) Rock music—from the lyrics; and (3) from the individual's peer group.

Apparently, however, teenagers do know why they should postpone sex. They said the reasons they should wait were because of pregnancy, the very fact that they were too young to have sex, and they could get a sexually transmitted disease such as AIDS.

In my opinion, all teenagers are too young to have sex. It seems to be the "big thing" for teens nowadays to get pregnant and then get married. This is a big mistake! They aren't even mature enough to take on the responsibility of a small child, much less an early marriage. Also, it is almost impossible for a teenage couple to support a child financially. You need to remember that without a high school and college education, it is very hard to get a good job in today's world.

Having a baby at an early age can not only ruin your life but it could also ruin your baby's. You wouldn't be capable of giving it a stable home or caring for all of its needs.

There is no doubt that something has got to be done. These staggering statistics have got to be changed. I don't have the solution, but perhaps this column will lead to a little more awareness on everyone's part. The problem is there, now what are we going to do?

Source: Laurel Boykin (October 1988). *Smoke Signals* (student newspaper of Oconee County, GA, Intermediate School). Volume 6, number 1, p. 2.

Source

Martha A. Brueggeman. (1986). React first, analyze second: Using editorials to teach the writing process. *Journal of Reading, 30*, 234–239.

SECTION FIVE

Presenting Subject Matter Spatially

The teacher may communicate subject matter to students in a variety of ways, ranging from telling about it with words to showing it with pictures. On the continuum between telling with words and showing with pictures are many possibilities for combining the advantages of both. Indeed, it is typical for the teacher to use some combination of language and spatial representation to explain and illustrate the content of a lesson. Although the teacher relies mainly on verbal means to deliver a lesson, much of the material is illustrated with presentational devices such as graphs and diagrams. Using space and pattern as well as language, the teacher can express conceptual information that could not be understood if it were expressed with language or pictures alone. The teacher can use words to name and comment on things and, at the same time, use nonlinguistic information to exploit the visual possibilities for understanding the material.

Language is basic to communication, but some things make a great deal more sense when there is a spatial dimension to the presentation. A spatial presentation not only offers an alternate access to material presented verbally but, more important, it provides additional information that shows how parts of the material are related. Unlike a strictly verbal presentation, a spatial presentation can be grasped all at once. Seeing simultaneously different aspects of material to be learned, students can integrate that material immediately into a comprehensible whole.

Numerous methods have been developed for teaching subject matter through spatial presentations. These include methods both for presenting subject matter directly by the teacher and for teaching students how to make effective use of spatial displays that are presented in textual materials. The instructional purposes served by these methods are to help students:

- *Visualize complex relations and interactions in the subject matter*
- *Search actively for relational ties among concepts*
- *Discover the usefulness of graphic displays*
- *Organize information hierarchically, where appropriate*
- *Read and review important information carefully*
- *Check the correctness of knowledge about the process, structure, and ways that aspects of subject matter are related*
- *Explore correspondences between concepts and their applications*
- *Identify essential vocabulary*
- *Attend to the organization of details and events in narrative material*
- *Recognize main ideas and important themes*

These are the purposes that the methods of this section are designed to meet.

45

Concept Mapping

Concept Mapping helps students translate lectures and written texts into graphic form. It assists students in visualizing complex relations and interactions, encourages critical thinking, and improves memory of new information. Concept Mapping is also useful for organizing information from several sources in preparation for writing.

As students create a spatial representation of an oral or written discourse, they symbolize and organize ideas in ways that force constructive decision making. They have to analyze and evaluate information, determine how to structure it, and then decide how best to turn the information into visual form. Through positioning and connecting information with lines, students can show relatedness of different sorts: example, feature, cause-effect, compare-contrast, sequence, and so on. Students can usually represent a large amount of information on a single piece of paper. Such a representation allows many pieces of information and their relatedness to be seen all at once. Thus, Concept Mapping provides an alternate, more efficient form of representing information than ordinary notetaking. This representation may stimulate the imaging of additional categories of information not given in the presentation itself.

Concept Mapping is appropriate for a variety of instructional situations. It can be used with individuals, small groups, or whole classes. It may be used with slow learners and with very young students if the teacher has time to work alongside them. Students who are experienced with the technique can use it in independent study and in writing assignments. Many mature and bright students say that Concept Mapping adds enjoyment as well as a measure of clarity to independent study tasks. Concept Mapping may be used effectively across the academic subjects. Most activities can be completed well within a 45- to 50-minute class period.

Procedure

Concept Mapping may proceed in several ways. It may be used before, during, or following an oral or textual presentation, and it may be used for any number of instructional purposes. The basic function of Concept Mapping itself is to reveal relatedness in information. With the procedure described here, the method can be introduced by the teacher and practiced by students until they can fashion an outline independently.

The best way to introduce Concept Mapping is with a text selection (preferably from students' textbook) on a topic with which students already have some knowledge. The teacher introduces the selection by placing on one side of the chalkboard a partial display of the material to be read. Included in this partial display may be the selection's topic and main ideas, or it may simply present the topic and slots labeled with the kind of information to be shown.

The teacher asks students to tell what they already know about the topic and lists their comments on the display in places where they seem to fit. Then the teacher directs students to read the selection in order to see if their existing knowledge about the topic is correct and to see if there is other information they need to know. While students read, the teacher places on the other side of the chalkboard the original partial display of the material, but without students' elaborations. When students finish reading, the teacher calls on them to finish this display with information gleaned from reading. Students compare the two and see the likenesses and differences in what they know, or thought they knew, and the text's presentation of the topic.

The teacher then assigns students to read another selection and, after reading, to construct a concept map of what they have read. Students may be asked to do this individually or in small groups. The teacher may provide a partial display that students may use as a guide or ask them to make a concept map from scratch. The teacher is likely to obtain better results from less able students if they are told the number of details to include on the concept map.

Discussion

Concept Mapping can be a powerful method of instruction because it makes use of students' spatial-visual abilities for understanding and remembering complex subject matter. Through Concept Mapping activities, students learn skills of organization that aid in the development of comprehension, critical thinking, and writing skills. Also, students' participation in learning is maximized, and the teacher can be available to react to students' needs as they work through the details of an assignment.

To teach effectively with Concept Mapping, the teacher needs to be familiar with the subject matter and be able to show how main ideas and their supporting details are related. Depicting relatedness of information in texts can become quite a cumbersome task if the selection is lengthy. To address this problem, an overview can be constructed with main ideas only, followed by a series of detailed concept maps.

▌ EXAMPLE

A sixth-grade social studies class is studying the geography of the United States. To introduce the state of Texas, the teacher has brought copies of a brief selection that contains identifying information about the state. The teacher presents the selection with a concept map activity.

Teacher: On the board, I've written the name of the next state we'll study – Texas. I've also placed around the name *Texas* labels of the kinds of information that give Texas its distinctive identity.

Sue Ellen: Oh, I know a Texas city – Dallas.

Ellie: And there's Houston, too.

Teacher: (writing these on the board) Good. What else do you already know about Texas?

Jet: They got oil there.

Teacher: (writing on the board) Oil. OK. Anything else?

Roy: When you think of Texas, you always think of cowboys. Texas is cowboy country.

Dale: Yeah. Its nickname is the cowboy state.

David: I think of the Alamo. Remember the Alamo!

Jenna: And, hey, Texas is the biggest state in the country.

Teacher: (continuing to write on the board) Anything else? OK. Let's read this short passage to find out more about Texas.

As students read, the teacher places the original partial display on the right side of the chalkboard. The display does not include students' comments. The teacher draws the figure of a five-point star around the name *Texas*, with each point extending to one of the labels for the state's distinguishing information.

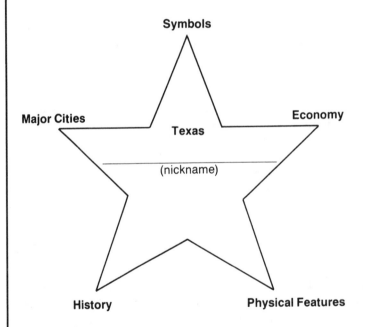

Teacher: Was what you already know about Texas correct?

Dale: It's nickname is not the cowboy state. It's the Lone Star state.

Teacher: Let's write that on the line for nicknames. Let's also put a big star around the name *Texas* to help us remember it's the Lone Star state.

Jenna: Texas is only the second biggest state. I was wrong.

Teacher: OK. We'll just put the correct information here on our revision.

Jet: What I said about the oil being there. That's right.

The discussion continues until all the details given in the selection are added to the concept map, whereupon the teacher divides the class into groups of three students each and assigns them to fashion a concept map with information they glean from a textbook section on the coastal plains region of Texas.

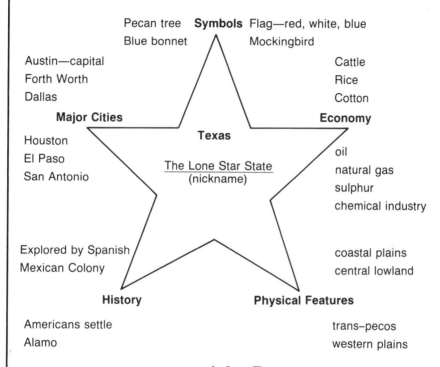

I Am Texas
by Joyce Maxwell

I am the second largest state. My tree is the pecan tree, which makes large shade. Squirrels like my tree because they like to eat pecans. My flower is the bluebonnet. They grow pretty along the highways. Another symbol of mine is the mockingbird, which you may see flying in all of my regions. My regions are the coastal plains, the central lowlands, the western plains, and the trans-pecos. Austin is my capital. My other big cities are Dallas, Fort Worth, Houston, San Antonio, and El Paso.

I was explored by the Spanish in the sixteenth century and colonized by them as part of Mexico. After Mexico became independent in 1821, large numbers of Americans came to me. At the Alamo, a great battle between the Americans and the Mexicans was fought for me.

Cowboys used to roam my plains, herding longhorns. Branding was used to show ownership of cattle that wandered over the vast country. Livestock ranching continues to be an important agricultural economy, along with cotton and rice farming. My chemical industries and my oil, natural gas, and sulphur deposits make up most of my economy.

My flag consists of three colors, which are red, white, and blue. It has one star on it. That is where I get my nickname, "The Lone Start State." I am Texas.

Sources

Jane L. Davidson. (1981). The Group Mapping Activity for instruction in reading and thinking. *Journal of Reading, 25,* 52–57.

Bob Gowin. (1981). *Educating.* Ithaca, NY: Cornell University Press.

M. Buckley Hanf. (1971). Mapping: A technique for translating reading into thinking. *Journal of Reading, 14,* 225–229.

Related Readings

Stephen Aldersley and Gary Long. (1980). *Networking: A technique for organizing what you read.* Rochester, NY: National Institute for the Deaf, Rochester Institute of Technology.

Edward Fry. (1981). Graphical literacy. *Journal of Reading, 24,* 383–390.

Linda Lee Johnson. (1989). Learning across the curriculum with creative graphing. *Journal of Reading, 32,* 509–519.

Jeannette L. Miccinati. (1988). Mapping the terrain: Connecting reading with academic writing. *Journal of Reading, 31,* 542–552.

Richard Sinatra, Josephine Stahl-Gemake, and Nancy Wyche Morgan. (1986). Using semantic mapping after reading to organize and write original discourse. *Journal of Reading, 30,* 4–13.

46

Story Mapping

Story Mapping shows how key elements of a story are organized. It serves to heighten students' awareness of story structure, to enhance their critical reading skills, and to improve their memory of story material.

Story Mapping is based on the idea that students' comprehension and memory of narrative material can be increased by creating a visual display of its important elements. The display makes readers' thinking about plot, characters, and setting visible. With a clear perception of how these elements are structured, students can discern relevant information and assign appropriate importance to various aspects of a story. It is on this kind of awareness that critical comprehension depends. Also, because information is easier to remember if it is organized, having a structure within which to place information about a story helps students remember it better.

This technique may be used across the elementary and secondary grades for any instruction that involves narrative material. It is especially well suited for teaching fictional literature in English and language arts classes, and it can be put to good use in studying narrative accounts in history classes. Story Mapping is one approach the teacher may take to present narrative material. It is perhaps best used, however, as a study activity in which students create and discuss their own visual displays in order to clarify and expand their thinking about narrative material.

Procedure

As a technique for presenting narrative material, Story Mapping is straightforward. The teacher jots down notes on the chalkboard about the narrative material as it unfolds. The information is positioned so as to show how it is related to other information. The teacher draws in connecting lines to show this relatedness and to show direction of the action. The teacher describes the in-process thinking that underlies the development of the map.

To teach students how to map narrative material for themselves, the teacher explicitly describes the procedure itself. The teacher introduces Story Mapping with a selection familiar to the students and explains the purpose of the technique with the rationale that seeing how a story is put together helps in understanding it. Making reference to the familiar story, the teacher briefly defines the story elements to be mapped. The *setting* describes the time and place in which the story unfolds. It also presents the *protagonist* and other *major characters*. The *problem or goal* introduces the question that the characters try to resolve or the result they are trying to attain. The *plot* comprises *episodes* or events that occur in the narrative. Simple stories may have only one event, whereas complicated stories have many. The *theme* of the story refers to an underlying message, idea, or moral that addresses universal human concerns. It usually requires an inference on the part of the reader. It usually refers to the author's overall purpose for writing the story. Themes are often related to love and friendship, good and evil, hope and resourcefulness, and the like. The *resolution* is the result of the characters' efforts to solve the problem or achieve the goal.

Having introduced the elements common to all stories, the teacher shows students an example of a map of the familiar story and explains the construction of the map to them. This explanation describes the teacher's own process of thinking that produced the map. Students are then directed to read a less familiar story. The teacher demonstrates how this story may be mapped by leading students through a discussion of its elements. The teacher's demonstration incorporates suggestions offered by students. At this point, the teacher may provide students with a partially drawn map to complete on their own. When students complete this map, they share the results. Finally, students are assigned to map a selection independently.

Discussion

Students are usually responsive to Story Mapping. They enjoy creating maps of their own, and if the purpose is effectively explained to them, they see it as a functional and relevant exercise. Story Mapping also increases students' interest in the stories they map. Low achievers are likely to benefit most from this procedure because it helps put abstract concepts into concrete terms that the student can use. It encourages inferential comprehension as it develops skills of sequencing, recognizing cause and effect, and predicting outcomes.

Story Mapping is easy to teach and easy to learn, if the teacher begins with simple stories and offers ample demonstration. Students may be stymied by complex stories and overwhelmed by stories with many characters and episodes. Some students may find it difficult to abbreviate map entries in order to keep it manageable and clear. Some students may also find it difficult to determine theme, which requires making an inference.

EXAMPLE

A high school English class is studying the elements of fiction. The teacher's aim is to teach students how to map these elements in diagrams of stories they read.

Teacher: You've probably noticed that when we talk about the stories in our anthology, I often sketch them on the board. What I sketch is called a story map.

Elise: It sure helps clear things up when a story gets complicated.

Teacher: It does help. A story map is more than a device that a teacher can use to explain a story. It's a tool that any reader can make in order to study a story.

Al: Can't we understand stories well enough just by reading them?

Teacher: You certainly don't always have to map a story to understand it. But as Elise says, it can help if the story is complicated. The way it helps is to sort out the parts of a story so you can see how the parts work together. Seeing how things are organized helps you see how things function.

Nathan: You've used story maps in teaching the stories in the class. I think I get the general drift of how you would make one, but I'm not sure I could make one as good as yours.

Teacher: What's important is that the map serves to increase your understanding, not that it be clever or measure up to someone else's map.

Amelia: How do you start?

Teacher: First you should be clear about what the basic elements of story are.

Ricardo: You mean like characters and plot and things like that?

Teacher: Right. Let's go over them. You've said characters. Every story has characters.

Elise: There's plot.

Teacher: Yes, there is plot. But when we think of plot, we should think of what makes a plot.

Loretta: You mean like the problem the characters face?

Al: And what the characters try to accomplish?

Teacher: Right. If there is no problem or conflict, there is no story. And for there to be a story, the characters have to be acting toward reaching a goal.

Ricardo: The things that happen are called events or episodes.

Loretta: And the way things turn out is called the resolution.

Teacher: You know your story elements well.

Nathan: Stories have a setting. They take place some where and at some time.

Teacher: Good.

Amelia: And there's what teachers just love to talk about–the theme.

Teacher: The theme–the underlying message or moral. When you make a map, you give the essential information about each of these story elements. To show you what I mean, let me show you how I would map a simple and familiar story.

The teacher presents a story map of the fairy tale "Cinderella," explaining why its story elements are placed as they are. Then the teacher assigns students to read an unfamiliar story that the class can map together. As students read, the teacher fashions a template of a story map on the chalkboard.

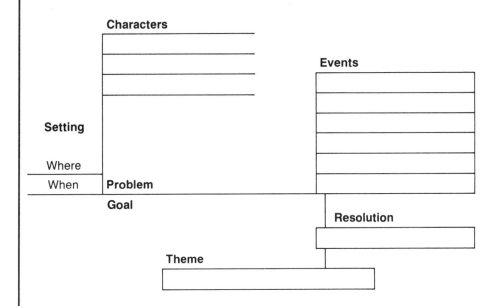

Teacher: It appears that everyone has finished reading. Let's try mapping this together. On the board, I've put the template of a map that we can fill in.

Ricardo: Filling in information about the setting will be hard to do. The story doesn't say anything about when the story took place.

Nathan: Nor about where it happened, really. It mentions a village called Peretola, but that's not where most of the action was.

Teacher: Given that the author was an Italian who lived during the fourteenth century, we have some clues about the setting.

Amelia: One of the characters was from Venice. The characters have Italian-sounding names. I think it's safe to say the story was set in Italy.

Elise: And it happened long ago.

Teacher: I think you're right. Where should I write that information?

Al: In the spaces at the far left.

Teacher: What about the characters?

Loretta: List them on the lines attached to the line called Characters.

Ricardo: There's Chichibio. He's the main character, so list him at the top.

Al: There's Currado.

Elise: And Brunetta.

Teacher: Good. So what problem did they face that made this a story.

Nathan: It was really only Chichibio who faced a problem. He angered his master, Currado, and faced being punished. . . .

Teacher: You've described the problem well, and you've clearly stated the goal.

Al: So write the problem above the line connecting the Setting and the Events box. Write, "Chichibio angers Currado."

Amelia: And under that line, write the goal: "Chichibio seeks to escape Currado's punishment."

Teacher: What happened in the story? What events took place?

Nathan: The first thing that happened was that Currado's hawk captured a crane, which Currado sent home for Chichibio to cook.

Loretta: Write that in the Events box.

Ricardo: Next, write that Brunetta persuades Chichibio to give her one of the crane's legs. . . .

Teacher: So Chichibio and Currado came upon cranes standing on one foot as they sleep. Is that another event to write down?

Loretta: You should write that as the Resolution.

Al: There's more to the resolution than that. Currado shouts at the cranes, that then walk on both feet before flying away. Chichibio says that the crane that had been cooked the night before would have also had two legs if Currado would have shouted at it. Currado sees the whole thing as humorous.

Teacher: OK. Good, let me just abbreviate that they find cranes standing on one foot and that Chichibio makes a joke.

Nathan: Is there a point being made here? Is there a theme?

Teacher: Good question.

Elise: I think it's that giving in to pressure to do something wrong can lead to a dreadful result later.

Ricardo: But the result was only Chichibio's dread. Nothing actually came of his offense.

Amelia: I agree. I think the theme is that we should not be offended by slight traspasses.

Al: There may be a bit more to it. Humor can help us see that some offenses are not serious enough to justify giving out a harsh penalty.

Several: Yes. That's the theme. Write it in the box underneath the Resolution.

The teacher enters this as the theme in the place provided on the map on the chalkboard.

Teacher: Good. I think you're ready to try mapping a story on your own. That's what you are to do with the next story beginning on page. . . .

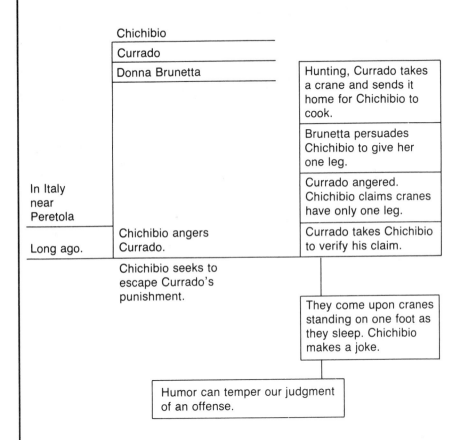

Neifile's Story (The Sixth Day)
by Giovanni Boccaccio, 1350

Currado Gianfigliazzi, always esteemed a gallant and worthy citizen, delighted much in hounds and hawks. Now he having taken a crane one day with his hawk, near the village of Peretola, and finding it to be young and fat, sent it home to his cook, who was a Venetian, and called Chichibio, with orders to prepare it delicately for supper. The cook, a poor simple fellow, trussed and spitted it, and when it was nearly roasted, and began to smell pretty well, it chanced that a woman in the neighborhood called Brunetta, of whom he was much enamoured, came into the kitchen, and, being taken with the high savour, earnestly begged of him to give her a leg. He replied very merrily, singing all the time, "Donna Brunetta, you shall have no leg from me." Upon this she was a good deal nettled, and said, "As I hope to live, if you do not give it me, you need never expect any favor more from me." The dispute, at length, was carried to a great height between them; when, to make her easy, he was forced to give her one of the legs.

The crane was served up at supper, with only one leg, whereat a friend whom Currado had invited to sup with him expressed surprise. He therefore sent for the fellow, and demanded what was become of the other leg. The Venetian (a liar by nature) answered directly, "Sir, cranes have only one leg." Currado, in great wrath, said, "What the deveil does the man talk of? Only one leg! Thou rascal, dost thou think I never saw a crane before?" Chichibio still persisted in his denial, saying, "Believe me, sir, it is as I say, and I will convince you of it whenever you please, by such fowls as are living." Currado was willing to have no more words, out of regard to his friend; only he added, "As thou undertakest to show me a thing which I never saw or heard of before, I am content to make proof thereof tomorrow morning; but I vow and protest, if I find it otherwise, I will make thee remember it the longest day thou hast to live."

Thus there was an end for that night, and the next morning Currado, whose passion would scarcely suffer him to get any rest, arose betimes, and ordered his horses to be brought out, taking Chichibio along with him towards a river where he used early in the morning to see plenty of cranes; and he said, "We shall soon see which of us spoke truth last night." Chichibio, finding his master's wrath not at all abated, and that he was now to make good what he had asserted, nor yet knowing how to do it, rode on first with all the fear imaginable; gladly would he have made his escape, but he saw no possible means, whilst he was continually looking about him, expecting everything that appeared to be a crane with two feet. But being come near to the river, he chanced to see, before anybody else, a dozen or so of cranes, each standing upon one leg, as they use to do when they are sleeping; whereupon, showing them quickly to his master, he said, "Now, sir, you yourself may see that I spoke nothing but truth, when I said that cranes have only one leg: look at those there, if you please." Currado, beholding the cranes, replied, "Yes, sirrah! But stay awhile, and I will show thee that they have two." Then riding something nearer to them, he cried out, "Shough! Shough!" which made them set down the other foot, and after taking a step or two they all flew away. Then Currado, turning to him, said, "Well, thou lying knave, art thou now convinced that they have two legs?" Chichibio, quite at his wits' end, and knowing scarcely what he said himself, suddenly made answer, "Yes, sir, but you did not shout out to that crane last night, as you have done to these; had you called to it in the same manner, it would have put down the other leg, as these have now done." This pleased Currado so much that, turning all wrath into mirth and laughter, he said, "Chichibio, thou sayest right; I should have done so indeed."

By this sudden and comical answer, Chichibio escaped a sound drubbing, and made peace with his master.

Source: Giovanni Boccaccio's "Neifile's Story" (the sixth day), *Tales from the Decameron,* New York: Washington Square Press. Reprinted with permission.

Sources

James F. Baumann and Peg Quigley Ballard. (1987). A two step model for promoting independence in comprehension. *Journal of Reading, 40,* 608–613.

M. Dianne Bergenske. (1987). The missing link in narrative story mapping. *The Reading Teacher, 41,* 333–335.

Dorothy J. Dixon. (1989). Story flow charts. *Journal of Reading, 32,* 456–458.

Laura Seidner Robb. (1989). Mapping the 'agonists. *The Reading Teacher, 42,* 549.

Ronald Schmelzer, Joyce Adkins, Cynthia Alsip, April Bales, Peggy Elliot, Gilbert Irvine, Rebecca Lavender, Barbara Taylor, Kimberly Trammell, and Janel Wheeler. (1989). Episodic mapping: A technique to help students understand and remember stories. *Kentucky Reading Journal, 11,* 8–11.

47

Semantic Mapping

Semantic Mapping lets students see how the defining features of a concept are related. Students are shown how to develop a diagram (map) for clarifying the meanings of subject matter concepts. In Semantic Mapping, students learn the uses of key vocabulary and organize their thinking for carrying out reading and writing tasks.

Students participate in the construction of a visual display that places a subject matter concept within a category (or network of categories), specifies its properties, and identifies examples. In the activity, students become familiar with the substance of the concept and the ways in which its elements are linked. They see how the general is linked with the specific within the concept and how the concept itself fits within a larger category of knowledge. With a diagram of an abstraction central to understanding the subject matter, students can orient themselves appropriately for carrying out study tasks attendant to it. Used before reading, Semantic Mapping activates relevant knowledge and supplies information students need for comprehending the text. Used after reading, Semantic Mapping refocuses attention on the main ideas presented in the text as students recall and graphically represent the information read.

Semantic Mapping is a highly useful approach to clarifying concepts in any academic subject. It is especially well suited for teaching concepts in literature, social studies, and science. It can be used to explain concepts in mathematics (but it would be of little value in teaching computational procedures). Semantic Mapping may be employed effectively in the elementary grades and beyond. It may be adapted for use with individuals, small groups, or whole classes.

Procedure

Semantic Mapping is used to illustrate concepts that are likely to be difficult for students to understand. The teacher initiates Semantic Mapping for each such concept by writing the term for the concept prominently in the middle of the chalkboard. The teacher asks students to think about the term and to say out words they associate with it. The teacher lists these word associations on one side of the chalkboard as they are given. The teacher or students may add words or phrases associated with the concept at any time during the lesson.

In a discussion of how the word associations are related to the concept being examined, each is transferred to a list under one of three headings that the teacher has written on the other side of the chalkboard: Class, Properties, and Examples. Once the word associations are transferred, the unordered list is erased and each of the three new lists is discussed in turn.

A label suggested by the list of words under the Class heading is written at the top of the chalkboard and above the focal term written at the middle of the chalkboard. The label is enclosed in a circle or box and a line is drawn to connect it with the focal term. By positioning the Class label above the focal term, the concept represented by this focal term is shown to be an instance of the superordinate Class set. Words from the Class list are placed around the Class label so as to show which words are components or subordinate features of others. Words that represent parallel instances of the concept being discussed are positioned so as to show their parallel status. This may be accomplished by listing other instances of the category on the left of the focal term and connecting each with a line up to the Class label.

To the right of the focal term, the teacher places words that represent Properties of the concept being mapped. The way in which these properties interrelate is shown with position relative to one another and with connecting lines. Beneath the central term, the teacher writes the Examples of the concept and draws lines to show their relatedness and relative standing.

Discussion

With Semantic Mapping, the teacher clarifies subject matter through working with students to diagram important concepts. As subject matter is presented in this way, students become informed about how to deal with a difficult concept. First, they analyze it according to feature categories for defining any concept (class, property, example), and then they examine the connections among the features. Semantic Mapping is informative for the teacher as well. In both the word association and diagramming activities, students reveal to the teacher what they know and do not know about the concept. With this information, the teacher may adjust the focus and emphasis of instruction. For example, students may need to know more about the general category to which a concept belongs before exploring the properties and examples of the concept itself in much depth.

Semantic Mapping is helpful for students across the range of academic ability, though it has most to offer students who have difficulty with analyzing abstract material. Given three major categories for placing information about a concept, students have a starting place for sorting their thoughts. Analyzing a concept into these categories first makes the diagramming task more manageable. Once a semantic map is constructed, it provides anchor points upon which further concepts can be introduced.

EXAMPLE

A high school English class is reading and discussing lyric poetry. In this lesson, the teacher's purposes are to present characteristics of the sonnet and to acquaint students with some well-known sonnets.

Teacher: Now, here's a sonnet that combines both the English and Italian forms. It's called a *Spenserian sonnet,* after Edmund Spenser.

Archie: I'm confused. I'm enjoying these poems and I do appreciate the skill of the poets, but I'm lost. I thought this unit was on lyric poetry, but we're reading poems that you call a lot of different names.

Elinor: I'm having the same confusion. Sometimes we call these poems *lyric poems,* and sometimes we call them other things like *ballads* and *odes* and *sonnets.*

Daniel: And these sonnets you call a lot of things: English, Italian, Shakespearean, Petrarchan.

Teacher: Well sonnets *are* lyrics, and so are ballads and odes, among others.

Elizabeth: Are lyrics sonnets, then?

Sid: Are sonnets ballads?

Teacher: You are confused. Let's see if we can get all of this cleared up.

The teacher writes the word *sonnet* in the middle of the chalkboard.

Teacher: I've written the term *sonnet* here in the middle of the board. On the side of the board, I'm going to write down what you say comes to your mind when you see or hear the term *sonnet.*

Archie: What comes to my mind is abbuh-abbuh-seedy-seedy-seedy.

Teacher: Uh ba-duh? I'd like to write that down, but I don't quite get what that has to do with the sonnet.

Archie: Abbuh-abbuh-seedy-seedy-seedy. You know, the rhyme scheme a-b-b-a-a-b-b-a c-d-c-d-c-d.

Teacher: Oh, OK. Sure. That's good.

Edna: There's also a-b-a-b c-d-c-d e-f-e-f g-g.

Teacher: Terrific memory, both of you. I'm impressed.

Sid: You gave us a quiz on it at the beginning of class today.

Wyatt: Fourteen lines.

Daniel: Love.

Elizabeth: "How do I love thee? Let me count the ways."

Daniel: "Shall I compare thee to a summer's day?"

Wyatt: Italian, English.

Edna: Petrarch, Shakespeare.

Elinor: Lyric poem.

Wyatt: Octave and sestet.

Daniel: Three quatrains and a couplet.

Sid: Iambic pentameter.

Archie: Odes and ballads.

Elizabeth: Romantic, emotional.

Teacher: Good. I think we have enough of your thoughts on this list to start getting the concept of sonnet straight. We can add words as we go.

The teacher has listed on the chalkboard the following unordered list of the students' free associations with the word *sonnet:*

> a-b-b-a a-b-b-a c-d-c-d-c-d
> a-b-a-b c-d-c-d e-f-e-f g-g
> 14 lines
> love
> "How do I love thee? Let me count the ways."
> "Shall I compare thee to a summer's day?"
> Italian
> English
> Petrarch
> Shakespeare
> lyric poem
> octave, sestet
> 3 quatrains and a couplet
> iambic pentameter
> odes
> ballads
> romantic
> emotional

Archie: But that list is as jumbled as my thoughts about sonnets.

Teacher: We're going to *un*jumble the list. We're going to sort out the concept about sonnets the way we would sort out any concept. We begin by putting information into categories—three major categories: class, properties, and examples.

Across the top of the left side of the chalkboard, the teacher writes the words *Class, Properties,* and *Examples.*

Daniel: Now you want us to tell you which words and phrases in the jumbled list to put under each of those headings.

Teacher: You know the direction we're heading. First tell me which of them to put under the Class heading.

Elinor: What do you mean by *class?*

Teacher: Class is the category of knowledge to which "sonnet" belongs. We would put here the more general category of poetry, as well as other kinds of poems that belong to that general category.

Edna: Oh, you mean like lyric poetry and different kinds of lyric poems?

Teacher: Right. I'll write "lyric poetry" under Class. What kinds of poems of the jumbled list are lyric poems?

Elinor: Ballads and odes.

Teacher: These are lyric poems because. . . .

The teacher defines lyric poetry, explaining that lyric poetry is itself one of the three great type-divisions of poetry, that it is identified by its properties of melody and unity of image, and that sonnets and the other kinds of poems named are examples of the forms of lyric poetry. As the discussion proceeds, the words and phrases from the unordered list are transferred to the columns under the three category headings:

Class	*Properties*	*Examples*
lyric poetry	14 lines	"How do I love thee?
ballads	octave + sestet	Let me count the ways."
odes	a-b-b-a-a-b-b-a c-d-c-d-c-d	"Shall I compare thee to a
	Italian, Petrarchan	summer's day?"
	3 quatrains + couplet	
	a-b-a-b c-d-c-d e-f-e-f g-g	
	English, Shakespearean	
	love	
	romantic	
	emotional	

Archie: Sorting this stuff into these categories helps, but I'm still confused about some things. Most of the Properties list is still a jumble to me.

Teacher: We have some more *unjumbling* yet to do. Through positioning the information from the category lists and connecting it with lines, we'll show how these bits of information about the sonnet are related.

Edna: Oh. We're going to use the category lists to make a diagram.

Teacher: Right. The kind of diagram we'll make is called a semantic map, because it shows how we can get at meaning by tracing paths that connect the different aspects of a concept. Let's begin by showing the class of poetry to which the sonnet belongs.

Wyatt: We said that it is a form of lyric poetry.

Teacher: So, let's write "lyric poetry" directly above the term *sonnet* and connect the two terms with a line. To remind ourselves how the terms are related, let's have the line show direction by making it an arrow and writing on this line the word *example*.

Sid: Other examples of lyric poetry are ballads and odes.

Teacher: All right. To show that these are other types of lyric poetry, that they are in the same class with the sonnet, we'll note them under "lyric poetry" and to the left side of *sonnet*.

Elinor: And then we draw an arrow line from "lyric poetry" to these types of poems.

Edna: And write the word *example* on the line.

Teacher: You're catching on. Now let's map the sonnet's properties.

Archie: That's a real jumble of stuff.

Teacher: It is, but I think we can manage it. All poems have three kinds of properties: form, subject, and mood. Let's draw three stems extending from the right side of the term *sonnet* and label each.

Elinor: One form is the English or Shakespearean sonnet.

Wyatt: The other form is the Italian or Petrarchan sonnet.

Teacher: Good. For each form I'll draw a line. I know there is information to put under each, so I'll provide space by separating them a bit. On the top line, I'll write the words *English* and *Shakespearean* with an equal sign between them to show that they're the same thing.

Elizabeth: And on the line below you should do the same thing to show that the Italian sonnet is the same as the Petrarchan sonnet.

Daniel: Both have fourteen lines.

Teacher: Right. All sonnets have fourteen lines, so I'll note that on the vertical line that connects these two different forms of sonnet.

Elinor: What makes these forms different is their rhyme scheme. The English sonnet is a-b-b-a c-d-c-d e-f-e-f g-g.

Teacher: I'll put that rhyme scheme on the line that I attach to the underside of the English sonnet line.

Sid: Three quatrains and a couplet.

Teacher: I'll attach a line below the rhyme scheme showing the three quatrains, label it, and below the end of the rhyme scheme I'll attach a label which I'll label "couplet." I'll also insert a plus sign to show that the couplet is a distinctive part of the poem that has been added to the quatrains.

Elizabeth: Do the same for the Italian form.

Wyatt: Put the rhyme scheme on a line you attach beneath the Italian sonnet line.

Elizabeth: And to that line attach two lines to show the octave and the sestet parts of the rhyme scheme.

Edna: Put a plus sign to indicate that the octave and the sestet are added together.

Teacher: Now, what shall we put for the subject of sonnets?

Several: Love, unrequited love.

Teacher: All right. I'll extend the stem for subject a bit and write in "love." What about the mood?

Several: Romantic. Emotional.

Teacher: That exhausts our properties list.

Archie: This has really helped to sort things out for me.

Daniel: What about the Examples list?

Teacher: We'll place things from that list beneath the term *sonnet*. And just as we indicated that the sonnet is an example of lyric poetry, we'll show that these particular poems are examples of the sonnet. We'll draw an arrow-line and label it *example*.

At this point the class has completed a semantic map of the students' existing knowledge of the concept sonnet. The teacher now moves to enhance students' knowledge of the sonnet by having them read the first part of the class anthology's

Semantic Map *Before* Reading

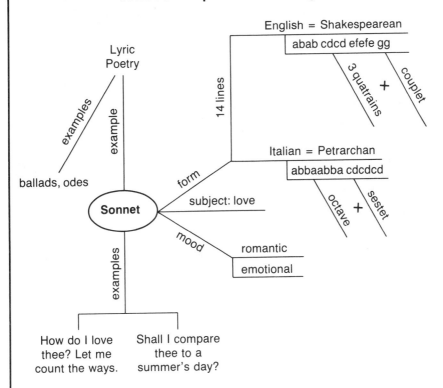

introduction to lyric poetry, which presents general information on lyric poetry and the sonnet. Following the reading, the teacher keeps the focus on the concept of sonnet by redirecting students' attention to the semantic map on the chalkboard.

Teacher: Before reading this segment in our anthology, we sorted out our thoughts about the sonnet by making this semantic map on the board. Now that we've done some reading, lets' modify the map. What did you read that we should add to our map?

Archie: There was more about lyric poetry. It's one of three major division-types of poetry.

Sid: The other major types are epic poetry and dramatic poetry.

Teacher: I'll write the word *poetry* above "lyric poetry" and draw an arrow-line to show that lyric poetry is a type of poetry. I'll label it *example*.

Edna: Beside "lyric poetry" you should write "epic poetry" and "dramatic poetry" and connect them with an arrow-line from "poetry," too. Label it *example*, too.

Elizabeth: Lyric is characterized by imagination, melody, and emotion.

Teacher: These are properties, so I'm mapping them to the right of "lyric poetry."

Elinor: The subject matter and mood vary according to the pattern of lyric poetry.

Teacher: What are these patterns?

Sid: We said earlier sonnet, ballad, and ode. They're already on the board. But we should add the elegy, song, and hymn. They're also examples of lyric poetry.

Teacher: What about the sonnet? What did the text say that we should add to our map?

Daniel: Mainly that there's a third form of sonnet—the Spenserian sonnet.

Edna: It combines the English and Italian forms.

Elinor: Like the English sonnet, it has three quatrains and a couplet. But it links the quatrains with its rhyme scheme—a-b-a-b b-c-b-c c-d-c-d e-e.

Teacher: I'll add the Spenserian form, note its rhyme scheme and that it combines the English and Italian forms.

Sid: I think we should change the way we show examples of sonnets. We should show them according to sonnet form.

Teacher: OK. Look up these sonnets in our anthology and check their rhyme schemes. Then tell me how to classify them.

Students examine the rhyme scheme of these sonnets and advise the teacher how to modify the semantic map. The teacher then recites the first line of a Spenserian sonnet that the class will read next. This sonnet is added to the map.

Lyric Poetry

Of the three type-divisions of poetry, the lyric is the most broadly inclusive. The epic restricts its concern to the recounting of history, and dramatic poetry is a vehicle for depicting situations. But the lyric is the medium of expression for the full range of human emotion and experience. The lyric is relatively brief. It is subjective poetry characterized by imagination, melody, and emotion. It attempts to create a focused and unified impression. The term *lyric* derives from the early Greek tradition of expressing emotion with the accompaniment of a lyre. Developed beyond the status of verse sung to the strains of a lyre, the lyric retains its melodic and rhythmic qualities. Over time, a variety of lyric patterns have evolved with the development of conscious artistry. The subject matter and mood vary with these patterns. Best known among lyric patterns are the sonnet, the ballad, and the ode. Also well known are the elegy, the hymn, and the song.

Semantic Map *After* Reading

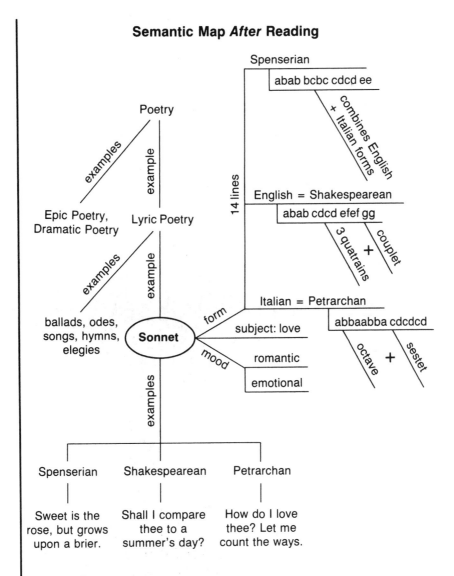

The Sonnet

The sonnet is synonymous with the contemplative love lyric. Well written, a sonnet creates a pleasant, musical effect. It is a form that places great demands on the technical skills of the poet. Its meter is iambic pentameter, and its rhyme patterns are fixed within a space of only fourteen lines.

The sonnet was introduced into English literature during the sixteenth century by Thomas Wyatt, who translated the work of Petrarch from the Italian. Still employed by skillful poets, Petrarch's form divides the sonnet into an octave and a sestet, abbaabba cdcdcd. The octave presents a problem and the sestet resolves it.

Elizabethan poets found the Italian form too restrictive and so developed their own form—the English form. The English sonnet consists of three quatrains and a couplet, abab cdcd efef gg. The quatrains make a statement that the couplet clinches. Shakespeare developed the English form of sonnet to its greatest perfection.

A third variation of the sonnet is one developed by Edmund Spenser, who combined the English and Italian forms. The Spenserian sonnet also consists of three quatrains and a couplet, but it links the quatrains with its rhyme scheme, abab bcbc cdcd ee, . . .

Sources

Joan E. Heimlich and Susan D. Pittelman. (1986). *Semantic mapping: Classroom applications.* Newark, DE: International Reading Association.

Dale D. Johnson, Susan D. Pittelman, and Joan E. Heimlich. (1986). Semantic mapping. *The Reading Teacher, 29,* 778–783.

P. David Pearson and Dale D. Johnson. (1978). *Teaching reading comprehension.* New York: Holt, Rinehart and Winston.

48

Vee Diagramming

Vee Diagramming is a procedure for bringing students to focus on a question or problem and to see how its conceptual and applied aspects are related. In the procedure, students are encouraged to take notice of how they use what they already know when they attempt to learn something new.

Subject matter is examined with the aid of a *v*-shaped diagram. A focal question or problem is noted at the point of the vee. Relevant conceptual statements are noted along one arm of the vee, and applications of these conceptual statements are noted in corresponding position along the other arm of the vee. Height on the arm of the vee indicates level of generality or abstraction.

The vee diagram makes obvious the subordinate/superordinate role of concepts relative to one another. Students can see the progressive specificity of a key concept as they read down the diagram, and they can see the subsuming qualities of higher-level concepts as they read up the diagram. Students attempt to understand the problem or question noted at the point of the vee by considering connections between concepts and applications of concepts noted across from each other on the arms of the vee. Reading back and forth across the arms of the vee, students move between the conceptual and practical dimensions of subject matter questions. Reading up and down the vee, students deal with the question at different conceptual and applied levels.

Vee Diagramming may be used in teaching most academic subjects, but it is especially useful in science and social studies. It is appropriate for high school and college students. It is best used in examining a question with discussion groups, but it can be adapted for use in delivering lectures to large groups.

Procedure

Vee Diagramming follows asssigned reading and assumes that students possess enough knowledge about the topic to discuss it. To initiate the procedure, the teacher states a problem or question that focuses on an event, object, or set of circumstances presented in the material being studied. As students tell what they know about the event, object, or circumstances, the teacher records the information they offer on one side of the chalkboard. Pointing out to students that they already have knowledge for dealing with the lesson's question, the teacher advises them that basic to using knowledge productively is to remain conscious of how best to organize their thoughts.

The teacher then places a large vee (V) on the chalkboard and beneath its point writes the lesson's question. Students are directed to draw a large vee (V) on a sheet of paper at their desks. The teacher explains that the purpose of the large vee is to serve as a device for diagramming students' thoughts about the question (written beneath the point of the vee). The teacher further explains that applied, factual information is to be written down on the right side of the vee and that conceptual information is to be written down on the left side of the vee.

First to be written on the vee diagram is the factual information written on the chalkboard. The teacher assigns students to place this information in some logical form at the right side of the vee, immediately above the question. Students may put the information in groups, an orderly list, or a map (spatial outline). While students carry out this task at their desks, the teacher carries it out at the chalkboard. If the information to be organized is complex, the teacher arranges it into a pattern in which position of information and connecting lines clearly show how features of the information are related.

After students have had time to organize and place the information on the vee, the teacher leads a discussion about how the information has been organized. The teacher explains why the information entered at the right of the vee on the chalkboard is arranged as it is, and students share explanations about how they organized the information. Following this discussion, the teacher writes on the opposite side of the vee a conceptual statement that summarizes or explains the factual information organized on the right side. The teacher explains the conceptual statement and its relation to the factual information.

The next step is to transform the factual information into statements that can be inferred from it. These statements are written on the right arm of the vee, immediately above the organized factual information. The teacher explains that the factual information suggests other information, which although not explicitly stated, can be taken from the facts that are given. The teacher provides an example and then elicits other statements that students can infer from the factual information. On the opposite arm of the vee, the teacher writes a concept statement that explains or summarizes the inference statements. Recorded at the next level up the vee, this concept statement represents a higher level of abstraction than the concept statement written beneath.

From the inference statements written on the right side of the vee, the teacher leads students to derive a conclusion and state it as a direct answer to the question written at the base of the vee. The merits of students' conclusion statements are discussed, and then the teacher writes one of the statements discussed on the right side of the vee, immediately above the inference statements. Directly opposite, on the left side of the vee, the teacher writes a concept statement that explains or summarizes the conclusion statement.

To complete the vee diagram, the teacher encourages students to speculate what the conclusion statement implies. At the top of the vee, on the right side, the teacher writes these as if-then statements or hypotheses to be explored in further study. The teacher and students continue to discuss the material, freely moving up and down and from one side of the vee to the other.

Discussion

Vee Diagramming serves as a useful tool for teaching students how knowledge in the subject is constructed and used. It visually separates the theoretical from the practical and the abstract from the concrete. Applying this tool to academic problems and questions, the teacher can probe connections between conceptual and factual content and thereby tighten students' understanding of how knowledge of the subject is put together. The vee diagram may be used to show how theories and principles explain observations. And it may be used to transform observations into conclusions and to convert conclusions into hypotheses. Serving these purposes, the vee diagram fosters in-depth consideration of subject area topics both in class discussions and in independent study assignments.

As with any tool, use of the vee diagram is limited by the sophistication of its user and by the task to which it is applied. The vee diagram can be used to sort the conceptual from the applied, but it cannot itself explain anything. The teacher must do that. Vee Diagramming is best used for teaching topics that involve a great deal of interplay between their conceptual and applied aspects. It is inappropriate for use with young students in the elementary grades.

EXAMPLE

A high school general science class is studying climate. Students have just read about global warming and now the teacher leads a discussion on the "greenhouse phenomenon." The objective is to have students follow the reasoning that connects facts of agricultural and industrial development to observations of global warming.

Teacher: As an old saying goes, "Everybody talks about the weather but nobody can do anything about it." Is that true, Carla?

Carla: According to our textbook, people might be able to influence the climate. I don't know about the weather.

Teacher: How so?

Carla: The earth's temperature is raised by our putting gases into the atmosphere. So people can raise the temperature.

Teacher: What does putting gases into the atmosphere have to do with raising the temperature?

Bob: The gases keep the earth from cooling off.

Teacher: Raising the earth's temperature and keeping it from cooling off seem to me to be two different things.

Joe: But our textbook says putting gases in the atmosphere causes the temperature to go up.

Joanne: It says more than that.

Teacher: What does the book say? You tell me, class, and I'll write it on the board.

Joanne: Industries that burn fossil fuels are increasing.

Monica: Burning fossil fuels puts carbon dioxide and ozone into the atmosphere.

Gary: Not to mention CFDs and nitrous oxide.

As students recite information given in the text, the teacher writes it on one side of the chalkboard. When students have completed reciting the text, the teacher moves to the center of the chalkboard and draws a large vee (V).

Teacher: Good. You have a firm grasp of the information presented in our textbook. That's important for productive thinking. And just as important is being aware of *how* you think with it, how you organize and reorganize your knowledge. Let's focus on a question that the information of the text would have us consider.

Beneath the point of the vee, the teacher writes out the question: What role do agriculture, industry, and deforestation play in global warming?

Monica: That's an easy question. Agriculture and industry dump lots of gases into the atmosphere.

Teacher: Basically, you're correct. But the question is, *How* does their dumping gases in the atmosphere affect temperature? Let's be clear about the reasoning involved in answering the question.

Gary: Is that why you've drawn that big vee on the board?

Teacher: Right. It should help us see the thinking behind the assertion that agriculture and industry contribute to global warming.

Carla: How?

Teacher: By sorting facts from concepts and showing how these facts and concepts are organized. We'll work together with the vee on the board, but you should develop your own vee diagram at your seat. So take out a sheet of paper and draw a big one on it. At the point of the vee, write the question I've written at the point of the vee on the board.

Bob: How does all the stuff written on the board go with the vee?

Teacher: Good question. That's the stuff we begin with. We take the facts that can help us answer the question and arrange them into a display that shows how they are related. We show relatedness by the way we position the information against other information and by lines we draw to connect the information.

Joe: In other words, we *map* the information. Right?

Teacher: Right. You place your map on the right side of the vee, toward the bottom. You place it here just above and to the right of the question.

Joanne: I'm not sure I know what you mean by mapping the information.

Teacher: That's all right. You can watch me develop a map at the board. It will be just one way, my own personal way, of showing how the information is organized. As soon as you catch on, you should begin a map of your own.

Gary: So right now, at our seat, each of us should map the stuff on the board at the lower right side of the vee?

Teacher: Yes, while I do the same thing at the board.

On the chalkboard, the teacher organizes the facts about global warming into a map at the lower right side of the vee. At their seats, students fashion their own maps. When the map on the chalkboard is complete, the teacher explains why it is structured as it is. Then, students compare their maps with the teacher's.

Teacher: OK. We've mapped our facts about increased agricultural and industrial development, increased deforestation, increased atmospheric gases, and increased temperature. There is a basic concept that can help us tie all of this together for the purpose of answering our question.

Joe: Atmospheric gases trap infrared radiation.

Teacher: Excellent. I'll write that down on the left arm of the vee, directly opposite of the mapped information.

Bob: Oh, I see. that's the concept that connects the facts. The more industry and agriculture, the more gases put into the atmosphere. The more gases put into the atmosphere, the more infrared radiation is trapped. The more trees cut, the less gas absorbed from the atmosphere. So there's even more infrared radiation trapped.

Teacher: That's right. Now, to answer the question, let's state a concept that will allow us to say what all of these facts have to do with global warming.

Monica: Increasing the amount of infrared radiation trapped in the atmosphere results in higher temperature.

Teacher: Good thinking. I'll write it on the left side of the vee, above the first concept we noted. Putting it above the first concept indicates that it's a higher-level concept in the reasoning process.

Gary: But why put it on the left arm of the vee?

Teacher: It's a conceptual statement. On the left side, we put statements of concept, principle, and theory. We keep that kind of statement separate from observations of actual occurrences.

Gary: So now, on the right side, we should write something about observations that have to do with global warming?

Teacher: Right. Given the facts we've mapped, and given the concepts we've stated, it seems reasonable to make an inference about the facts.

Climate is significantly affected by the amount of gases that trap infrared radiation in the atmosphere.

If current trends continue in agriculture industry and deforestation, temperature will continue to rise. Polar ice caps will melt. Oceans rise. Shorelines change. Weather patterns shift.

Increasing the amount of infrared radiation trapped in the atmosphere results in higher temperature.

The rise in the earth's temperature is due to an increase in infrared-trapping gases produced by agriculture and industry. Deforestation has reduced absorption of these gases.

Atmospheric gases trap infrared radiation.

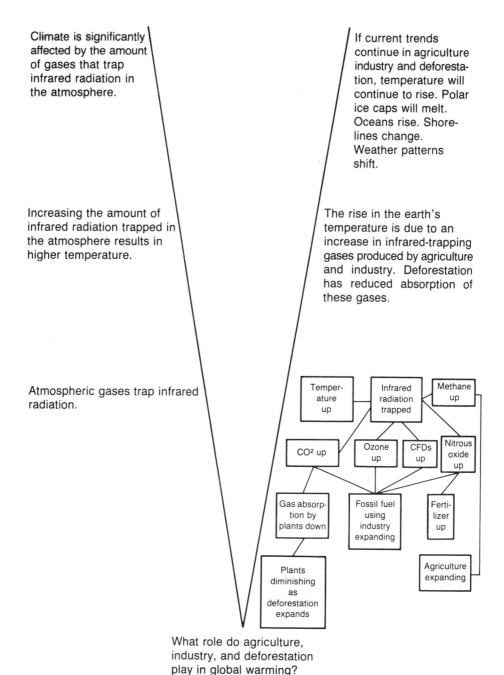

What role do agriculture, industry, and deforestation play in global warming?

Bob: The rise in the earth's temperature is due to an increase in atmospheric gases produced by agriculture and industry.

Teacher: Good. To show that inference arises from the facts we've mapped, I'll write it above that mapped information. And to show it as an inference that would be consistent with the second level concept, I'll write it directly across from the statement of that concept.

Carla: Industry and agriculture continue to develop. Deforestation is not slowing down. Does that mean the earth is bound to get hotter and hotter?

Joanne: And if it does, won't that cause the polar ice caps to melt?

Joe: And the ocean levels to rise and shorelines to change?

Teacher: These are speculations about things that could occur. Go ahead and name some more possibilities and I'll list them at the upper end of the vee's right arm.

In the discussion that follows, it is observed that the dominant concept is that amount of infrared-trapping gases in the atmosphere significantly affects climate. This concept is written at the upper left of the vee.

Global Warming

The earth is warmed by sunlight. Clouds and ice reflect some of the light, and clouds trap some of its heat. Excess heat is radiated from earth as infrared energy. In recent history, industry and agriculture have produced large amounts of gases that trap infrared energy. Deforestation has diminished absorption of carbon dioxide, the gas that accounts for the most infrared energy trapped in the atmosphere. As a result, less infrared energy has escaped the earth's atmosphere and the earth's temperature has been rising.

Carbon dioxide in the atmosphere is the chief contributor to global warming. For hundreds of thousands of years, carbon dioxide generated naturally by plants and animals remained at a stable level in the atmosphere. A minute trace of approximately 200 parts per million kept the earth's average temperature to about 60 degrees Fahrenheit. Without this carbon dioxide in the atmosphere, the temperature would have averaged some 20 degrees cooler. The carbon dioxide level varied slightly, but it never rose above 280 parts per million until the end of the eighteenth century. But as the burning of fossil fuels increased during the Industrial Revolution, the carbon dioxide level began to rise. Today, the amount is approaching 350 parts per million.

An increase in the amounts of other gases is also contributing to global warming. Methane has risen with population growth. Generated by decomposition and incineration of organic matter, methane from landfills and agriculture has increased by over one percent during the past decade. Chloroflourocarbons (CFDs) in the atmosphere have increased by about 5 percent annually. This increase corresponds with the increased use of CFDs for refrigeration, solvents, and plastic foam. Nitrous oxide is on the rise due to the widespread use of nitrogen-based fertilizers and fossil fuels, especially gasoline. Ozone is also increasing rapidly with increased burning of fossil fuels. These gases are much more effective at blocking the escape of the earth's heat than is carbon dioxide. Soon the combined effect of these gases will exceed the effect of carbon dioxide.

The effect of the increased amounts of these gases in the atmosphere is already apparent in the earth's warming trends. The warming is greater in winters than in summers. It is greater at higher latitudes than near the equator. The lower atmosphere is warming, while the upper atmosphere is cooling. The 1980s saw the hottest years on record. Climate has changed before, but the changes have taken place slowly over many centuries. In recent history, climate has changed dramatically in just a few decades.

Sources

Bob Gowin. (1981). *Educating*. Ithaca, NY: Cornell University Press.

Joseph D. Novak and Bob Gowin. (1984). *Learning how to learn*. Cambridge, MA: Cambridge University Press.

49

Inductive Towers

Teaching with Inductive Towers fosters the development of inductive reasoning. The method has students gather relevant facts from material being studied, transform the facts into interpretations, draw conclusions, and derive a theory or value statement.

An inductive tower provides students with a memorable structure for visualizing how inductive thinking works. At the base of the structure is a foundation of concrete, factual information. On this foundation stand higher levels of abstract propositions. Students become familiar with the structure through experience in building inductive towers. Construction begins with gathering information at the concrete, factual level. The next level of the tower is formed of interpretations of the factual information. These are interpretations for defining relations, formulating hypotheses, and making predictions. From these interpretations, conclusions are drawn to form the third tier of the inductive tower. For the highest level of the tower a single theory or value statement is induced. With a structure for placing thoughts hierarchically, students can examine their thinking part by part, within and across levels of generality. The process leads students to question their own assumptions and beliefs.

Building an Inductive Tower calls for considerable abstract thinking and reasoning. For this reason, the procedure is best used with high school and college students. It is an effective method for teaching literature, philosophy, science, and social studies. The method can be used to explain to large groups the reasoning that underlies conclusions, theories, and values that have been derived inductively from observed phenomena. It is more effectively used, however, with activity groups of four to six students. The activity may span several class periods.

Procedure

The teacher introduces the procedure by demonstrating the construction of an inductive tower on a small scale. The teacher's example is one that students can easily grasp. The purpose of this introduction is to show students what they are expected to do and what the outcomes will be like in upcoming activities that build inductive towers. The tower-building activity itself takes place in four phases: recording the facts, transforming the facts into interpretations, drawing conclusions, and formulating a theory or value statement.

In the first phase of tower building, the class is divided into task groups of four to six students each. The teacher assigns the task groups to collect as many facts about the topic being studied as they can find. The facts are taken from texts, personal experience, lectures, or classroom experiments. Each task group develops a list of the facts they find and keeps a record of the source of each. It is with these facts that students lay the foundation of the inductive tower. Fact gathering is usually the lengthiest phase of the activity.

In the next phase of tower building, the teacher works with students as they begin to interpret the facts they have collected. Together they discuss the facts in order to find linkages among them and to come to agreement about how to group them. This often requires compromise and deal making. For each group of facts, students formulate an interpretive statement such as a prediction or hypothesis.

As tower building moves into the third phase, the teacher works with students to reach an even higher level of thinking about the material. The approach taken in this phase is essentially the same one taken for interpreting the facts in the second phase. Now, the interpretations themselves are discussed and brought together into groups. Again, differences in opinion and perspective are resolved through compromise and deal making. The purpose here is to induce conclusions, generalizations, principles, and rules that can form the third tier of the tower.

The final phase in building the tower is to develop a theory or value statement for the top tier. Following the pattern for building the two tiers below, students arrive at this statement through discussion. It is a statement that captures the essence of previous interpretations and conclusions. As such, it can serve as a theme or thesis statement for a written report of the topic should the teacher assign one.

Discussion

Inductive Towers provide a visual device for making sense of the mass of information on a topic. The technique imposes order on the information and gives students a system for analyzing a problem or question. To construct an inductive tower, students work methodically toward a goal. They put facts together, interpret them, and draw conclusions in order to explain or judge material being studied. Working in groups, students listen to the opinions of others and reach compromises. In the process, students stand to develop a critical attitude toward statements that express theories or values.

To be effective, the activity takes close teacher guidance. Without such guidance, a number of difficulties may arise. Students may overlook or omit relevant information. They may mix interpretations with facts and leapfrog logical steps in thinking through the material. Students who most need practice in interpreting facts and drawing conclusions may allow other students to do the thinking. Shy or quiet students may acquiesce to assertions made by more dominant students.

EXAMPLE

A high school social studies class is studying global ecology. Students wonder how people with the same set of facts about the eco-system arrive at different opinions about it. To demonstrate the process by which values and conclusions are induced from facts, the teacher has divided the class into task groups. The teacher takes each task group through a sequence of gathering facts and making interpretations.

Teacher: Tropical rain forests are important to the world ecology.

Marcia: Rain forests are part of nature, but what makes them so important?

Teacher: More than you might think. I have some newspaper clippings that will answer your question and probably raise others. I'd like this group to read these clippings to learn some facts about the rain forests.

Once students have read the newspaper clippings, the teacher has students recite the facts. Then the teacher assigns them to list the most important facts and to note beside each which newspaper clipping is the source.

Teacher: All right. Let's see how we might interpret these facts. Let's try to put them into groups and then state generally what each group of facts says.

Bert: Is that like saying what they have in common?

Teacher: In a way it is, because they have to have enough in common that it is possible to make a single statement that can cover most of the facts.

Jean: Oh, then, scientists' predictions about disaster goes with 50 million acres of trees getting cut each year.

Clark: Oh, no. The 50 million acres of trees getting cut goes with 40 percent of the deforestation happening in Brazil, because those are both facts that tell about the amount of deforestation.

Jean: I think the fact that they earn $7,000 from fruits and rubber a year goes with their earning $3,000 a year from wood.

Jim: That obviously goes with their earning a living from the forest.

Sherry: What also goes with those things is that people will have to leave once the forests are cut.

Teacher: Obviously you have differences of opinion about how to group the facts. You'll have to reach some compromises. That means you will have to let your classmates have their way on grouping some things so they will let you have yours on some. In other words, you'll have to make some deals.

Jean: Well, I do see Clark's point for putting 50 million acres of deforestation with 40 percent of it happening in Brazil. But I think things I said about how much money they get go together. And what Jim said about natives earning income from the forest goes with it.

Clark: I'll go along with that.

Sherry: But what I said about people having to leave after the forests are cut means that it's more economical to harvest fruits and rubber, not wood.

Jean: I see what you mean, in the long run.

Teacher: In stating your reasons for grouping the facts as you have, you made some interpretive statements.

Jean: You mean like the facts about earning a living from the forest suggest what Sherry said: It's more economical to harvest fruits and rubber, in the long run?

Teacher: Right. Go ahead and make an interpretive statement for each group of facts that you put together.

Students continue grouping facts and generating statements to interpret each group. As students work, the teacher lists the titles of the newspaper articles on the lower part of the chalkboard.

Teacher: OK. Now tell me your fact groups and the interpretive statement you have for each. First, tell me your fact groups and I'll write them here above this box where I've written the titles of the newspaper articles you read.

Marcia: Our first grouping was about all the deforestation that's going on.

Bert: Yeah. We put two facts in that group: 50 million trees are cut each year, and 40 percent of those are cut in Brazil.

Teacher: Good. I'm writing down each fact and you'll notice I'm enclosing each group of facts in a box. Now what was your interpretive statement for these facts?

Jim: "Extensive deforestation is occurring all over the world."

Marcia: Yes. We had to talk about that. Even though one of our facts states that 40 percent of the deforestation is taking place in Brazil, there's still a lot of trees being cut everywhere else.

Teacher: Good. Interpretations don't have to fit the facts precisely. Notice I'm writing your interpretive statement above the two fact boxes and that I'm also enclosing *it* in a box. I'm connecting these boxes with lines to show that your interpretive statement arises from the facts.

Bert: It's like you're making a diagram.

Teacher: It *is* a kind of diagram, or will be. It will show how your thinking about the subject works. It will show how your thinking starts with facts, from which you derive interpretations. From these interpretations, more abstract levels of thought will be added to the diagram. When it is finished, the diagram will resemble a tower.

Jim: Shaped like a pyramid?

Teacher: Sort of, but really more like the Eiffel Tower. You'll see.

Students continue to report their fact groupings and interpretive statements, which the teacher adds to the tower diagram on the chalkboard.

Teacher: The way I've diagrammed what you've told me, we have begun our tower with nine boxes of facts to serve as its foundation and, above these boxes, four boxes containing interpretive statements.

Clark: Hey, it *is* beginning to look like a tower.

Teacher: Now let's build another tier. Concentrate on the interpretive statements. How can they be put in groups? What more abstract or general statement could you make to cover each grouping?

Sherry: Two of the interpretive statements are about the economic effects of deforestation.

Bert: And the other two are about damaging the eco-system.

Jim: So, draw lines connecting these two pairs of boxes the way you draw lines to show how the boxes of the facts are connected.

Teacher: OK. What can we induce from the first pair? What more abstract or general statement can we produce from the fact interpretations in these two boxes?

Clark: You could say: "Poor countries should harvest fruits and rubber instead of wood."

Marcia: You could say that for one of the boxes–the one about it being more economical to harvest fruits and rubber–but it's too narrow to cover the other statement about worldwide deforestation.

Sherry: I agree. Since one statement suggests the need to restrain deforestation and the other is about the rain forest economy, how about this statement: "Restraint is needed to preserve the rain forest economy."

Several: Yes. That works.

Teacher: Excellent. I'll write that statement above the two statements that it covers.

Clark: I have a statement you could make on the basis of the other two interpretive statements: "Destroying rain forests damages the worldwide eco-system."

Several: That's it. That's the conclusion you draw.

Teacher: Excellent again. And I'll write this statement above the statements that it covers.

Jim: Draw boxes around these two statements and draw lines the way you did for the layers beneath.

Teacher: Now let's put the top on our tower.

Sherry: Here we just make a more abstract statement that could be made from the two statements we just made, right?

Teacher: Right. Try to come up with a statement that expresses a guiding principle.

Clark: The two statements we just made are about economy and ecology, so it should cover both.

Bert: And all of this points to the need to use the rain forests more wisely.

Marcia: I've got it: "Using rain forests wisely is advantageous both economically and ecologically."

Several: Yes. That fits.

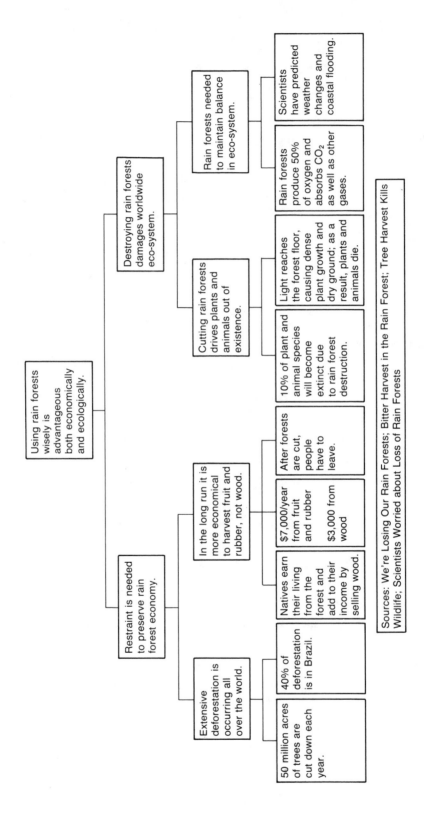

Using rain forests wisely is advantageous both economically and ecologically.

Restraint is needed to preserve rain forest economy.

Destroying rain forests damages worldwide eco-system.

Extensive deforestation is occurring all over the world.

In the long run it is more economical to harvest fruit and rubber, not wood.

Cutting rain forests drives plants and animals out of existence.

Rain forests needed to maintain balance in eco-system.

50 million acres of trees are cut down each year.

40% of deforestation is in Brazil.

Natives earn their living from the forest and add to their income by selling wood.

$7,000/year from fruit and rubber

$3,000 from wood

After forests are cut, people have to leave.

10% of plant and animal species will become extinct due to rain forest destruction.

Light reaches the forest floor, causing dense plant growth and dry ground; as a result, plants and animals die.

Rain forests produce 50% of oxygen and absorbs CO_2 as well as other gases.

Scientists have predicted weather changes and coastal flooding.

Sources: We're Losing Our Rain Forests; Bitter Harvest in the Rain Forest; Tree Harvest Kills Wildlife; Scientists Worried about Loss of Rain Forests

We're Losing Our Rain Forests

Every year the world loses an area of tropical forests almost as big as the state of Washington. On the basis of data collected with satellites and ground sensors, scientists at the World Resources Institute have estimated that about 50 million acres of tropical forests are stripped each year. About 20 million acres of forest are destroyed every year in Brazil. Although Brazil is the country with the greatest area of annual deforestation, sizable tree harvests take place in many other countries, including the United States.

Bitter Harvest in the Rain Forest

More and more tropical rain forests are being harvested. Historically, the forests have been the mainstay of tropical economies. Fruit and rubber have provided a livelihood for people of the forest. On the average, they earn about $7,000 per year harvesting rubber and fruit. Now this economy is being destroyed for relatively short-term gains. Large companies pay a tidy sum for the wood. By selling trees, natives can make over $3,000 per year without having to work for it. But once the forests are gone, these people have to find other ways to live and make a living. For most, this means that they have to move away.

Tree Harvest Kills Wildlife

Harvesting the wood of the rain forest destroys not only the trees that are cut but other life as well. Living things that depend on the trees directly are obviously put in danger. But plants and animals that depend indirectly on trees are also put in jeopardy. With the natural canopy removed, light reaches the ground. This has the effect of drying out the ground and causing dense growth of some species of plants. This in turn chokes and crowds out many other species of plants. By the end of the century, nearly 10 percent of all plant and animal species will become extinct due to rain forest destruction.

Scientists Worried about Loss of Rain Forests

Scientists who study the atmosphere are seriously worried about the destruction of tropical rain forests. Over 50 percent of the world's oxygen is generated by these rain forests. Little by little, deforestation is choking off the supply of this life-sustaining gas. At the same time, less and less carbon dioxide and other man-made gases are absorbed by the rain forests. The immediate consequence is that the earth's temperature rises. The long-term consequences are significant changes in weather patterns and severe coastal flooding that will result from the melting of the polar ice caps.

Source

John H. Clarke, James Raths, and Gary L. Gilbert. (1989). Inductive towers: Letting students see how they think. *Journal of Reading, 33,* 86–95.

50

Pyramiding

Pyramiding is useful for teaching students how to organize subject matter hierarchically. When students organize material into superordinate and subordinate information structures, they can communicate it more effectively and can remember it more clearly.

In Pyramiding, students process information actively. As they put it into order, they search, discuss, arrange, categorize, and label. Through these processes, students come to see the subject matter as a system of related facts and ideas. They see which facts and ideas control and which ones serve to support others. Students can organize and place new information they encounter within the frame of reference they construct. When they need the information, students have easy access to that which is high in the thought structure. This information, in turn, provides access to its associated subordinate information.

Pyramiding may be used in academic subjects whose content lends itself to hierarchical arrangement. It may be especially indicated for teaching topics in science and social studies. And it may be used successfully in a range of instructional situations. It is excellent for fortifying instruction given to remedial students, and it helps average and superior students pull together material that is complex and abstract. Pyramiding is obviously suitable for upper-grade students, though middle-grade students may find it helpful as well.

Procedure

After students have read a chapter section or short article, the teacher initiates Pyramiding by having students offer facts taken from the reading. The teacher writes each fact on a large index card, one fact per card. Then, using magnets, the teacher displays the cards randomly on the chalkboard for everyone to see. The teacher calls on students to sort the cards into groups and arrange the groups in one horizontal line on the chalkboard. This line forms the base blocks of the pyramid.

Now the teacher chalks in the next elevation of the pyramid and solicits labels for the groups on the base line. The labels students offer are written into the blocks of the second tier. Then the teacher draws one large block for the third tier and, without filling in this block, proceeds directly to draw the top block of the pyramid. At this juncture, the teacher asks, "What is the whole thing about?" Reducing students' response to one or two words, the teacher writes the overall subject in the top block. Finally, the teacher asks students to summarize all of the information in a single sentence which, once agreed upon, can be written in the large box on the third level. Students copy the pyramid in their notebooks for reference when they study.

Discussion

Pyramiding has several positive features. It can be used for teaching virtually any topic ordinarily taught in school, and it requires only minimal preparation. Students enjoy it, whether Pyramiding in groups in class or individually at home. It encourages active reading and, following reading, the production of a system of cues for retrieving information.

Pyramiding also has obvious limitations. Handling index cards and placing them with magnets can become awkward. The activity can be time consuming. And for the time invested, the return is likely to be limited to fostering memory of high-level information.

EXAMPLE

A seventh-grade social studies class is learning about nomads of the desert. The teacher wants students to know how nomads live and to understand that their survival in the desert depends on cooperation and group loyalty. The class has just finished reading a brief textbook section on the Bedouins.

Teacher: Now that you've read the textbook section on the Bedouins, who can tell us some facts about this nomadic people?

Ann: The sheik is the leader.

The teacher writes this fact on an index card and, using magnets, displays it on the chalkboard.

Teacher: Who knows who helps the sheik make decisions?

Alicia: The council of elders.

Tad: It said that the men are camel herders and warriors.

Teacher: (writing these facts on index cards and placing them on the chalkboard) Yes, it did say that, Tad. How about the women and children?

Emery: The women cook and watch the flocks. The children start learning their job when they are seven.

Laura: People cannot survive in the desert if they're alone, so they have to rely on groups.

Teacher: What are the groups that the Bedouins rely on? What groups does a Bedouin belong to?

Michael: His family, his clan, and his tribe.

Bert: Those groups have to train the young and look after each other.

Tad: A bunch of families make up a clan, and clans are led by nobles.

Teacher: What is the combination of several clans called?

Several: A tribe!

The teacher has written each of these facts on a separate index card and placed it on the chalkboard for the class to see.

Teacher: Alicia, Bert, and Laura, please come up to the board and put these facts about the Bedouins into order. Arrange them into groups and put them on a horizontal line across the board.

These students take a brief time at the chalkboard to discuss the grouping possibilities. Finally they decide on three groups: (1) person alone cannot survive; family, clan, tribe; take care of others; (2) men–camel herders and warriors; women–cook, tend flocks, care for children; children–begin training at age seven; and (3) families form clans led by nobles; clans form tribe; sheik rules tribe with help of council of elders.

Teacher: All right. That's a logical way to group these facts.

The teacher draws blocks above each group.

Teacher: Who can think of labels for these groups?

Michael: The first group says how important groups are to the Bedouins. Let's call it "Group Importance."

The teacher writes "Group Importance" in the block above the first group.

Emery: The second group is about the role of individuals according to whether they're men, or women, or children.

Ann: Then let's label it "Individual Roles."

Tad: The third group is about who's in charge of the tribe. Maybe we should call it "Group Leaders."

Teacher: Let's think about that one. There are facts about leaders, but within the tribal hierarchy.

Tad: What's that mean, *hierarchy?*

Bert: It means that some people are more important than others, and then there are people who are even more important than they are.

Teacher: In this case that's what *hierarchy* means. It refers more generally to an arrangement of things, any things, according to their importance.

Tad: OK, then let's label the third group "Hierarchy of the Tribe."

Ann: How about "Tribal Hierarchy"?

The teacher finishes writing in the group labels in the blocks of the second tier, draws above them a large block, and then draws still another block at the top of the pyramid.

Teacher: What is this textbook section about?

Alicia: Nomads.

Tad: Bedouins.

Bert: Tribes.

Teacher: It *is* about all those things. But one of them is more appropriate than the others. We *are* studying about nomadic people of the desert. And nomadic people *do* form tribes. This textbook section was about one nomadic people, the Bedouins.

Laura: So let's call it "Bedouins."

The teacher writes "Bedouins" in the block at the top of the pyramid.

Teacher: What does our textbook emphasize most about the Bedouins?

Bedouins								
The Bedouins know the importance of a group for survival and so work as group members and respect the decisions of their leaders.								
Group Importance			Individual Roles			Tribal Hierarchy		
person alone cannot survive	family, clan, tribal loyalty	take care of others	men are camel herders and warriors.	women tend flocks, cook, care for children	children begin training at age seven	families form clans led by nobles	several clans make a tribe	ruled by sheik with help of council of elders

After several minutes of discussion, the class agrees on a statement that summarizes the point made by the textbook section on the Bedouins.

Several: The Bedouins know the importance of a group for survival and so work as group members and respect the decisions of their leaders.

Bedouins Cooperate to Survive in the Desert

Every Bedouin knows that an individual alone cannot survive long in the desert. The Bedouin knows that it is only by living in groups that survival in the desert is possible. Thus, Bedouins are intensely loyal to family, clan, and tribe.

Within these groups, Bedouins are trained to perform tasks that serve the needs of others. As early as age seven, boys begin learning their roles as warriors and camel drivers. At the same age, girls begin training to tend flocks, take care of children, and cook.

Bedouin groups are highly organized. Families form clans, and clans form tribes. Each clan is led by a noble, and each tribe is headed by a sheik. The sheik rules the tribe with the help of a council of elders.

Sources

Suzanne F. Clewell and Julie Haidemos. (1983). Organizational strategies to increase comprehension. *Reading World, 22,* 314–321.

Carol Solon. (1980). The pyramid diagram: A college study skills tool. *Journal of Reading, 23,* 594–597.

51

ConStruct

The ConStruct procedure helps students see how complex concepts in a text are related. ConStruct is short for concept structuring, an activity that gets students involved in the search for the relational ties among concepts. With greater understanding of the concepts, students can remember them more readily.

The procedure is based on three principles, which teachers should observe in order for students to be successful with their reading assignments. First, prereading instruction helps summon students' knowledge relevant to the lesson and sets the stage for learning from the reading. Second, concepts are best understood when they are related to one another. By constructing a graphic representation of the concepts, students actively pull these concepts together. Third, understanding comes before remembering. The graphic representation aids students' understanding and recalling concepts.

The ConStruct procedure can be used with individual students, small groups, or large class groups. Once the procedure has been learned, it can be used effectively by individuals to study on their own. With variations, the technique can be taught at different levels of students' development, beginning at an age when students first encounter complexity and technical vocabulary in texts. Putting things into categories and making basic outlines are often taught as early as the third grade.

Procedure

To begin the procedure, the teacher tells students that together the class is going to study from the text and how they are going to study it. They are going to diagram its content. The students are going to read each section of the text repeatedly (three times) in order to get different kinds of information. The teacher will take this information and organize it into a diagram on the chalkboard. The diagram will represent ways that the subject matter might be visualized.

For the first reading, the teacher assigns the students to read the text section rapidly. Students are to skim the text, attending to titles, subtitles, introductory and summary paragraphs, first sentences, graphs, pictures, and boldfaced words. With this initial survey, students get an overview of the passage and can help the teacher begin to construct the diagram of its content. At this time, the diagram will consist of only the major topic and any outstanding subheadings. (See the first figure of the Example.)

Next, the teacher assigns students to read carefully in order to try to understand the concepts. Students are not to try to remember details, but to read them to help in understanding the concepts. Eliciting from students information they gain from this second reading, the teacher extends the diagram on the chalkboard. (See the second figure of the Example.)

For the third reading, the teacher has students reexamine any part of the text that was not fully understood before. At this time, students can scan the text for details that should be in the diagram or add information that might have been missed in the previous readings. Again, the diagram is elaborated. (See the third figure of the Example.) Skimming over the completed diagram at this time serves to reinforce understanding and to make recall of the concepts easier.

Discussion

Students often have difficulty understanding the technical vocabulary and concepts presented in texts. They have problems recalling explanations, causes and effects, and other kinds of relations. A visual outline can help remedy these difficulties. By *seeing* how technical terms and the concepts they represent are related, students are helped in understanding and remembering difficult subject matter that they encounter in reading.

Teaching with the ConStruct procedure initially requires taking class time for reading material that might otherwise have been assigned for homework. The procedure cannot be taught quickly. With two classroom sessions per week, the time needed for students to become proficient in its use is usually about 10 weeks. Patience is important.

EXAMPLE

A high school science class is studying the human circulatory system. The teacher's objectives are to trace the flow of blood through the body and to describe coronary, pulmonary, systemic, renal, and portal circulation.

Teacher: I know that many of you are having difficulty reading and understanding this chapter of your science book. So, instead of assigning this for homework, we'll work on it in class.

Mandi: I never read homework anyway.

Todd: Yeah, it's boring.

Teacher: Reading a science book is sometimes difficult because of the unfamiliar words and details, and, as Todd says, it can be boring if you don't understand the words you're reading. One way to increase your understanding of what you read is to visualize it. Let's try to visualize the material in our text on the circulatory system. To help you see the material, I'll put on the chalkboard a diagram that outlines the information that you tell me is in the text. Read only the title, first and last sentences, and boldfaced words. Be sure to look at any pictures.

Students skim the section for about a minute.

Teacher: Now that you've surveyed this passage, what is it about?

Several: Circulation of the blood.

Teacher: All right, let's place Circulatory System as the heading for our outline on the board. What else did you find in this passage?

Kara: The heart.

Teacher: Good, Kara. Let's add that to our outline as a subheading.

Keith: But, outlines have like Roman Numerals I and II and . . .

Teacher: You're right, but our outline will be shorter, and instead of making it with Roman numerals and sentences, let's make it more like a tree with a main idea or trunk and side branches. Now is there anything else that we need to add to our outline?

David: It also told about pulmonary circulation.

Teacher: Great, David. We'll let pulmonary circulation be another subheading. Now, are there any more?

Several: No.

With the information offered by students, the teacher has begun the diagram on the chalkboard:

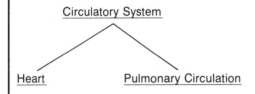

Teacher: Now go back and read the passage again, carefully this time, to find out about the heart and pulmonary circulation.

Teacher: (after about 3 to 5 minutes) What did you find out about the heart?

Mandi: It contracts, pumping blood through the whole body.

Teacher: Good. Let's add that to our outline. Did anyone find anything else?

Josh: Blood comes in the right atrium and then to the right ventricle.

Bernard: Then it goes to the pulmonary arteries to the lungs.

The teacher records these observations on the outline on the chalkboard.

Teacher: Where does the blood go after it leaves the lungs?

Samekia: It comes back to the heart, the left atrium and left ventricle.

Teacher: And then?

Keith: All over the body.

Teacher: Good! Now what about the pulmonary circulation?

Mary Anne: That's the blood that goes to the lungs.

Teacher: Yes, but what happens to the blood in the lungs?

Samekia: The blood picks up oxygen and loses carbon dioxide. Then the blood comes back to the heart in the pulmonary vein.

Teacher: That's right, Samekia.

Using the information students have gleaned from their more careful reading, the teacher develops the diagram:

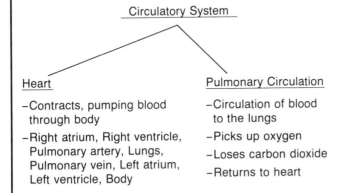

Circulatory System

Heart

−Contracts, pumping blood through body

−Right atrium, Right ventricle, Pulmonary artery, Lungs, Pulmonary vein, Left atrium, Left ventricle, Body

Pulmonary Circulation

−Circulation of blood to the lungs

−Picks up oxygen

−Loses carbon dioxide

−Returns to heart

Teacher: Now, let's go back over the passage to see if we've missed any important details. Scan it quickly for details.

Amy: (after about a minute) What's a valve?

Teacher: That's an important question, Amy. Let's look back at that sentence.

Amy: Oh, it prevents blood from flowing backwards the wrong way.

The teacher adds this information to the diagram.

Teacher: Good, have we missed any more details?

Everyone: No!!

Teacher: All right. Now let's follow this same procedure in reading the next short passage. Skim it quickly for main ideas.

The class proceeds through the next section of the text in the same way, surveying, discussing, reading, and adding to the diagram until the material is completed. At this time the teacher has students go back over the completed diagram, recalling the concepts outlined. The completed diagram contains all the important details from the text sections. The students use this diagram to review the concepts and to help them trace the flow of blood through the various systems of the body. The finished diagram looks like this:

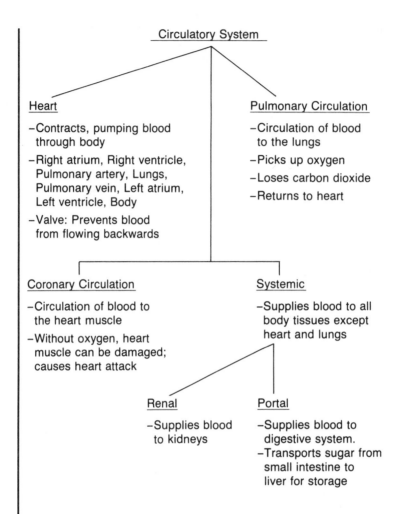

Circulatory System

Heart
- Contracts, pumping blood through body
- Right atrium, Right ventricle, Pulmonary artery, Lungs, Pulmonary vein, Left atrium, Left ventricle, Body
- Valve: Prevents blood from flowing backwards

Pulmonary Circulation
- Circulation of blood to the lungs
- Picks up oxygen
- Loses carbon dioxide
- Returns to heart

Coronary Circulation
- Circulation of blood to the heart muscle
- Without oxygen, heart muscle can be damaged; causes heart attack

Systemic
- Supplies blood to all body tissues except heart and lungs

Renal
- Supplies blood to kidneys

Portal
- Supplies blood to digestive system.
- Transports sugar from small intestine to liver for storage

The Heart Pumps Blood through the Circulatory System

Each time the heart beats, it pumps blood through the **arteries.** The blood flows from the larger arteries through the smaller arteries to the **capillaries** and all parts of the body. The blood circulates back to the heart through the **veins.**

Pulmonary Circulation

Returning to the heart, blood enters the right **atrium.** When the right atrium contracts, it pumps blood through a one-way valve into the right **ventricle.** The right ventricle then pumps blood into the **pulmonary artery.**

Through the pulmonary artery the blood flows to the capillaries of the lungs, where it releases carbon dioxide and takes in oxygen. Through **pulmonary veins** the oxygen enriched blood returns to the heart. It flows into the heart's left atrium.

When the left atrium contracts, blood there is pumped through another one-way valve into the left ventricle. When the left ventricle contracts, oxygen-enriched blood is forced into the **aorta.** The contraction of the left ventricle is stronger than the contractions of the other chambers of the heart. When it pumps blood into the aorta, the pressure is great enough to force blood on to the capillaries and all the cells throughout the body.

The heart's contractions can be heard with a **stethoscope.** The contractions make a lub-dub sound. The lub sound is made by the ventricles' contracting and the valves' closing. The dub sound is made when the ventricles relax and the valves to the aorta close.

Coronary Circulation

Coronary circulation refers to the flow of blood through the tissues of the heart itself for the purpose of nourishing the cells of the heart's tissues. Without oxygen, the heart muscle can be damaged and cause a heart attack. From the aorta stem two main **coronary arteries.** Through these coronary arteries, one on each side of the heart, blood flows downward into smaller arteries and then into capillaries and the heart tissues. Through coronary veins blood returns to the right atrium.

Systemic Circulation

Through the systemic system blood flows through the body. From the heart and aorta blood moves into smaller arteries and capillaries, exchanging nutrients for waste materials in the cells. Two important aspects of the systemic system are **portal circulation** and **renal circulation.**

Portal circulation includes the network of blood vessels for the digestion of food in the small intestine and the **portal vein** that passes through the liver. Food enters the blood in the blood vessels of the small intestine. Through the portal vein, some of the sugar is transported from the vessels of the small intestine to the liver for storage.

Renal circulation includes the network of vessels that pass through the kidneys. For each kidney there is an artery, from which capillaries branch out and join again to form veins. Through the veins, blood returns to the heart.

Source

Joseph L. Vaughan, Jr. (1982). Use the ConStruct procedure to foster active reading and learning. *Journal of Reading, 25,* 412–422.

52

Issue Web

The Issue Web takes a diagrammatic approach to organizing and refining students' critical thinking about a controversial topic. It is a discussion/debate activity in which students construct a web (a diagram) of arguments in support of both pro and con sides of an issue. Students are encouraged to consider both sides of the issue as they interact with peers and develop the web. Students use the web to analyze literature on the issue and to organize the content of critical essays they write.

The Issue Web has students derive evidence from a text, clarify arguments, and interact with classmates. Before coming to a conclusion on an issue, students see arguments and facts noted on a diagram as well as hear them presented in class discussion. Both the web and the discussion bring divergent perspectives into the open. The web shows the extent to which arguments are supported with evidence and makes imbalances in the arguments apparent. Through a dialectical process augmented with a visual aid, students come to a reasoned conclusion.

Issue Web is appropriate for high school and college-level composition, literature, philosophy, and social science classes. It is a whole-class activity, but it may be modified for use with small groups or individuals.

Procedure

The teacher introduces a controversy presented by the material being studied. Posing a question that has students take either a pro or con stand, the teacher elicits different points of view on the controversy. Following a brief discussion of the controversy, the teacher assigns students to read a selection relevant to the issue discussed. The teacher hands out a web starter to each student and directs the class to develop it into a full-blown web, showing arguments and evidence for both sides of the controversy.

Students are told to take account of evidence presented in the text as well as information they may know from personal experience. After students have had time to read the selection and get a start filling out their web, the teacher solicits students' help in developing a class web at the chalkboard or on the overhead. Inviting students to make suggestions for completing the class web, the teacher leads a discussion that explores both sides of the question posed at the beginning of the lesson.

As the question is discussed and the class web is developed, the teacher points out imbalances in the arguments. Some arguments may lack evidence, and some arguments on one side of the issue may lack counterarguments or other offsetting arguments on the other side of the issue. Having benefit of the class web, students may add information or otherwise modify their individual webs. When both sides of the issue have been thoroughly presented and the web has been constructed, the teacher has students consider possible conclusions about the questions. The teacher writes these in the space provided beneath the question.

The teacher then has students derive possibilities for a main idea from the conclusions suggested. The teacher writes these on the web in the "Thesis" space provided above the question. The teacher directs students to write a single main idea on their individual webs. It may be one of the main ideas on the class web or the student's own conception of the main idea. Finally, students are assigned to use the web to write a composition that explores the issue.

Discussion

Students construct a study device that brings many different facets of an issue immediately before their eyes. It is a device that allows students to see how arguments and evidence are related and to evaluate the adequacy of the evidence for and against a position on an issue. Constructing the web is a flexible process in which thoughts are recorded as they emerge, not as they occur in a logical or chronologically correct sequence. The pro and con sides of the web usually develop together since most students think reactively. Arguments stated for one side of an issue suggest counterarguments to be inserted on the other side. Beyond helping students thoroughly analyze controversial issues, the web provides a valuable tool for helping move students away from writing strictly in the narrative mode and toward composing critical essays in expository form.

The teacher can expect students to differ in the extent to which they construct their individual webs. Some students may not be able to make a web at all. This is likely to be the case with young students who have not previously seen the process demonstrated. Average- and low-ability students may need to observe the development of a web several times before they can handle developing one themselves. Able students usually need only watch the process once to catch on to it.

EXAMPLE

A high school sociology class is studying the role of institutions of higher education in society. The focus of the lesson is on women's colleges. The question before the students is whether women's colleges continue to be needed.

Teacher: So, the question is whether colleges exclusively for women continue to serve a necessary function in society.

Mildred: It's self-evident that they do.

Teacher: Self-evident?

Mildred: Sure. They offer women the choice of whether to go to college where guys are or to go where they don't have to mix with guys. Having choices like this is what a free society is about.

James: But the guys don't have *any* choice about attending colleges that are for women only.

Rona: Why would they even want a choice like that?

James: For reasons having to do with convenience and expense. Maybe one of those colleges is in their hometown.

Paul: And there's another, more important reason. They may *just want* to go to a particular college. They should be free to make that choice.

Delia: But there are all-men's colleges that don't allow women.

Teacher: Before we go on, we need to remind ourselves that the question we're considering is whether women's colleges continue to serve a useful social purpose.

Mildred: That's what we're talking about. Keeping freedom of choice in society.

Paul: But you're talking about freedom of choice only for women.

Teacher: The problem of conflicting freedoms is an interesting one. But there are other problems related to the issue.

Mildred: Yes, there are.

Paul: I'll say.

Teacher: As you read the textbook segment on women's colleges, take note of the arguments and supporting evidence on both sides of the question: "Do women's colleges continue to serve a needed function in society?" After you've read the selection, we'll explore the issue together by making a diagram of the arguments and evidence on both sides of the question. You'll make your own diagram, and the class will make one together.

Delia: You mean we're going to draw a picture of the controversy about women's colleges?

Teacher: A diagram, like a picture, does represent things visually. But a diagram can be used for dealing with abstractions. A diagram can help us see how abstract things are related. It can help us see a whole web of interconnected abstractions.

Delia: So what we'll draw is a diagram that shows the web of arguments and evidence on both sides of the question about the social need for women's colleges?

Teacher: Exactly. To get you into the task, I have a starter web for you to develop as you read.

The teacher hands out a starter-web to each student. The students silently read the textbook segment "Women's Colleges."

Teacher: On the board, I've begun a web for exploring the controversy about women's colleges. Let's develop it as a class. How shall I begin to build the web?

Tony: The selection gives three main arguments against women's colleges. And there are three branches extending from the *NO* stem. So, I guess you write those three arguments on the three *NO* branches.

Teacher: What are the three *NO* arguments?

Paul: One is that women's colleges are an anachronism. Write that on the top branch of the *NO* side.

Tony: On the middle branch on that side, write that keeping women's colleges is inconsistent with women's demands for gender equality.

James: And on the branch beneath that, write that there are no social or academic advantages for the students.

Delia: But on the other side, be sure to write all three of the counterarguments.

Teacher: Which are . . . ?

Delia: That males control coeducational institutions, that the existence of women's colleges denies no opportunities to males, and that women's colleges have an outstanding record of accomplishments.

Teacher: All right. I'm writing those counterarguments on the *YES* branches of the web.

Tony: But we need to add why women's colleges are an anachronism. The selection gives two reasons.

Teacher: All right. On the top branch of the *NO* side of the web, I'll attach two lines and write your reasons on them.

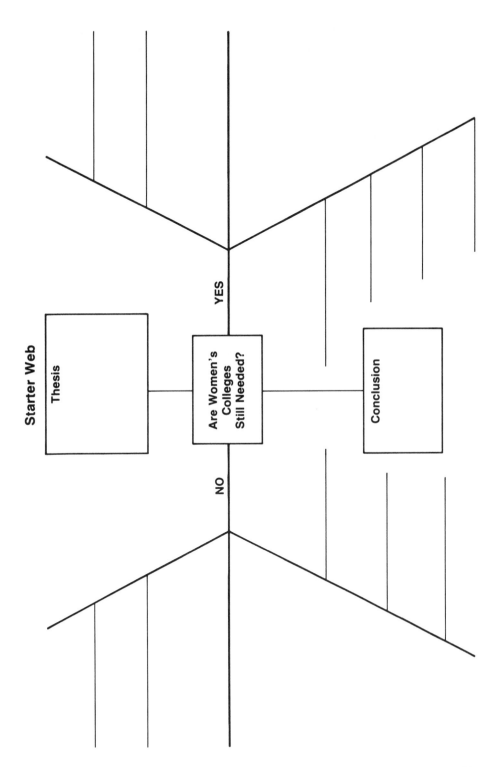

Starter Web

Thesis

Are Women's Colleges Still Needed?

YES

NO

Conclusion

Tony: The reasons are, one, that women have access to the full range of opportunities in higher education and, two, that women have access to the best universities in the world.

Rona: But be sure to write the two reasons that support the counterargument.

Teacher: OK. What are they?

Rona: That men try to dominate whatever discussions they're in and that women's colleges teach women how to be assertive and compete with men.

Students continue to offer information, which the teacher adds to the web on the chalkboard.

Teacher: There are arguments and evidence on both sides of the question about the social need for women's colleges. But I notice some imbalance between the two sides of our web. There are no supporting reasons for the argument that keeping women's colleges is inconsistent with women's demands for gender equality.

Delia: That's right. But the counterargument on the *YES* side is supported with two reasons.

Rona: Also, we should all take note that the argument about the record of accomplishments for women's colleges is backed up with four pieces of evidence. The argument on the other side just has three more arguments to go with it, but no evidence.

Following some class discussion on the worth of arguments versus evidence, the teacher encourages students to draw possible conclusions.

Teacher: Obviously a case can be made for either side of the question. What are we to think, given the web we've constructed?

James: Even though women's colleges have served a useful social purpose in the past, they will have less and less to offer as women participate more fully in society.

Teacher: OK. I'll write that as one possible conclusion here in the box beneath the question.

Mildred: I would come to a quite different conclusion: The role of women's colleges has changed with greater educational choices available to women, but women's colleges will continue to render important service to society.

Teacher: I'll also write that down as a possible conclusion.

The teacher writes other possible conclusions offered by students. The teacher then turns attention to the web as an aid to writing a composition that considers the arguments on both sides of the question about women's colleges.

Teacher: The web can be a useful tool for writing a composition. It can help you keep track of the things you want to say on both sides on an issue, and it can suggest how you might want to present those things. An effective composition develops a main idea, a thesis.

Rona: What main idea would we develop using this web?

A Student's Web Completed

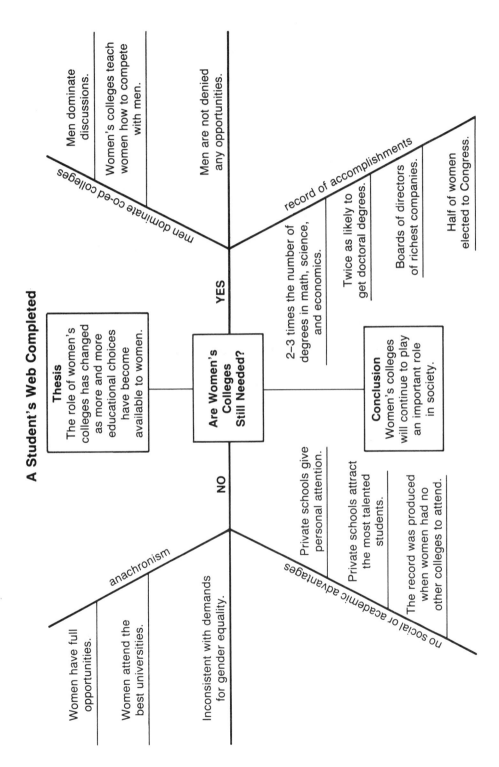

Thesis
The role of women's colleges has changed as more and more educational choices have become available to women.

Are Women's Colleges Still Needed?

YES

men dominate co-ed colleges

Men dominate discussions.

Women's colleges teach women how to compete with men.

Men are not denied any opportunities.

record of accomplishments

2–3 times the number of degrees in math, science, and economics.

Twice as likely to get doctoral degrees.

Boards of directors of richest companies.

Half of women elected to Congress.

Conclusion
Women's colleges will continue to play an important role in society.

NO

anachronism

Women have full opportunities.

Women attend the best universities.

Inconsistent with demands for gender equality.

no social or academic advantages

Private schools give personal attention.

Private schools attract the most talented students.

The record was produced when women had no other colleges to attend.

Teacher: That's a question I should have *you* think about. You've already suggested some possible conclusions. These conclusions tell you where the composition is headed.

Delia: So the conclusion we're going to reach gives us the main idea?

Teacher: It suggests a thesis statement, which will govern your thinking as you write, and which will tell your reader clearly what you want to say.

The teacher has students suggest possible thesis statements, which are written above the web's central question. Finally, students are assigned to write a composition on the place of women's colleges in society. Students are reminded to refer to their webs. One student's web is shown as an example on page 293.

Women's Colleges

Women's colleges have traditionally been small, privately operated institutions. They were established during the nineteenth century, when women had limited access to higher education. With the disappearance of barriers to the admission of women to most institutions of higher education, the pool of students seeking entry into all-female colleges has significantly diminished. Shrinking enrollments have been accompanied by heavier financial burdens. During the 1970s, many women's colleges became coeducational either by dropping the women-only restriction or by merging with men's colleges. Since 1960, the number of women's colleges dwindled from over 300 to fewer than 100.

Critics of single-sex colleges question whether there should be any women's colleges at all. They argue that women's colleges are an anachronism. Women today have access to the full range of opportunities in higher education, including access to the best universities in the world. The critics point out that retaining colleges that exclude men is inconsistent with women's demands for removing gender barriers from traditionally all-male colleges, military schools, and social clubs. The critics see no particular academic or social advantage to be gained by students who attend colleges for women only.

Defenders of women's colleges say that in coeducational institutions the men are still in control. When men and women participate together in group activities, men dominate the discussion. Men control the topic of discussion, take more turns speaking, and talk longer. In classes at all-women's colleges, women receive support and encouragement. They get the experiences they need to become assertive and to compete with men.

Proponents of women's colleges see no inconsistency in excluding men from their institutions and at the same time insisting on equal access to traditionally all-male institutions. They argue that men are denied nothing when they are denied admission to women's colleges. But when women are denied admission to men's colleges, they miss opportunities to become part of social networks that can later enhance their professional careers. Also, denying women access to men's social clubs keeps females out of places where business is often transacted informally.

Champions of women's colleges point with pride to a tradition they believe worth maintaining. They cite impressive statistics. Students at women's colleges are two to three times as likely to earn undergraduate degrees in male-dominated disciplines such as in the physical sciences, mathematics, and economics.

Graduates of women's colleges are twice as likely to earn doctoral degrees. They are six times as likely to serve on boards of directors of the richest companies in the nation. Almost half the women elected to Congress have been graduates of women's colleges.

Although the record is undeniably extraordinary, critics of women's colleges doubt that it has anything to do with admitting women only. Students at small, private institutions enjoy a great deal of personal attention. And these schools attract bright, affluent students who would do well in any environment. And, impressive though it is, the record of accomplishments by graduates of women's colleges was produced in an era when women had few opportunities to attend top universities.

Now things are different. For women, educational and career opportunities are widening. For higher education, resources are becoming scarce. Times have changed, and the change will inevitably affect the future of women's colleges.

Source

James Duthie. (1986). The web: A powerful tool for the teaching and evaluation of the expository essay. *History and Social Science Teacher, 21,* 232–236.

Related Reading

Donna Alvermann. (1987). Strategic teaching in social studies. In Beau Fly Jones, Annemarie S. Palincsar, Donna S. Ogle, and Eileen G. Carr (Eds.), *Strategic teaching and learning: Cognitive instruction in the content areas* (pp. 92–110). Elmhurst, IL: North Central Regional Educational Laboratory.

53

Graphic Information Lesson

The Graphic Information Lesson (GIL) enhances students' understanding of subject matter while it leads them to discover the usefulness of graphic displays (charts, diagrams, graphs, etc.). It encourages students to read carefully and to review important information. The GIL moves students from the literal comprehension of graphic aids toward more inferential and evaluative levels of interpretation.

The lesson is designed so that students integrate the information of graphic displays with a prose presentation. As students process the information in graphic displays, they go over the information presented in the prose. Students synthesize information taken from the prose and apply it in interpreting the graphic material, and *vice versa*. Students see how information from the two sources is sometimes overlapping and sometimes complementary. As students make greater use of graphic material in study, they come to think more divergently about the subject matter.

The GIL is used in instruction that involves texts that are augmented with graphic displays, importantly including mathematics, science, and social studies texts. The method is especially useful for teaching that shows relatedness, difference, and change in the material. Students should be at the upper-elementary grades or above. Although it is possible to use the method with individual students, it is more effectively used with groups of 10 to 20 students. Groups of this size are large enough to allow several interpretations to be expressed, yet small enough to include all students as significant participants in the activity.

Procedure

The Graphic Information Lesson begins after students have read a text segment augmented with one or more graphic aids. The teacher asks students to tell how the information presented in the graphic aids relates to information given in the prose. If students answer with literal-level information, which they usually do, the teacher accepts these answers with encouragement to make inferences and to connect the information of the graphic display with the prose. As much as possible, the teacher has students evaluate the helpfulness of the graphic aids. This may include commenting on the purpose and usefulness of any caption or title in a graphic aid.

Next, students are presented graphic aids that the teacher has made up for the lesson. Some of these graphic aids contain accurate information, but some of them contain inaccurate information. The teacher asks students to explain why each graphic aid is believable or unbelievable. Students give the page numbers and cite information in the prose that supports their explanations.

Finally, the teacher assigns students to create their own graphic aids for understanding the material being studied. Students present their graphic aids to the class and defend them by referring to the prose content they help clarify. The teacher may assign a follow-up activity that has students choose the text's most helpful graphic aid and defend their choice in terms of the graphic aid's accuracy and clarity.

Discussion

The GIL provides a systematic approach to evaluating the depiction of information in graphic aids. It has students identify and use significant information in graphic aids, but equally important, it has students seek to understand how graphic aids clarify and extend a prose presentation. Students not only come to understand the material thoroughly, but they also learn to examine graphic aids closely and critique their effectiveness. Deciding on graphic aids' accuracy stimulates discussion productive of subject matter learning. Creating original graphic aids builds skill and confidence in communicating the subject matter to others.

To use GIL effectively requires more preparation than for most lessons. The teacher has to be familiar with the content, organize it well, and identify vocabulary that needs to be taught. Time and imagination are needed to create additional graphic aids for students to examine. These are not limitations that should discourage teachers from using GIL. It is, after all, but an alternative method for teaching subject matter, and one that is to be used occasionally.

EXAMPLE

A high school geography class is studying the Gulf Coast region of the United States. The class has just completed reading a textbook segment on Mississippi's oyster economy.

Teacher: After reading our text, I don't know whether I'll be eating any Mississippi oysters. Think you'll be having any, Bill?

Bill: They do seem to be getting scarce.

Kay: And yukky.

Teacher: Oh?

Bill: The harvest is way down since the early 1980s.

Kay: And nastier.

Teacher: And nastier, yes. How much has the oyster harvest fallen off, Andrea?

Andrea: The text says it's down from 4.1 million in 1983 to 100,000 pounds a year.

Teacher: How much was the harvest before 1983?

Dianne: The text doesn't say. It only says it peaked in 1983.

Teacher: Check the graphs–"Oyster Harvest."

Dianne: In 1982, about 2 million pounds were taken.

Teacher: And before that?

Dianne: Less than a million pounds. Looks like about 800 thousand pounds.

Teacher: And before that?

Alvie: It looks like it varied from year to year between 200,000 and 600,000 pounds.

Teacher: Looking at both the graphs and the text, how would you characterize the trend in oyster fishing before 1983?

Bill: The text says it was "on the rise" and that it had been important "over the past several decades." To me, that means that over the past decades oystering was on a steady increase. But the graphs don't exactly show that.

Teacher: What *do* they show?

Bill: In 1982 and 1983, the harvest shot up like a rocket. Before that, the oyster take may have been on a gradual rise in the whole Gulf of Mexico, but not in Mississippi. There, the harvest was a little up and down over the years since 1970.

Teacher: The text says that after 1983 the harvest dwindled. How much did it dwindle and how fast?

Alvie: At first glance, it looks as if it came crashing down fast. But for three years it was still almost twice as high as it had been before 1982. Then in Mississippi it fell to its 1971 low and has remained there. In the rest of the Gulf, it never fell below its highest mark previous to 1982. And, in fact, it has been climbing.

Teacher: Excellent analysis. But what accounts for the sudden drop in the mid-1980s for both Mississippi and the entire Gulf? And why has it stayed low?

Bill: Could be the weather, or overharvesting, or pollution. The text doesn't pin it down.

Teacher: Let's compare some of the graphs. Let's first compare the graph showing the estimate of oysters available against the weather and water salinity graphs.

Gregg: From 1970 until 1990, the precipitation steadily decreased. The salinity levels correlate exactly with the precipitation levels over this time.

Teacher: Interesting, but of what significance is this correlation?

Gregg: The text says this would cause an increase in oyster predators, but there's no information about oyster predators specifically.

Teacher: OK, go ahead.

Gregg: Anyway, the weather and salinity trends have been steady, and, until 1983, there was a correlated trend in amount of oysters available. It was decreasing as precipitation decreased and salinity increased. Then there was a very sharp decrease. But the number of oysters came back up almost to as many as before.

Teacher: Now look at the oyster harvest graphs. If you compare the oysters available with the actual harvest, what seems apparent?

Carol: The harvest only takes a small portion of them.

Teacher: OK. Now, comparing the weather and salinity graphs against the harvest graphs and the oyster availability graph, what do you think is the effect of the weather and water salinity on the oyster harvest?

Kay: Although the weather affects the total number of oysters available, it really has little or no effect on the harvest.

Teacher: I would agree. What does that leave us to infer about the reduced harvest?

Carol: Of the three causes mentioned in the text, overharvesting and pollution have reduced the oyster harvest.

Teacher: OK, but let's sort this out. Which has accounted for the harvest reduction?

Bill: Probably both. I mean, at one time overharvesting really zapped oyster fishing. But then, at another time, pollution zapped it.

Teacher: I think you're right, but be more explicit. What do the graphs tell us?

Bill: The 1982 and 1983 harvests cut the total number of oysters almost in half, and the 1984 harvest nearly wiped them out in Mississippi.

Teacher: Then what happened?

Kay: They began to recover. And, as Gregg says, they bounced back to their previous number.

Teacher: So what does that lead you to think?

Kay: There are plenty of oysters, and yet the harvest has remained low. To me, that means pollution has made a whole lot of the existing oysters unfit for harvesting.

Teacher: What about pollution before 1984, Gregg?

Gregg: It's hard to say. Maybe the pollution reached unacceptable levels at that time due to population growth and industrial expansion on the Mississippi coast. Or maybe the pollution was ignored and the oysters were harvested anyway.

Teacher: I agree, it is hard to tell with the information given us. About the information that *is* given us, how important is the information in the graphs?

Carol: The graphs repeated some of the written information, but they gave other information that helped us understand the situation. The written information didn't really give enough information to get an accurate picture.

Teacher: What do you mean?

Carol: The written information is factually correct, I suppose, but it is misleading. I mean, it names three things that could affect oyster harvesting, but the graphs show only two things have had any real effect.

Kay: And the written information might leave you thinking that it's the weather and oystermen themselves to blame for the low harvest, as much as the pollution. But when you look at the graphs, you see that overharvesting had an effect for only two or three years. It's really just the pollution to blame after that.

Teacher: Did the graphs tell us all that?

Gregg: Not straight out. But they told us enough so we could come to a more correct understanding of the oyster situation in Mississippi. I mean, oyster harvesting is on the rise elsewhere in the Gulf. It's Mississippi that can't control its pollution.

Alvie: Or it's Mississippi that watches for polluted oysters more carefully.

Teacher: Graphs don't tell us everything. But, I think you're saying that they do tell us a great deal. We have to examine them carefully and think about their information. I've made up some additional graphic aids for this text segment for you to examine.

The teacher hands out a sheet showing the three Venn diagrams (which are shown on the next page). After students have had time to examine them, the discussion resumes.

Teacher: Which of the three diagrams can you believe?

Bill: I'd like to say that diagram A doesn't work at all.

Teacher: Why not?

Bill: It's inaccurate. It shows sewage and city run-off accounting for less than half the pollution. The text says they account for well over half.

Teacher: OK. What about the other two?

Bill: Both show sewage and city run-off making up over half the pollution. But diagram B does not show how much each contributes to the pollution.

Dianne: But B is consistent with the text, which doesn't tell that information either.

Teacher: Assuming diagram C is correct, which is more informative?

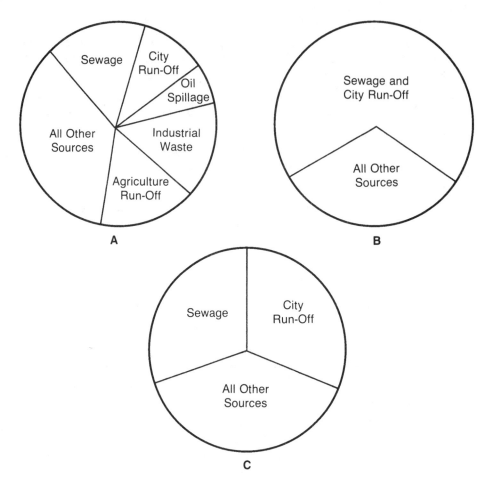

Dianne: C.

Teacher: OK, here are three more graphic aids. Which among them are believable?

As the lesson proceeds, students comment on the believability of still other graphic aids the teacher has developed. As a closing exercise, the teacher assigns students to create their own graphic aids for information not shown in the text's graphic displays. Students produce graphs that show prevalence of oyster predators and pollution content of Mississippi coastal waters.

Mississippi's Oyster Economy

Over the past several decades, oysters have been a significant part of the economy of the Mississippi Gulf Coast. But oyster harvesting is not what it used to be. Bad weather, pollution, and overharvesting have reduced the catch of oysters in the coastal waters of Mississippi, as in other areas of the Gulf Coast.

In recent years the area's weather has become relatively dry. This has increased the salinity of the water. In the saltier water, snails and other oyster predators have flourished.

Annual Precipitation and Average Salinity Levels of Mississippi's Coastal Waters

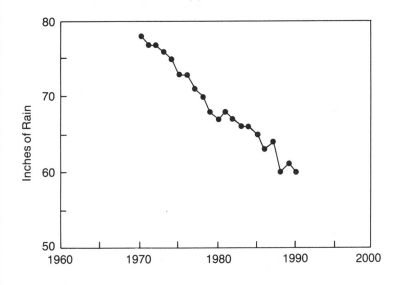

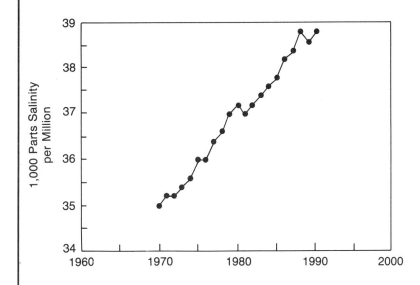

Due to pollution, well over half of the Gulf water from Florida to Texas is closed to shellfish harvesting at least part of the year. The pollution has several sources, but it is effluent from sewer systems and run-off from cities that make most of the oysters unfit for harvest.

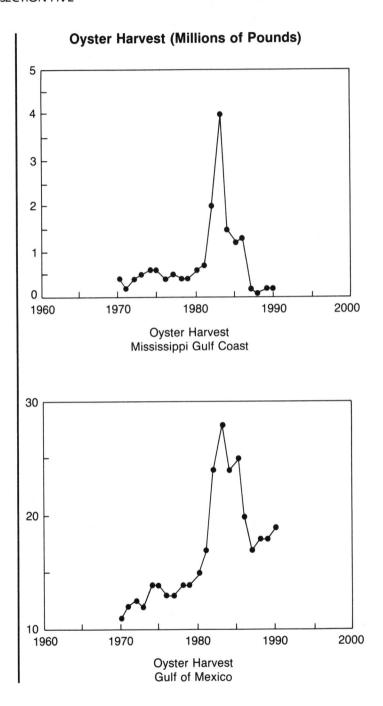

Oyster Harvest (Millions of Pounds)

Oyster Harvest
Mississippi Gulf Coast

Oyster Harvest
Gulf of Mexico

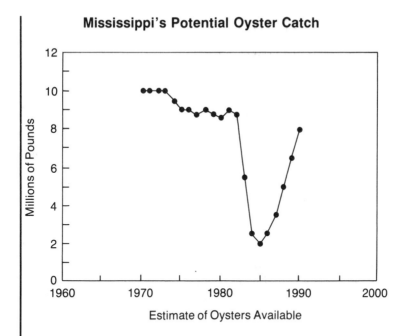

Mississippi's Potential Oyster Catch

Estimate of Oysters Available

Until the early 1980s, the oyster economy was on the rise. It peaked in 1983, when about 4.1 million of pounds of oyster meat were harvested. An oysterman could make up to $700 a day. After that, the oyster harvest dwindled. In 1987, the harvest was only about 100,000 pounds. Today, an oysterman is lucky to make $100 a day.

Source

David Reinking. (1986). Integrating graphic aids into content area instruction: The graphic information lesson. *Journal of Reading, 30,* 146–151.

54

Visual Reading Guide

The Visual Reading Guide (VRG) has students organize their thoughts before reading and studying a topic. It is a preview activity in which students note the main idea and details of visuals, interpret critical vocabulary, identify major concepts, and select important themes in the material to be studied. It provides guidance for reading and writing activities and contributes to the development of generalizations, attitudes, and value choices.

The VRG prepares students for studying a topic by having them see important aspects of the content in advance. Students are presented with visuals and directed to respond to them in a structured way. This alerts students to significant aspects of the material, arouses their expectations, and gives them a sense of direction for studying. Not only do students get a sense of what the content is about, but they are put in a better position to organize their thinking and to set appropriate study purposes.

The Visual Reading Guide is designed for social studies lessons that involve reading materials containing visuals such as pictures, cartoons, charts, graphs, or maps. It may also be used effectively in other classes that involve reading materials containing visuals such as these. The VRG is appropriate for students in the middle and secondary grades. The method may take as much as two class periods.

Procedure

The teacher prepares for the lesson by identifying concepts in the text that are illustrated by visuals. The VRG is used to introduce these concepts before having students read.

The procedure begins with giving students index cards for each visual essential to understanding the content and concepts developed in the text. The teacher asks students to inspect the first visual and to create a title for it, which they are to write on the first line of the index card. Students are asked to share the titles they have created and to justify the title with information in the visual.

Next, the teacher asks students to say what they think the visual's main idea to be. The teacher lists students' responses on the chalkboard or the overhead. Class discussion is directed toward bringing students to consensus about the main idea, which students explain in a sentence they write beneath the visual's title. A sentence might read: "This picture is about _____ ." Students are then asked to write under this main idea sentence at least two details they observe in the visual.

Now, the teacher asks students to write a question they would like to be able to answer about the visual. This question is written below the details. The teacher may have to give examples of possible questions. A simple example is a true-false question; such a question can then be used to show students how to formulate a question that calls for a more thoughtful answer.

Finally, the teacher introduces students to important vocabulary terms either illustrated by the visual or conceptually related to it. The teacher indicates the page where students will first read each term. The teacher provides a clear example of the meaning of each word. The teacher may also find it useful to analyze each word into root words, prefixes, and suffixes. Attention may also be given to synonyms, homonyms, or alternate meanings.

This procedure is repeated for every visual the teacher judges important to understanding the material presented in the text. (If there are many such concepts, the teacher is selective and places the concepts in priority.) Students are directed to refer to the cards as they read the assigned text. As they read, they are to answer the questions they have written on their cards. Students may turn the cards over and outline information, jot down notes, or write questions about troublesome words or ideas they encounter in the reading.

Discussion

For most students, understanding and learning are facilitated by presenting subject matter through visual means. The effectiveness of visuals accompanying prose material can be heightened by the VRG. With the VRG, the teacher focuses students on important concepts and has students themselves set some of the purposes for reading. Students can use the completed index cards later for studying. The cards are also useful for writing assignments, particularly for developing paragraphs: The visual's title and main idea become a topic sentence; the details develop the topic sentence in following sentences; and notes taken during reading fill out the paragraph.

EXAMPLE

A ninth-grade world history class is beginning its study of the Middle Ages. The teacher's objective is to introduce feudalism of Western Europe. To prepare for the lesson, the teacher has identified visuals in the text that help explain concepts related to feudalism.

Teacher: To start our reading about the system of feudalism that developed following the fall of the Roman Empire, let's take a look at the three illustrations in this section of our textbook. And let's write down the important information of these illustrations on index cards.

The teacher distributes index cards, telling students to take three cards each. As the cards are handed out, the discussion proceeds.

Teacher: Although illustrations sometimes merely dress up the text, usually they signal important concepts and provide helpful information.

Gwen: The first illustration in this section is a time line.

Teacher: That's right. It's a time line. On the top line of one of your index cards, write a title for this time line.

Art: It already says "The Middle Ages."

Teacher: Yes, but you can probably think of a title that tells more completely what this time line is about.

Elaine: The time line also shows the word *feudalism* in all capital letters, so that's an important part of what this time line is about.

Merle: Even though it says "The Middle Ages" at the top, that's just telling when feudalism existed. And this section *is* about feudalism.

Lance: I think a good title would be "Feudalism Time Line."

Several: Yes, good.

Teacher: All right. Beneath the title, write a complete sentence that states the time line's main idea.

Vivian: The title already gives the main idea, doesn't it?

Teacher: It does indicate what the time line is about, but it doesn't indicate what the time line tells us. We need a complete sentence to do that.

Elaine: The time line shows the Middle Ages as the historical period and feudalism as something that existed during the Middle Ages.

Gwen: How about this: Feudalism and the Middle Ages are the same thing.

Elaine: That's not what I was getting at. The Middle Ages was the time period and feudalism was what was happening. They're not the same thing.

Gwen: I guess you're right.

Elaine: So I think the main idea could be: Feudalism existed through the Middle Ages.

Gwen: Yes. That's much better.

Several: We like that.

Teacher: I do, too. Write that down beneath the title. Now, let's try to pick out at least two important details in the time line. These details should support the main idea statement.

Merle: Feudalism lasted from about 700 A.D. until after 1500.

Teacher: All right. It lasted from the eighth century until the early sixteenth century. That's one important detail to write down.

Art: I guess the broken line means that feudalism wasn't solidly in place during the time indicated. So, it looks as if feudalism began to disappear in the 1200s.

Teacher: That's an important detail, too. So write that down.

Vivian: Underneath the other detail?

Teacher: Yes. Now, what question does the time line raise?

Lance: That things were happening around the thirteenth century that would cause feudalism to begin to disappear?

Teacher: That's an excellent question.

Merle: Also, did the fall of the Roman Empire have anything to do with the rise of feudalism?

Teacher: Another excellent question. On your index card, beneath the two details, write down one of these questions.

Vivian: Could we write down both questions?

Teacher: Sure. The questions help us form purposes for reading. Reading to answer these questions are both good purposes for reading.

Art: So, are you saying that usually we would just write down one question we have about the illustration, but we could write down more?

Teacher: That's right. Now, one more thing to write on the index card. Are there any words in the illustration, in the time line shown here, that you don't know or need to know more about?

Art: Feudalism. This whole textbook section is about feudalism and I don't even know what *feudalism* is.

Several: Me neither.

Teacher: So, underneath the question you've written, write down the word *feudalism*. If you needed to know about other words shown in the visual, you would write them down, too.

Lance: Do we fill out index cards the same way for the other two illustrations?

Teacher: Yes. So when you begin to read you'll already have some idea about what you're going to read. And you'll have purposes and questions in mind. When you read, you'll take notes on the reverse side of the cards. But we still have cards to fill out for the other two visuals.

Feudalism Time Line

Feudalism existed through the Middle Ages.

  A. From 8th century to 16th century.
  B. Began to disappear during 13th century.

What caused feudalism to begin to disappear during the 13th century? What did the fall of the Roman Empire have to do with the rise of feudalism?

feudalism

The Feudal System

The feudal system was an economic and political system.

  A. Land, labor, loyalty, and protection were traded for each other.
  B. A structure with king at top, noblemen/vassals in middle, and serfs at bottom.

  How did the feudal system work?

The Homage Ceremony

The homage ceremony sealed the land tenant's loyalty to the suzerain.

A. Tenant kneels before the suzerain.

B. Tenant places hands in the hands of the suzerain.

What was the homage ceremony like? What part did it play in feudalism?

homage, tenant, suzerain

Feudalism of the Middle Ages

Feudalism was the dominant political and military system of Western Europe during the Middle Ages. Essentially, feudalism was an arrangement whereby land was given in exchange for military and other services. It was a system that provided social order, justice, and protection against attack. It was out of feudalism that national states of Western Europe later arose.

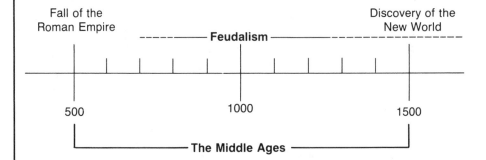

Feudalism came about during the time of disorder and barbarian invasions following the collapse of the Roman Empire. Afraid of marauding bands, people turned to their strong neighbors for protection. They were willing to pay in order to take safety in the neighbor's stone castle. Payment was usually made in the form of land, which the protector allowed the former owners to use during their lifetime.

Over time, the land tenure arrangement became an arrangement among a class of men who had acquired hereditary rights to hold land. These men were called noblemen. Land holding among noblemen was hierarchical. A nobleman held land in exchange for loyalty and service to a more powerful nobleman, who in turn held the land he had granted in exchange for loyalty and service to an even more powerful nobleman.

Each nobleman was a vassal to a more powerful nobleman who was his lord. At the top of the hierarchy was a king. In theory, the king owned all of the land parceled out among the noblemen. In the feudal system, the role played by noblemen was largely to ensure a measure of law and order and to provide a military force.

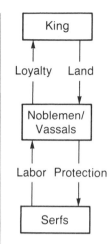

The Feudal System

At the bottom of the system were the serfs. They were not permitted to leave the land, but neither could they be removed from it. They lived on the land and worked it. When the land changed hands, they remained on the land and worked for the new landlord. The feudal economy depended largely on the work of the serfs.

The feudal system depended on adherence to a set of principles and practices by noblemen. According to these principles and practices, a nobleman could hold land and exercise power only by becoming a vassal to a nobleman superior in the feudal hierarchy. Each land holder swore allegiance to an overlord in the homage ceremony. In the ceremony, the future vassal pledged to be the lord's man and to perform military service. In return, the lord promised to treat the vassal with honor and to permit him to possess a feodum as long as he fulfilled his feudal duties. . . .

In the homage ceremony the land tenant takes an oath of loyalty to the suzerain.

Source

Harry Stein. (1978). The visual reading guide (VRG). *Social Education, 42,* 534–535.

Author Index